THE
HO MODEL RAILROADING
3RD EDITION HANDBOOK
ROBERT SCHLEICHER

Published by

krause
publications

700 E. State Street • Iola, WI 54990-0001
Telephone: 715/445-2214

Please call or write for our free catalog.
Our toll-free number to place an order or obtain a free catalog is 800-258-0929
or please use our regular business telephone 715-445-2214
for editorial comment and further information.

ISBN: 0-87341-608-2
CIP 92-53147

Printed in the United States of America

CONTENTS

PART I GETTING STARTED

PART II PLANNING, BENCHWORK, TRACKWORK & WIRING

PART I: GETTING STARTED

CHAPTER 1

Model Railroading

THE ONLY DIFFERENCE between a set of toy trains and a real railroad in miniature is your own state of mind. If that surprises you, you are not alone. If you thought the difference between the two might be the scenery, the number of track switches, or the size of the layout, you are right, because that's the way it appears to the eye. When you look at the illustrations on these pages and in model railroading catalogs and magazines, you will see all the things that can make a model railroad. Even the most realistic layout can still be seen as a toy train set if those who build it and operate it think of it as only an adult toy or a grownup plaything. That is why your state of mind is important. If you become totally involved, if you can convince yourself that you are creating and operating a real railroad in miniature, then you really are doing just that. Of course your particular railroad will not have many of the problems that a real one has, so in a sense it's still a model. But keep in mind that it can be a perfect model, or replica, of the real thing.

Creating a real railroad in miniature is an art. Just like any other art form, such as painting or sculpture, it requires skill and imagination. In effect, you become an artist because your technique and style combine to establish your own personal signature. In this book you will find explanations, descriptions, and advice on how to apply the art of model railroading to your toy trains and how to create a layout that is fine enough to be classified as art.

A BRIEF HISTORY OF THE HOBBY

Model railroading has been a hobby for at least as long as toy trains have been made, and that's more than 100 years! Tens of thousands of true railroads in miniature have been built during that time, and the men and women who built them have learned some very cunning tricks. Many of those tricks are collected and described for you on these pages.

The pioneer model railroaders had a difficult time because they had to go through the painstaking process of building every piece of their railroads. Imagine how few part-time artists there would be if they had to make their own paints and stretch their own canvases.

THE EARLY MODEL RAILROADERS

Although the greatest advances in the art of model railroading have occurred during the past fifty years, lessons have been made available to almost anyone only during the last twenty years or so. The early model railroaders had no publications to turn to for advice except those books and magazines that described the real railroads of the time. Most of the clever adaptations of real railroading to our miniature railroads were first used and perfected in the 1930s. That aspect of the art of model railroading, then, is not really new; but it is new in that it is finally being rediscovered by hobbyists and craftspeople. The few really clever model railroaders of the 1930s devised most of the methods of operating their miniature trains like real ones because there was no other source of advice except that offered about the real railroads. The concept of using insulating gaps to allow two-rail track like the real railroads, rather than the toy trains' three rails, was also developed then, as were switching operations and timetables and a host of other model-railroading methods and concepts.

Much of the realism we take for granted today was developed by several modelers who used museum dioramas as their inspiration. The museum models were among the few that were built with everything to the same scale. In other words, the people were matched in proportion to the size of the trees and the doors in the buildings and in the passenger cars. The proportions of a scale model are virtually identical to those of the real thing. These early modelers were the first

ones to make a model railroad appear realistic to the eye.

MODEL VERSUS REAL

Very few model railroads in the 1930s looked or operated like real railroads. It was so difficult to build a scale model with the right proportions that most of those modelers didn't have enough time, energy, or inspiration left to operate their models like the real thing. However, a number of other modelers were operating their three-rail toy train sets almost exactly like real railroads. Men like the late Watson House, John Page, Minton Cronkite, Al Kalmbach, Harry Bondurant, and Linn Westcott ran trains over their three-rail layouts with switching and timetable operations that were almost identical to the real thing. It was the late Frank Ellison, however, who was one of the first

Fig. 1-1. The romance of real railroading. A Great Western Railroad train struggles upgrade on the front range of the Rockies, circa 1955—photo from the collection of Harold K. Vollrath.

model railroaders to combine the art of running a model railroad like it was real and the art of true scale miniatures into one system. Mr. Ellison was also the first to describe it in the model railroad books and magazines published just before and after World War II. And it was he who made model railroaders aware that they were indeed practicing the art of railroading in miniature; he was even willing to share with his readers the true significance of the painting or sculpture-like quality of the hobby that can make it a true art form.

PLASTIC TRAINS

The real breakthrough in technology, which allowed almost anyone to enjoy the art of railroading in miniature, came with the much-maligned plastic models of the late 1950s. In the pre-plastic age, it took about a week's worth of evenings to build every car or every structure, and it often took a month to assemble a locomotive. The alternatives were relatively expensive brass models or the ready-to-run toy trains. Plastics allowed the manufacturer to include even more detail than the wood and metal model kits. The plastic models were sold either ready-to-run or took two or three nights to assemble. The use of plastic also allowed the manufacturers to produce more of their products in less time, so the selling price was lower. These lower prices resulted in even more sales, and that, in turn, resulted in even lower prices. Even at today's inflation-boosted prices, you can buy a complete ready-to-run train set for less than the price of a single locomotive in the 1950s, and the locomotive and cars in that set look more like the real thing, run more like the real thing, and are more reliable than most hand-assembled kits.

KITS AND READY-BUILT MODELS

The availability of inexpensive kits and ready-built model railroad products gave almost every model railroader the means to construct a truly artistic setting for his realistic models and to oper-ate his miniature layout like a real railroad. Space, rather than time or skill, became more of a limiting factor to the creation of a miniature railroad empire. Fortunately, the experience of other model railroaders, together with the reliability of small-scale models, such as HO scale miniatures, has often solved the space problem. The compact "shelf" layout designs, larger layouts that can be disassembled for moving, and the efficient use of space to allow the creation of a true empire in an area as small as 4 x 8 feet, have made model railroading a hobby accessible to everyone.

STATE-OF-THE-ART RAILMODELING

There have been a number of significant advances in model railroading just during the past five years and those are all included in this edition of the HO MODEL RAILROADING HANDBOOK. Today, you can buy plastic freight cars, passenger cars, diesel and steam locomotives with separate handrails and ladders and brake lines, Kadee-style working magnetic knuckle couplers, and paint and lettering schemes precisely matched to specific prototypes. You can buy this equipment either as kits or ready-to-run and for prices that, with inflation factored in, are no higher than the HO scale plastic toy trains produced by Tyco and others in the sixties. Look for cars and locomotives in Life-Like's Proto 2000 series, Bachmann's Spectrum series, Athearn's Genesis series, and models by A-Line, Ertl, InterMountain, Kadee, Kato, Red Caboose, and some of the Atlas models for examples of the best-detailed, ready-to-run models ever produced. The medium-priced car and locomotive models with molded-on ladders, grab irons and air lines from Accurail, Athearn, Atlas, Bethlehem Car Works, Centralia Car Works, Con-Cor, E & C Shops, Detail Associates, Details West, Eastern Car, Tichy, MDC, Stewart and Walthers are far better replicas than the models of a decade earlier.

Fig. 1-2. The 7 x 8-foot Burlington Route is built using the latest techniques for blue foam benchwork, r-t-r track with roadbed, Digital Command Control, shaped blue foam scenery, and felt Grass-That-Grows scenery texturing.

And most of these kits and ready-to-run (r-t-r) models have knuckle couplers that can be operated by magnets. The majority of the original toy train cars of the sixties and seventies are still available, but with upgraded trucks and operating knuckle couplers, and the older steam and diesel locomotives are also available, but with new chassis featuring modern motors and drive trains. The Tyco cars, locomotives and buildings are now offered by IHC. Bachmann and Mantua have most of their cars and locomotives in full production as upgraded models.

TWO MODEL RAILROADS

There are two complete model railroads in this book, built from the plans shown in Chapter 20 for the 9 x 9-foot Burlington Northern (Figure 20-3) and the 7 x 8-foot Burlington Route (Figure 20-5). The Burlington Northern layout is set more or less in the early seventies, when the major real railroads were merging. The Pennsylvania Railroad and New York Central became Conrail, and the Great Northern, Northern Pacific, Spokane Portland and Seattle, and the Burlington became the Burlington Northern. The Burlington Northern layout was built using nothing but toy trains that, when the layout was built, were all available from Tyco. I use the word toy because, although nearly all of the equipment was based on specific prototypes and built to scale, the couplers were mounted on the trucks, the details were thick to withstand children's rough use, there were few separate parts, and the color schemes ran a rainbow of both real and imaginary decorations. Most of those locomotives are still offered by IHC, but with updated chassis. IHC also sells most of the cars and rolling stock that were originally Tyco, but with more subdued real railroad

Fig. 1-3. The 9 x 9-foot Burlington Northern layout was built using traditional techniques of open-grid bench-work, sectional track, block control, plaster-soaked paper towel scenery shapes, and real earth and ground foam scenery texturing.

paint schemes. Similar products are also available from Bachmann and Life-Like. That layout also uses the traditional open-grid benchwork shown in Chapter 5, with sectional track shown in Chapter 7, a power pack for each train with electrical blocks and wiring shown in Chapter 9, and paper towels, soaked in Hydrocal plaster scenery, from Chapter 15. Scores of model railroaders still prefer most of these traditional techniques when building their model railroads.

The Burlington Route layout utilizes the newest proven construction techniques and models. It is set in the 1959 era, when the Chicago, Burlington and Quincy were known as the Burlington Route. This layout is built with a lightweight table using thin plywood and blue insulation foam, with scenery shaped from the same blue insulation foam, textured with state-of-the Grass-That-Grows felt and a new technique using Scandinavian tumbleweeds and fine ground for trees (all in Chapter 17). The trains on the Burlington Route can be controlled with just two wires connected to a Digital Command Control power pack that allows up to 10 trains to operate on one track. The cars and locomotives you see are mostly ready-to-run models, but there are also top-level products with separate ladders and intricate details. You might be interested to know that, with inflation factored in, these state-of-the art models cost no more than the Tyco trains did in their day. You can still buy toy trains from manufacturers like Bachmann, IHC, Life-Like and Model Power and the prices are roughly twice what they were in the seventies which, again factoring in inflation, is about one-fifth the cost of the original Tyco products. The state-of-the-art Burlington Route layout can be completed in less time, with less mess than the original Tyco layout, and the resulting layout is far more realistic as are the models you see operating on the layout.

KEEP IT SIMPLE

Today, anyone can practice the art of model railroading. The incredible array of inexpensive products and easy-to-learn techniques gives you the freedom to concentrate on whatever aspect of the hobby you find most pleasing. You can, for example, assemble just a few simple building kits and use ready-built structures so you have more time to enjoy the actual operation and add details to the scenery. Please do not feel that you must master every technique in this book in order to build a model railroad. Most chapters include enough information so you can specialize in that area of the hobby and need apply only a few of the techniques from the other chapters to those specific areas. The locomotives, rolling stock, trackwork, wiring, structures, and scenery on the 9 x 9-foot layout in Chapter 16 appear throughout the book, but they are included only as examples, with the layout itself an example of a combination of all the elements of the hobby. It takes an experienced model railroader at least two years to build a layout as complete as those seen in the illustrations. However, most of us would want to take even more time for such a project. The goal of any model railroader is to have fun first and foremost; and the old-timers are those who are wise enough to know that their layouts will really never be finished.

TACKLING THE PROJECT

Don't be appalled at the thought that a model railroad is a project with no end; in fact, this aspect is what makes this hobby so exciting and rewarding. A model railroad is truly a growing and living thing. When it stops growing, most model railroaders tear the layout apart and start another, building on the lessons and experience they collected from that first creation. Every genuine model railroader has built at least two layouts for whatever reason or excuse he or she cares to offer. One of the most valuable lessons this book can provide, then, is that your first model railroad should be for practice. The practice layout is the one you can use to try, at the very least, some of the techniques and tips from every chapter of this book. Then you'll know what ones you like and what ones you would rather touch on lightly.

There are two complete model railroads included in this edition: The 7 x 8-foot Burlington Route is pictured with locomotives and rolling stock from the late fifties. That layout is built with the easiest methods developed including lightweight benchwork and scenery described in chapters 6, 16 and 17. It has the new E-Z Track with built-in roadbed that snaps together as shown in Chapter 4. It also has Digital Command Control, described in Chapter 9, that allows you to run two or more locomotives on the same track with no special wiring. The 9 x 9-foot Burlington Northern is shown with BN green locomotives and rolling stock from the late sixties and later in most photographs. The layout is constructed with the traditional open-grid benchwork sectional track and roadbed, a power pack for each train (and electrical gaps for each block) and plaster and paper-towel scenery in chapters 5, 9, 15 and 17.

A GOOD-EYE VIEW

It's difficult, indeed, to convince even yourself that you're not playing with trains when you're crawling around on your hands and knees chasing them around the floor. It's also very hard on the equipment, because the floor is the final resting place for every bit of dust, lint, and debris in the room, and those oil-coated gears can pick up and absorb every particle. Dust and lint also land on the track itself and form an insulation layer that not only stops the flow of electricity but also the progress of the noon freight. That set of problems was particularly acute with the older sectional track shown in Chapter 7. The new Bachmann E-Z Track and Life-Like Power-Loc track (described in Chapter 4) with built-in roadbeds have

overcome the dirt and lint problem, so you can operate on the floor or have track that can be rearranged on a tabletop without nailing it down.

You can purchase a 1/2-inch-thick piece of C-C grade 4 x 8-foot plywood, two 2-inch thick 2 x 8-foot pieces of blue extruded-Styrofoam insulation board, and four screw-on legs or 2 x 4s and sawhorse brackets for about the price of a train set. I recommend the sawhorse brackets and 2 x 4s because they'll allow you to raise the layout all the way to your chest, which is where it belongs. Most of the screw-on table legs are so short that they'll only lift a 4 x 8 piece of plywood to your waist, and that's really only half the way up to miniature railroad from a toy train.

Fig. 1-4. You can buy rolling stock, locomotives and vehicles to model any era, including the late fifties, like the scenes on the Burlington Route layout.

You can view the train at eye level at every angle with just a slight bend of your knees. The layout is still low enough, however, so you can see it all and, of more importance, reach at least halfway across the table. Position the 4 x 8 layout so you can reach at least three sides. Any attempts to reach across a 4-foot miniature railroad will only result in a very sore back or some very flattened models. The plywood and the 2 x 4s can be used (recycled) on your next layout too, so nothing will be wasted.

BUILDING AN EMPIRE

This practice model railroad empire in 4 x 8 feet will also need at least two turnouts (switches) and a few pieces of track in addition to the circle or oval supplied with most sets. Bargain packs of track that often include a pair of turnouts and some extra track section are available to simplify the purchase. Be sure you buy track with built-in roadbed, like Bachmann's E-Z Track©, Life-Like's Power-Loc© track, or Atlas True Track© for this first layout. You can use the plans that come with the pack of track and

turnouts or you can use one of those described in Chapter 3 if you want something more complex than an oval with a couple of stub-end sidings. It's your model railroad; if a simple track plan suits your fancy, then stick to it and spend some extra time on the trains themselves, the structures, on scenery, or just in perfecting your knowledge of operations. The advice of a half-century's worth of model railroaders' mistakes is valuable, so try everything in every chapter of this book on your 4 x 8-foot layout.

For instance, don't assume that you dislike real railroad operation until you've tried it, and don't think fashioning scenery is too hard until you spend an afternoon with felt, spray paint, dirt and ground foam rubber (as shown in Chapter 17). You might want to postpone the purchase of Digital Command Control power pack for two-train operation, particularly if you've decided on a simple track plan with two or three turnouts. Do try the walkaround control system, though, so you can see what it feels like to stay with your train rather than just watching it come and go. Try

Fig. 1-5. The Waybill system of operation in Chapter 19 allows every car to carry a load just like the real railroad cars.

it all and you'll have the confidence to build that second model railroad to the perfection level you'd promised yourself for the first layout.

Model railroading is one hobby where you can only learn by doing; all I can do for you is show you the easiest possible methods and some typical results. These will serve as models to help judge how good a modeler you are becoming and will become over the months and years ahead.

DO'S AND DON'TS FOR NEW MODEL RAILROADERS

- Do try different layout designs on the floor (if you have track with built-in roadbed like Bachmann's E-Z Track or Life-Like's Power-Loc track) before deciding on the size and type of tabletop you want.
- Do create your own world or copy a real one. Duplicate reality or create a fantasy, or combine fantasy and reality. Remind yourself, if you must, that this is fun!
- Do lay the track directly onto the tabletop or roadbed, with no up or down grades for the first layout you build.
- Do keep that first layout simple, with no more than six turnouts and no reversing loops or other track configurations that can cause wiring complications.
- Do build any layout with strong enough benchwork or tables so you can add or delete entire sections of track without destroying the remainder of the layout.
- Do try to imagine that the trains are real and operate them at the relatively slow speeds of real trains. This will increase both the realism of the scene and create the illusion of a larger layout.
- Do try to limit your purchases of locomotives to 8-wheeled or smaller diesels and 53-scale-foot or shorter freight cars if you have only 4 x 8 feet or less of layout space. The shorter equipment looks more realistic on the tight curves.

- Don't nail or glue the track to the tabletop until you have operated for a month or two to see whether you want to change the track arrangement.
- Don't purchase 12-wheeled or larger diesels, 86-scale-foot-freight cars, or 85-scale-foot passenger cars for a 4 x 8-foot layout. Save them for the time when you can have an around-the-wall layout with 24-inch or larger radius curves.
- Don't use the over-and-under trestle sets on any model railroad. The steep up and downhill grades cause derailments, and the track is both unstable and toy-like.
- Don't take model railroading so seriously that it becomes a task or chore with unreasonably high standards of fidelity to prototype or detail.
- Don't try to build the more complex layouts on your first try. Consider that first layout a practice run and just enjoy trying everything.
- Don't try to operate trains, even passenger trains, as though they were racing cars.
- Don't ever consider a layout to be finished or so perfect that you are not willing to change it. Even the real railroads change track alignments and locations as their equipment and traffic change.

CHAPTER 2

Inspiration

AMERICA LOVES TRAINS. They are a large and romantic part of American heritage, and they remain in our history books—if not completely in contemporary American life—to remind us how our nation grew and expanded westward in years past. Trains were the key that opened the great American West. The sight of seemingly mountain-size, monolithic cubicles zigging and zagging down a twisting and turning stretch of track, guided by only those tiny flanges, is awe-inspiring. A train is so tall, so wide, and so infinitely long that it almost seems to be more a part of nature than a man-made contrivance. The train may be more of a symbol of everything that is America than the bald eagle. If you stand a few feet from a passing train, you cannot help but have an emotional experience. A train can carry you a few miles or it can take you across the country, but time and distance are merely relative. Many Americans' fondest memories are of spending nights in berths of trains while the country clickety-clacked its way beneath them, or of having meals in the dining car while watching the panorama of American cities and wheat fields, small towns or huge mountain ranges, or of just standing in the protection of dad's huge hand while the earth shook under the might of a passing locomotive. It doesn't even matter whether or not you have taken a trip on a train, for almost every person feels some trace of nostalgia about them.

TOY TRAINS

Toy trains also can evoke a feeling of love from a person, particularly a young person. There's something very exciting about a string of brightly colored cars following that engine wherever those two shiny steel rails might lead it. And it's thrilling in a way that's completely different from the experience of watching a real train. A toy train is one of the few toys that duplicates real life with the fairyland of action and color and the fantasies of adventure. A toy train is the dream of real railroading brought to life, and it can be as lovable as a bear cub, even if the real thing may be as frightening as a grizzly bear. Because toy trains are a kind of living magic, it is almost impossible not to love them.

ROMANCE AND ADVENTURE

Model railroading combines the lovable aspects of real-life railroading with all the charm of the toy train. No wonder it's one of the most popular hobbies today. What else can make dreams come alive in three dimensions, and in living color and action? The hard work of real railroading can be ignored to include the movements and environment that are the rewards of that work. Model railroading, in the best sense of any art, captures only the romance of real railroading. The model railroad world is that absolutely perfect environment we can only dream of in our day-to-day lives. As a world, it's a wondrous place to escape to, and it offers what television and books can only promise. The model railroad world, however, is one that demands the involvement of the builder. This is a participatory pastime. In modern terms, model railroading is similar to watching virtual reality three-dimensional television, where the

Fig. 2-1. The reality of real railroading is captured, in Abbott, on the 7 x 8-foot Burlington Route layout, built with ready-to-lay E-Z Track and ready-to-run locomotives and rolling stock.

sets, the actors, and the scripts are created by the viewer. In some ways, you really can bring dreams to life.

THE MAGIC WORLD OF MODEL RAILROADING

A magician is one who makes dreams of the impossible appear to be not only possible, but probable. He creates the illusion through the power of suggestion that you are, indeed, seeing what you would like to see. The model railroader needs a very similar bag of tricks to make his or her toy trains appear so realistic that they invoke the feelings we have for both real railroads and for toy trains. Many of the illustrations on these pages, and particularly those in the color section, are supposed to do just that: to give the impression of real railroading without losing the hint, at least, that the models began as toys. The effect that should be achieved on a model railroad is the same one that is created at Disneyland or Disney World, where you imagine you are boating through real caverns at the same time you know you are surrounded by only toy figures.

It is very easy to get carried away with the idea that you are running a real railroad, because you can use real railroad freight bills and order forms and much of the stuff that makes running a real railroad a job. Model railroading should be more than a job, it should be fun (and it is, even for me). The experienced model railroader often gets caught up in his own act, so to speak, and will build a few cars or structures that literally have every board and bolt and rivet that was on the real thing. This expert, caught in the whirlpool of realism, finds he cannot make his entire model railroad totally realistic and still find time to run it. Model railroading is fun when you can achieve a balance between realism and operation. You may like one more than the other, but don't let yourself get so involved in building that you don't have time to operate, or, conversely, don't get so caught up in its operation that you don't have time to

Fig. 2-2. The "magic" of a mirror doubles the apparent size of Alliance on the 9 x 9-foot Burlington Northern layout in Chapter 20.

create a reasonably realistic world for those operations.

This book is similar to magic books in that it reveals the secrets you need to create the illusion that your toy trains are real. The magic, here, is that you can build model railroads just as realistic as these because the models themselves are available ready-to-run, right down to track with roadbed. Two trains can operate on the same track with each under your total control, there are automatic working-knuckle couplers and breathtakingly realistic scenery made from materials as common as felt and weeds. The techniques are simple and most use materials you can buy in any town—it's what you do with those ready-to-run trains and basic materials that makes a model railroad. If you follow the examples you see here, you'll find you can capture that romantic thrill of real railroading, and it's no more magical than the stage magician's magic because you'll know all the secrets.

THE APPRENTICE MODEL RAILROADER

You cannot learn to build or to operate a model railroad by just reading one, two, three, or even a dozen books; you can learn only by applying the basic lessons to your own model railroad. Everything about model railroading falls into the learn-by-doing category. I have tried to show the simplest possible ways of doing everything you'll want to do to create a real railroad in miniature. I have also been particularly careful to select materials that are both inexpensive and readily available in hobby, toy, lumber, hardware, fabric and craft stores. You can obtain those materials and use them in the ways you see on these pages. Nobody was ever a born model railroader; each of us has to practice the simple techniques for painting, weathering, track laying, wiring, and the like to teach ourselves how to do it.

Most of the photographs in the book, with the exception of those of real railroads, were taken in my own workshop. Most of the model railroad photos were taken on either the 7 x 8-foot Burlington Route or the 9 x 9-foot Burlington Northern layouts illustrated in Chapter 20. There are no contest winners here, just average models that have been assembled and painted by average model railroaders especially for this book. Frankly, the 7 x 8-foot and 9 x 9-foot layouts in Chapter 20 are far too complex for a beginner or even for a group or club of beginners; rather, these are layouts you should consider as dream layouts that you could try for your second or third model railroad. Any of the buildings on that layout and all the scenery and wiring and operation ideas can be applied to the simpler 4 x 8-foot layouts in Chapter 3. Or, following the ideas in Chapter 4, you can expand that 4 x 8-foot layout into something as complete as the 7 x 8-foot Burlington Route layout as described in chapters 6 and 16. The technique of running trains around one or two ovals or a Figure 8 connecting one siding with the next, via rail, is another that can be used on any layout. Real railroads connect one town with another; a model railroad can connect one siding with another and each of them can be called a town to effectively match the function of a real railroad.

THINK SMALL

A completely finished and detailed layout like the one in Chapter 16 is the dream or goal of most model railroaders. Before I discuss how to create a layout like that, it would be helpful to see just what a railroad in miniature might be like.

HO SCALE

Imagine that you're an HO scale person, which means you're only 1/87 of your own size. You might wonder, at this point, why HO scale? HO scale is by far the most popular scale for model railroading; more than 75 percent of the hobbyists build in that scale. The only other scales that have more than 5 percent of the 350,000 or so model railroaders' attention are N scale (1/160 the size of the real thing), O scale (1/45 to 1/48 the size of the real thing) and G scale (also called Gauge 1, approximately 1/24 scale).

N SCALE

The tiny N scale locomotives and cars are fine if you want to run very long trains, because they do allow you to capture the train aspect of real railroading in a relatively small space. It is difficult to keep the track and wheels clean enough for stall-free operation in N scale, and the price of cars and locomotives may be as much as double those you see on these pages. The proportions of N-scale equipment are not as close a match for the real thing either; the rails and wheel flanges are several times too large, and the distance between coupled cars is far too great. The size of N-scale models, relative to your size, makes it advisable to build layouts large enough for long trains; an N-scale version of the Burlington Northern empire should be at least the same size as the 9 x 9-foot HO scale version.

O SCALE

O scale is primarily for experienced modelers who like to get really close to the models to enjoy their mass and bulk. O scale is only twice the linear size of HO, but it takes up four times the surface area and eight times the volume. An O scale version of the Burlington Northern layout would completely fill a two-car garage. The cost of the wood, plaster, track, and rolling stock could easily be eight times that of the HO scale layout, and the construction time might well be proportionally longer. HO scale models generally have as much visible detail to the naked eye as O scale models, and HO models are small enough to allow an empire in a space about equal to that needed for an N scale layout. If you're cramped for

space, then build a small, shelf-style layout, such as that in Chapter 20 (Figure 20-6), rather than going into N scale. If you like the bulk of O scale, then raise your layout to eye level and you'll find HO scale equipment looks quite large enough.

ALLIANCE TO EMMETT, ALL ABOARD

You can follow our trip by train from Alliance to Emmett over an imaginary branch of the Burlington Northern by looking at the illustrations in the color section. A satellite view of the layout and a track plan is illustrated in Figure 20-4 in Chapter 20, and a schematic diagram of the route is included in this chapter.

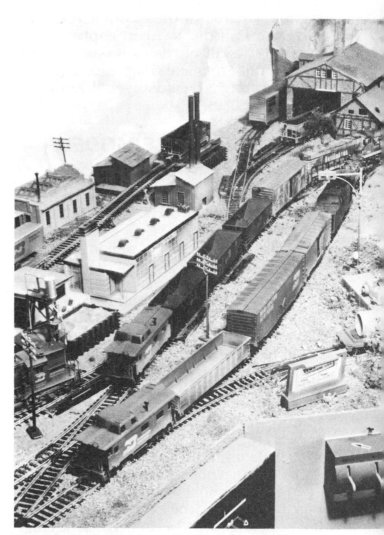

Fig. 2-3. Most freights on the 9 x 9-foot Burlington Northern begin their trips in Alliance yard. Our diesel-powered pedlar freight is scheduled out ahead of the steam-powered freight.

Both should provide more than enough reality to allow your imagination to see what real railroading in miniature is all about. Use the schematic diagram in conjunction with the track plan in Chapter 20 (make a photocopy if you need to) and you will be able to see what direction our train must take at each switch in order to travel over a two-loop layout connecting towns imaginary miles apart. Our train will travel very briefly over the crossed lines on the schematic diagram twice in its journey over the road. With the exception of those few feet of track, our flanged wheels will pass over the same rails only once as we travel from Alliance to Emmett on the Burlington Northern.

AN IMAGINARY JOURNEY

Imagine the town of Alliance as a place that might have a population of 30,000 people. It could be located in any state. Imagine it in southern Illinois if you wish, but it could be anywhere with a simple change of railroad names and colors on the locomotives. Alliance is a center of small manufacturing plants and feed mills. It is also a collection point for towns from miles around to load and unload trailers from piggyback flat cars and other lcl (less than carload) freight at the American Express Co. plant or at the Alliance Freight Station and its team track. Concrete pipe and other construction materials, fuel, seed, and lumber for the furniture factory are just a few of the commodities that arrive in Alliance by rail.

An endless string of coal-filled hopper cars are emptied at the electrical power-generating Alliance Company plant on

Fig. 2-4. Our train stops at Bedford, on the Burlington Northern layout, to find out whether any trains are scheduled on the Santa Fe interchange track into the tunnel.

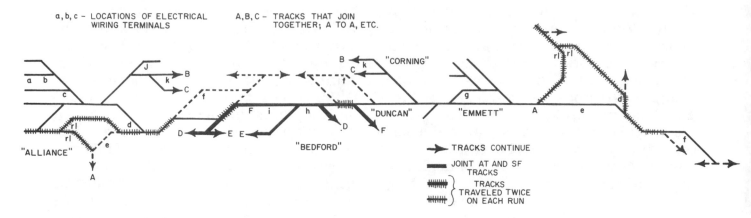

Fig. 2-5. The track on the 9 x 9-foot Burlington Northern can be traveled in a point-to-point route that duplicates the stops made by a real railroad. This is a schematic view of the complex track, unraveled to show that point-to-point route.

Fig. 2-6. The train en route to Alliance and Points East travels past the Duncan Grain Elevator twice—but not on the same tracks.

the outside of the town. The Burlington Northern has a connection or interchange with the Union Pacific just far enough away (track j) from town to keep the Union Pacific from serving local industry. There is also an engine house, fuel-oil facility, water tower (left over from the days of steam), and sand house at Alliance to service the locomotives used on the line. The few remaining steam locomotives receive their tender loads of coal by hand-shoveling at the Alliance Fuel trestle or directly from the coal mine at Corning. There is also a wye at Alliance to turn locomotives, cabooses, or passenger cars.

POINTS EAST

Trains are scheduled out of Alliance as rapidly as the line can handle them (see Chapter 19 for Sequence-Timetable operations) for Bedford, Corning, Duncan, Emmett, and Points East. The first stop will be the Santa Fe Interchange at Bedford, so our train rolls right past Duncan and its tiny grain elevator as though it doesn't exist (Figure 2-6). There's a Santa Fe freight train waiting on our right for us to clear the joint main line (actually the layout's inner oval) between Bedford and Duncan and Train 9 (from Points East - the holding siding "f" at Duncan) waiting to enter Emmett on our left. Bedford has no interchange traffic, so our train will continue east through a short tunnel and back past the Duncan Feed & Fuel grain elevator (Figure 2-7). The mine at Corning is always switched before dropping off or picking up any cars for Duncan on that Points East holding track "f". Our train has three loaded hopper cars for the Corning Mine and three empties are waiting there for us to pick them up. While we're switching, the

Fig. 2-7. The Burlington Northern boxcar (just visible above the station) will have to be pushed ahead of our locomotive so that we can take the siding to let the Amtrak local onto the main line out of Emmett.

steam-powered Train 5 for Emmett has left Alliance and is following our path to Bedford and beyond.

Emmett is our next stop, and we're scheduled to arrive there in time to meet the Amtrak streamliner. There's a passing siding at Emmett, but a car at the trailer train freight dock must be pushed away ahead of our locomotive to clear the main line for the Amtrak

passenger train (Figure 2-8). Our waybills tell us that the stock car in our train is supposed to be dropped off at the cattle pen outside of Emmett. There, a loaded hopper of coke is to be picked up at the coke ovens in Emmett. The series of train movements needed to perform those operations are illustrated, step by step, in Chapter 14. The load of coke won't be ready until our re-

Fig. 2-8. The second trip past the Duncan Grain Elevator routes the train toward the turnout that leads back to the Corning Mine.

Fig. 2-9. The three empty hopper cars are swapped for three loaded ones at the Corning Mine as the train heads for Emmett.

turn trip from Points East, so we can proceed on through Emmett after the Amtrak train leaves and after we spot that boxcar back at the Emmett Trailer Train platform.

MEETING THE SCHEDULE

The series of meets with other trains, the switching operations, and the use of waybills are just part of the real railroad action that has been condensed to model railroading. The work of meeting the deadlines of a real railroad timetable has been eliminated by simply scheduling trains as quickly and as often as you can operate them. The work of making out paperwork for waybills and switch lists has been reduced to just handling some playing cards and plastic envelopes, which is discussed in Chapter 19. The magic ways to have loaded freight cars are described in the Loads-In/Empties-Out section of Chapter 19. All these ideas will help to make even a simple oval with two sidings as much fun to operate as our Burlington Northern 9 x 9-foot branchline empire. You can, incidentally, perform nearly all of these operations on the smaller, and easier to build, 7 x 9 foot Burlington Route layout (Figure 20-5).

Fig. 2-10. A modern-era intermodal stack train of containers (all Athearn kits) pulled by a General Electric Dash 8-40BW diesel (a Walthers r-t-r) pulls past the Abbott station on the 7 x 8-foot Burlington Route layout.

PART II: PLANNING, BENCHWORK, TRACKWORK & WIRING

CHAPTER 3

Track Planning

THE PURPOSE of a model railroad is to simulate as many of the movements of a real railroad as possible within certain space limitations. The only difference you might notice between the track plans in this book and the layouts you might see in toy or department stores at Christmas time is that these layouts seem to have more than their share of stub-end sidings. The locations of the other switches have been selected because they can be used to route trains over a track system that is like the real railroads. Each of these layouts is designed to be used with point-to-point operation. The model trains that move over these tracks, like the real trains, will be bound for some distant town, rather than just running in circles. These miniatures will be running from one point to another; hence the term "point-to-point". The five 4 x 8-foot layouts in this chapter may look like only double-track ovals and Figure 8s with a few extra switches and sidings. These layouts, however, have a purpose like the prototype's, thanks to careful track planning.

A MATTER OF SPACE

Two conflicting desires are present in most model railroaders' minds. Each of us wants to build our railroad as much like the real ones as possible—and to operate it that way. Each of us also wants to see trains run and run and run. It's okay to watch a switch engine or a pedlar freight move cars in and out of sidings, but at least half the trains should still be running, or at least appear to be. You'll have to balance your list of priorities with the amount of space you have available. Most of the ready-to-run track sections and turnouts (switches) are inexpensive enough, so it will be space, rather than money, that will probably be the limiting factor. Remember, you can often select a rather complex track plan that can be started with just a simple oval or Figure 8 and extended with switches and track as quickly as your budget allows. If you happen to have the almost limitless space of an empty basement, a complete spare room, or a garage, you'll have to restrain yourself and build a smaller first-time layout before attempting to fill the larger space with benchwork, track, and scenery.

I suggest that you consider the following priorities before you create or select the track plan for your first layout.

1. Try to have at least four turnouts so you can include a passing siding as well as a facing-point and a trailing-point stub-end siding, such as those described in Chapter 19.

2. Do not feel you have to have enough length of storage tracks to hold every one of your cars and locomotives. Only 40 percent of the length of all the passing sidings and stub-end sidings should be filled with cars and locomotives. You need the empty factor in order to give the trains enough room to maneuver so they can switch. Keep any extra cars or locomotives on shelves beneath the layout.

3. Try to include at least one stub-end siding near the edge of the table. This can serve as a Fiddle Yard so you can maintain a 40-percent-full rate by hand-carrying cars and locomotives from storage shelves or drawers (rather

than from storage tracks) to and from the layout. You may want to include a two-, three-, or four-track Fiddle Yard (such as the one in Figure 20-6 in Chapter 20) inside an existing or specially built cabinet. The extensive Fiddle Yard trackage will allow you to have complete trains that appear and disappear from the scene during operating sessions (as they leave and arrive at those hidden Fiddle Yard tracks). The contents of those trains can be fiddled by hand before each operating session in order to arrange whatever variety of freight or passenger trains you might want to schedule on the layout.

4. I recommend that you arrange the layout so that there will be at least one possible route that is an oval or a Figure 8. This will allow continuous operation of the trains. Obviously, real railroads don't run around in circles; they have hundreds of miles of space.

5. You should arrange some of the sidings to allow point-to-point operation like the real railroads.

TWO HO TRACK SYSTEMS

Nearly all HO scale train sets are now supplied with track sections that have a built-in plastic roadbed and ballast that snap firmly together. Bachmann's E-Z Track is the most common track because Bachmann sells more train sets than any other firm, but there are also a lot of Life-Like train sets with their similar Power-Loc track and some hobby dealers carry the Atlas True Track©. In this book I often refer to these track systems with built-in roadbed simply as E-Z Track, and that is the track I used for the Burlington Route 7 x 8-foot railroad, which is made with blue Styrofoam and appears on the cover and elsewhere in this book. For simplicity, I refer to the older track systems with only rails and ties, but no roadbed or ballast and shown on all the track plans in this book, as sectional track systems.

These new track systems with built-in roadbed are illustrated in Chapter 4.

E-Z Track, Power-Loc track and True Track all have track sizes that match the sectional track shown in all the plans in this book. In fact, you can connect almost any brand of sectional track with these newer systems with built-in roadbed, but that interchangeability will work effectively only if the track is nailed or glued to a tabletop so the sectional track can be supported with cork roadbed. Also, note that the Atlas True Track relies on the rail joiners to hold the track together with small tabs in the plastic roadbed to aid alignment. To be most effective, True Track should be nailed or glued to a tabletop rather than used on the floor or as portable and movable track. None of the track with roadbed systems interface with one another except where the rails join. It is possible to provide interfaces between E-Z Track, Power-Loc track or True Track and sectional track with cork roadbed as shown in Chapter 4, but I would recommend that you pick one brand for the entire layout.

The only plans in this book that can be built with E-Z Track, Power-Loc track or True Track are the layouts in Figures 3-1, 3-2 and 3-3 in this chapter and the Burlington Route plan 20-5 in Chapter 20 (and illustrated throughout the book). The turnouts in these three systems are designed with full-length curved track sections. The older sectional track turnouts, like those illustrated in Figure 3-6 and in all the plans in this book, have a separate 1/3-curve track section. Those 1/3-curve sections are marked with a W on all the track plans, but that track section is actually an integral part of every E-Z Track, Power-Loc track and True Track turnout. The photographs in 4-10, 4-11, 4-12 ,4-1 and, 4-14 show how to use a razor saw to cut an E-Z Track turnout to produce this 1/3-curve section. Frankly, cutting one of these switches should only be attempted if you are mounting the track permanently on tabletop.

The lesson here is to use only plans designed expressly for E-Z Track, Power-Loc track or True Track with these

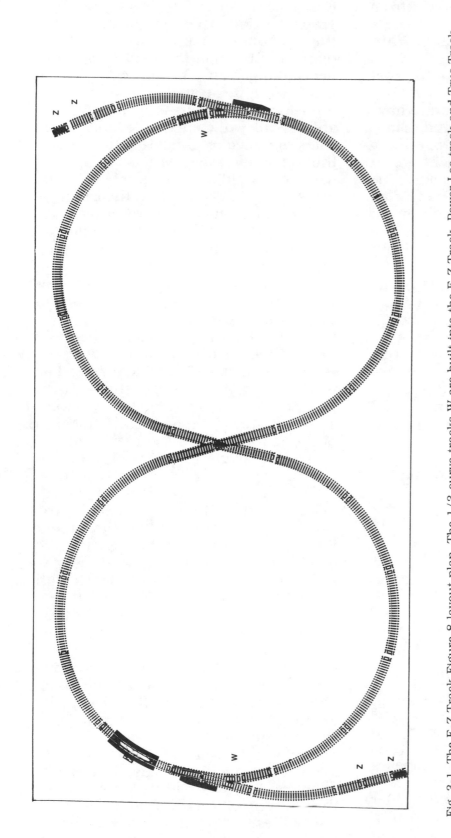

Fig. 3-1. The E-Z Track Figure-8 layout plan. The 1/3-curve tracks W are built into the E-Z Track, Power-Loc track and True Track turnouts. (See Figure 9-9 for the key to track symbols.)

Track Sections Required

3-inch straight Z	4
Bumper track	2
30-degree crossing	1
Full 30-degree curve	21
Curved terminal track	1
1/3 curve (10 degree) W	2
Right-hand turnout	2

brands of track. Bachmann's *Model Railroading Made E-Z with Bachmann's E-Z Track* book includes 20 track plans. Life-Like and Atlas have booklets included with their train sets that have other plans. The Bachmann book describes some of the geometry of their system that you must follow to design track plans with E-Z Track. Briefly, if you add any straight track sections to one side of a curve, you must add that same amount to the other side of the curve to maintain the geometry of the system so the track sections will align properly and lock together firmly. You can build any of these plans with conventional sectional track, but you can not use E-Z Track, Power-Loc track or True Track to build most plans designed for conventional sectional track. Do note that plans 3-1, 3-2, 3-3 and 20-5 are drawn using conventional track, however, that 1/3-curve is included at each switch. When you assemble these plans with E-Z Track, Power-Loc track or True Track, you simply ignore those 1/3-curve sections because they are already part of each turnout.

4 X 8-FOOT E-Z TRACK PLANS

THE E-Z TRACK FIGURE-8 PLAN

The Figure 8 is one of the most interesting of all the possible model-railroad track plans because it gives the effect of many trains crossing at a single point. The effect is somewhat more credible and more realistic than watching a train work its way around and around an oval. The Bachmann E-Z Track system offers two crossings with built-in roadbed and ballast, a 90-degree crossing and a 30-degree crossing. The 90-degree crossing can be used to build simple Figure-8 layouts that can be developed into something as complex as in Figure 3-5, if you do not include any of the curved switches or the Reverse Loop Section.

The E-Z Track 30-degree crossing is the length of 1-1/3 sections of conventional straight track and a special Figure-8 track plan is required to fit the curves to that 30-degree crossing. If you follow the layout design rule for these track systems, you must add track to the opposite sides of the two curves of the Figure 8 to compensate for the extra length of the 30-degree crossing. In this case, about 1-1/2 inches are needed in each curve and the only place to get that short a piece of track is to take advantage of the design of the E-Z Track turnout and add a turnout to each curve at the positions shown. The turnouts in this plan, then, are not optional, nor can they be located anywhere else on the curves. You can add additional turnouts, but, if you add one to one side of the curve, you must add another turnout positioned 180 degrees around the curve on the opposite side of the circle. This particular plan requires a minimum of 3 feet, 6 inches by 6 feet, 9 inches so it will fit well within a 4 x 8-foot area.

4 X 8-FOOT E-Z TRACK MAIN LINE

The track plan in Figure 3-2 shows how to make a double-track main line layout in a minimum 4-foot-wide space. The inner oval on this plan includes a diagonal cutoff track that makes a reverse loop for turning whole trains. That inner oval is also the minimum size to include a reverse loop. The arrows on the plan indicate where insulating rail joiners must be installed for two-train operations. Conventional power packs should be used to avoid electrical short circuits on the reverse loop. The use and installation of these rail joiners is explained in Chapter 9. If you want to avoid using these gaps, do not include the diagonal track across the oval. Avoid the need for the other two insulating gaps (at each crossover) by using one of the Digital Command Control power packs described in Chapter 9, or simply do not install the two crossover pairs of right and left turnouts on the far left of the plan. The plan is designed with all 18-inch radius curves. You can substitute 22-inch radius curves on the right end by leaving out the matching pair of 3-inch straights on the long straight

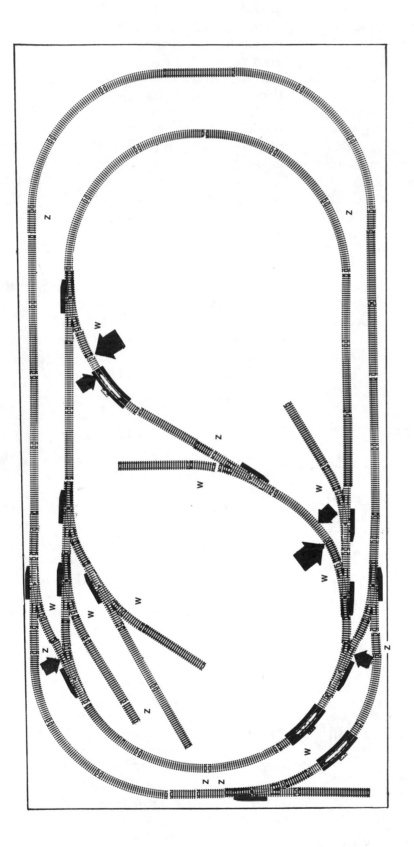

Fig. 3-2. The 4 x 8-foot E-Z Track Main Line layout plan. The 1/3-curve tracks W are built into the E-Z Track, Power-Loc track and True Track turnouts. If the layout is built with Life-Like Power-Loc track, two 3-inch straights must be substituted for the 9-inch straight at P. (See Figure 9-9 for the key to track symbols.)

Track Sections Required

9-inch straight	22
3-inch straight Z	12
Full 30-degree curve	20
1/3 curve (10 degree) W	12
Curved terminal track	2
Right-hand turnout	2
Left-hand turnout	10

edges of the oval and one of the two 3-inch straights at the far right end of the outer oval.

THE E-Z TRACK BURLINGTON ROUTE

This plan can be used so trains can be operated in the complex patterns described for the 9 x 9-foot Burlington Northern layout in Chapter 20. It is a simple 4 x 8-foot variation of the 7 x 8-foot Burlington Route E-Z Track layout in Figure 20-5 that is featured throughout this book. The 4 x 8-foot plan in Figure 3-2, does not have the 1 x 3-foot extension of the L-shaped layout in Figure 20-5, and it does not have that layout's wye to reverse locomotives. The plan in Figure 3-2 does, however, have a reverse loop cutoff running diagonally across the layout so complete trains can be reversed. It also has six industrial sidings that can be used to serve a coal mine, a power plant and other industries. It also lacks the connections for the Loads-In/Empties-Out operations between the mine and power house described in Chapter 19. If you want to include those types of operations, you can remove the diagonal reverse loop track and substitute two curved through sidings on the inner oval like those in Figure 20-5. This plan can also be used to duplicate the Point-to-Point Run operations described later in this chapter for the layout in Figure 3-4.

Since this plan does not include a 30-degree crossing, it can be built with Power-Loc track if a third piece of 3-inch straight (or simply a single 9-inch straight in place of the three 3-inch pieces) is used at the far left end. Also, two pairs of 3-inch straight track sections can be substituted for the 9-inch straight track sections marked P on the plan. This layout can be built as shown with Atlas True Track.

THE 4 X 8-FOOT E-Z TRACK FIGURE 8 WITH WYE

This 4 x 8-foot plan in Figure 3-3 is a development of the Figure 8 for E-Z Track, with one side of the 8 connected with two turnouts to produce a reverse

loop. The plan also has a passing siding added to one end and two additional stub-ended sidings. Each of these turnouts is necessary to maintain the geometry of the plan, so you can add turnouts but you cannot leave any of the four sidings out or the track will not align properly. This is the closest possible design to the Out-and-Back plan in Figure 3-5 that can be assembled with E-Z Track, Power-Loc track or True Track within a 4 x 8-foot area. It can, however, be operated as an Out-and-Back by using the passing siding as the originating and terminating town as described for Figure 3-5.

4 X 8-FOOT SECTIONAL TRACK PLANS

The layout plan in Figure 3-4 is a simpler plan than the oval in Figure 3-2. The plan in Figure 3-4 cannot be assembled using E-Z Track, Power-Loc track or True Track because these systems do not allow the type of crossover turnouts shown at E and F. You could, however, simulate all of the operations possible on this layout using the plan in Figure 3-2. This layout appears to be nothing more than a double-track mainline oval, but it has far greater possibilities. The plan could be shortened to as little as 4 x 6 feet, but you would have to eliminate the switch to H. The trackage is angled, relative to the sides of the table, to improve the effect of trains running along a table edge. By angling the track, the train is moving toward or away from the edge, and this lends a far greater sense of reality to your operation.

THE MAIN LINE

This plan is designed so either one or two trains can be operated at the same time. One train can be circulating on the outer oval while the second runs on the inner oval and switches the sidings. For realistic operation, however, the layout can be used as a point-to-point run for a single train, beginning at siding A and traveling through the cross-

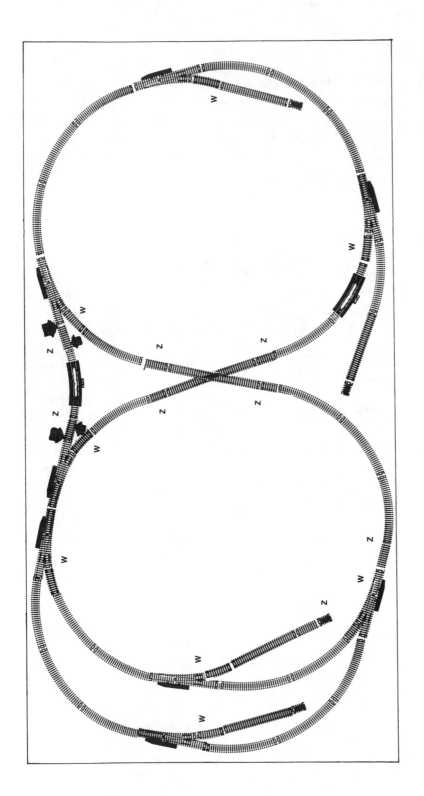

Fig. 3-3. The 4 x 8-foot E-Z Track Figure 8 with wye layout plan. The 1/3-curve tracks W are built into the E-Z Track, Power-Loc track and True Track turnouts. (See Figure 9-9 for the key to track symbols.)

Track Sections Required

9-inch straight	4
3-inch straight Z	8
Bumper track	4
30-degree crossing	1
Full 30-degree curve	23
1/3 curve (10 degree) W	8
Right-hand turnout	4
Left-hand turnout	4

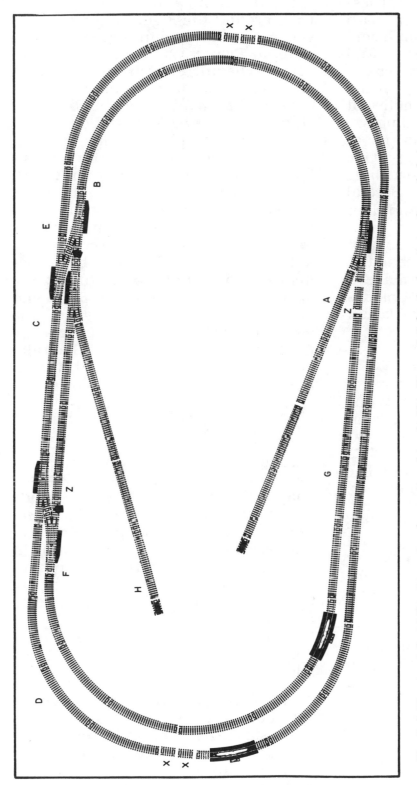

Fig. 3-4. The 4 x 8-foot Main Line plan for sectional track. (See Figure 9-9 for the key to track symbols.)

Track Sections Required

9-inch straight	24
3-inch straight Z	2
2-inch straight X	4
Bumper track	2
Full 30-degree curve	22
Curved terminal tracks	2
Right-hand turnout	3
Left-hand turnout	3

over from B to C, around the outer oval through D and E, and over the cross-over to F, for a trip halfway around the inner oval to G and B, and the final destination siding H. The train's path would then be reversed, but not before the locomotive used the run-around switching maneuvers at the two cross-overs, thus placing the caboose at the rear of the train and the locomotive at the front for the trip back to siding A.

Additional curved turnouts in at least two of the corners could provide other towns and industrial-switching possibilities along the way. Several turnouts could be added at A and H for locomotive holding tracks and additional industries. There's even room for a passing siding at A (such as that at A on Figure 3-5), which could make it more of an independent town. A mountain ridge down the middle of the layout would separate A and H visually.

THE FIGURE-8 PLAN FOR SECTIONAL TRACK

The layout plan in Figure 3-5 is one of the best I have seen using conventional sectional track for the popular and practical 4 x 8-foot space, which is the site for most first-time layouts. The only drawback to this layout, however, is that you cannot see two trains in motion and sit back and watch them like you can with the layouts in Figure 3-2 and 3-4. The layout is drawn with just enough terminal tracks and gaps for operating one train (the gaps on the reversing section are there just for that feature, as described in Chapter 9). The long siding A to B, as well as the siding F, could become a separate block, so you could operate one train switching in either of those areas while a second train circulated around the Figure 8.

OUT-AND-BACK

This layout (Figure 3-5) is also designed for point-to-point operation from A through B, C, D, and E (in that order) to F. A run-around or passing siding at both A and F allows the train to operate engine-first on the return

trip to A, and to be rearranged or switched for an engine-first trip back to F. If you want to add some mileage on the route from A to F, circulate the train around the Figure 8 (just as you would circulate around either or both ovals in Figures 20-5 and 20-6) until you're scheduled to have it arrive at A or F. The advantage of this layout, as compared to many others, is that it includes a reversing-loop section so you can turn complete trains around hands-off. The reversing loop would allow you to operate to and from A, with F as a town along the way. The route would begin at A and proceed through B, C, D, and E to G, and from G on back to B, around into the reversing-loop section through E, D, and C, before going back to B and into A. This type of operation is called Out-and-Back, and its advantage is that most of the switching operations, including placing the locomotive at the front of the train, are only done in one large yard (at A on this layout).

DO-IT-YOURSELF TRACK PLANNING

You can create your own track plans by taking advantage of the simple snap-together feature of most brands of HO scale sectional track. Each section of track is part of a geometric system based on 9-inch pieces of straight track (or fractions thereof) and on 10- and 30-degree segments or sections of a 360-degree circle of track. If you use a 30-60-90-degree plastic triangle to help plan your trackwork, you'll be far more likely to get those critical track alignments right.

TRACK PLANNING WITH E-Z TRACK

You can use this system to design layouts using E-Z Track, Power-Loc track or True Track, but I would not recommend it. These track systems with built-in roadbed and ballast demand much more precise alignment of the track sections than conventional track because the roadbed interlocks mechanically. Really, there's no need to use cut-outs to plan

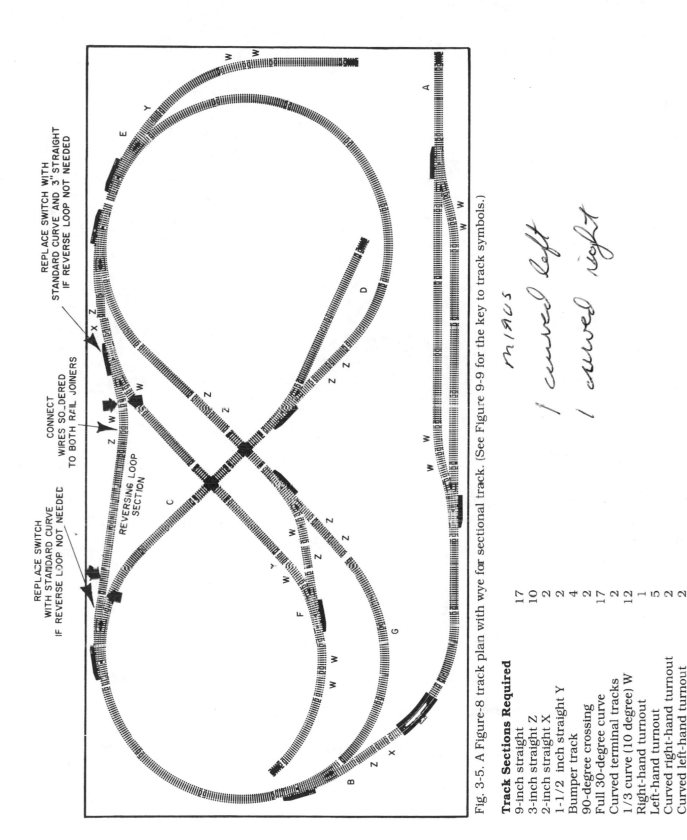

Fig. 3-5. A Figure-8 track plan with wye for sectional track. (See Figure 9-9 for the key to track symbols.)

Track Sections Required

9-inch straight	17
3-inch straight Z	10
2-inch straight X	2
1-1/2 inch straight Y	2
Bumper track	4
90-degree crossing	2
Full 30-degree curve	17
Curved terminal tracks	2
1/3 curve (10 degree) W	12
Right-hand turnout	1
Left-hand turnout	5
Curved right-hand turnout	2
Curved left-hand turnout	2

minus

1 curved left

1 curved right

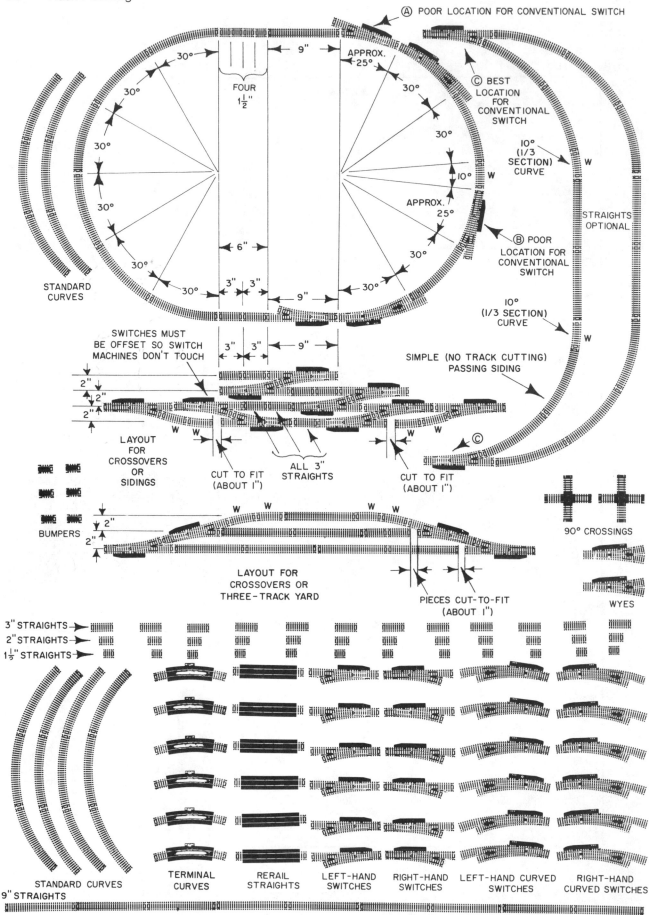

Fig. 3-6. Scale track sections and track geometry basics for copy-and-cutout track planning using sectional track.

with these systems because it is far easier to simply use the track itself. Just remember the rule of design with these systems: If you add a switch or straight track on one side of a circle or oval, you must add a matching piece of track on the opposite side to maintain the geometry and alignment.

USING TURNOUTS

The turnouts in the E-Z Track and True Track system use the same geometry as those in these sectional track cutouts. Each turnout has approximately 1-1/2 inches of extra length through the curved portion of the turnout (see Figure 4-9 in Chapter 4). Thus, when you replace a piece of curved track in, say, an oval with a turnout, you actually add 1-1/2 inches to the oval and that distance must be compensated for by adding another turnout to the opposite side. An alternative is to use two turnouts on one side of the circle or oval and to add a piece of 3 inch straight track on the opposite

side, 180 degrees around the circle. The Life-Like Power-Loc turnouts do not use this system; the turnout is the same length through either the curved or the straight portion. You can, then, replace any piece of Power-Loc curved track, even on an oval or circle, with a Power-Loc turnout and the geometry and alignment of the system will be maintained.

REDUCE TO SCALE

All the plans in this book are reduced to a scale of 1 inch to the foot, which means that each foot on the layout is just 1 inch on the plan, and each inch on the layout is but 1/16 inch on the plan. A draftsman's triangular ruler has one side marked in 1-inch scale, or you can use the 1/4-inch marks on any ruler for measuring 3-inch increments on these plans. Use the drafting triangle or ruler to pencil in the outline of the available area you have for your layout. If you're looking for something for a 4 x 8-foot board, just trace the outline of the table

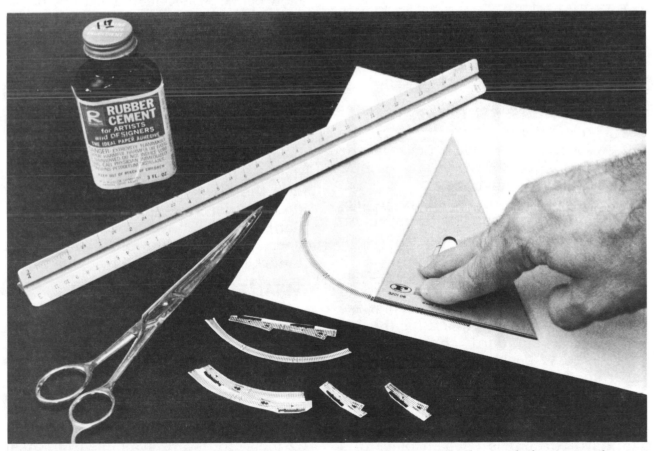

Fig. 3-7. Use a ruler and a 30-60-90-degree triangle to obtain accurate track plans with the copy-and-cutout scale track sections in Figure 3-6.

in Figures 3-2 or 3-3 and design your layout within that space; the track plan in Figure 20-6, in Chapter 20, is the 5 x 9-foot size of a ping pong table, so you can trace it to provide an outline if you have that size table available.

TRACK SECTIONS

The track sections in Figure 3-6 can be photocopied, then cut out with scissors and glued down with rubber cement. This means that you can plan what track you need before you buy it. When you cut the track sections apart, keep the ends (where the rail joiners would be) perfectly even with the ties, but don't worry about how close you trim on the sides of the ties. The object is to get an idea of how well the track will fit together. Use the 30-60-90-degree triangle to align the ends of the curves. The paper track plan may not be a perfect replica of what you will actually build because there may be some areas where small filler pieces of track might have to be used (such as the 1/2W and 1/2Y sections in Figure 20-6). You can avoid having to cut these fillers and have a more accurate track alignment if you pay attention to the geometry of the system.

ALIGNING TRACK SECTIONS

The oval, the passing siding on the left, and the yard-style tracks in the center of Figure 3-6 are there to show you how the conventional sectional track pieces must be fitted for perfect alignment and where slight misalignments might have to occur. The standard turnouts (either remote-controlled or manual) are best placed in areas where a 9-inch straight section would normally go. The curved portion of these turnouts is a perfect match for the 18-inch-radius standard curved tracks, but the curve begins about 1-1/2 inches from the single track end of each turnout. Two standard turnouts on the right end of the oval show you how this can create a misalignment when the standard turnout is used in place of a curved track. Each standard turnout is

supplied with a single piece of 3-curved track (10 degrees of a circle-marked W on the plans). The curved sides of those standard turnouts are the length of a standard curve track section, but there is still that 1-1/2 inches of straight track to be accounted for.

If you can use two turnouts in a half-circle curve, such as the one on the right of the oval, then just one of the 1/3 curves will almost compensate for the portions of the circle that those short pieces of straight track fill. A slight misalignment in a curve will be made that way because you are actually lacking about 10 degrees worth of curved track. Follow the rule that if you must use a turnout to replace a piece of curved track in the middle of a curve (where there are curved tracks on both ends of the turnout), use one of the curved turnouts. Another rule is to use the standard turnouts only to replace a piece of straight track. The turnouts at either end of the passing siding to the far right will allow perfect track alignment. Any of the curved pieces of track on the left of the oval could be replaced with a curved turnout without affecting the geometry or the alignment of the track in any way.

When you add a piece of straight track (or a turnout or 90-degree crossing) to one side of an oval, you must add exactly that length of straight track to the opposite side in order to maintain track alignment. Many track configurations have the 180 degrees of track that create an oval (including any Figure-8 plan), so you'll have to watch for them when you're working out a track plan and when you are actually laying track.

PARALLEL SIDINGS

You may find it helpful for both track planning and actual track-laying to draw the center line of the track with a pencil. Each of the r-t-r curves is 18 inches from the center of the track, with the exception of the 22-inch-radius curves on the outside of the curved turnouts. Curved track sections with a 22-inch radius are available from most manufacturers of HO scale track, but they are not shown in any of the plans for sectional track in this book. (Those 22-inch radius curves were, however, used on a slight modification of the layout, the Burlington Route, in Figure 20-5 and pictured on the cover and throughout this book.)

Parallel straight tracks can be spaced 2 inches center-to-center. The 3-inch straight-track sections will often fill in the gaps, but some places will need little 1-inch pieces of filler track. Note: I do not recommend that you try to cut a piece of filler track that short. In most cases, you can add the length of the adjacent track to the required cut-to-fit filler in order to increase the length. You may have to make a short piece of flexible track, using the techniques shown in Chapter 7. The filler tracks shorter than 1-1/2 inches just aren't strong enough, and, since you have to cut one to fit in any case, you might as well make it long enough so that it will have plenty of strength. You can squeeze a large number of sidings into a small space if you align the switches and/or the two 1/3 curves (W on all the plans for layouts) as shown on Figure 3-6.

CLEARANCE

It's best to check very tight track-planning situations with actual pieces of track and, if necessary, with structures you might want to include as shown in Chapter 14, Figures 14-12 and 14-13. You don't need to build the entire layout, just the area where you expect to have tight clearance problems. Always try to leave room at the end of any passing siding for at least one locomotive, and, if switching must be done on switches with facing points toward that end, allow room for a locomotive and your longest car. The far upper left corner in the town of Alliance on the track plan in Figure 20-3 and at Abbott on the track plan in Figure 20-5 are examples of confined area where a minimum car-and-locomotive length is needed. You can often gain a few extra inches in such tight areas by using conventional track rather than bumper tracks at the end of the stub-end siding. You can just glue on some plastic ties cut from old track sections or use the bumpers shown in Chapter 7, Figure 7-21. The real railroads often use a method to stop cars from rolling off the ends of tracks.

PLANNING UPHILL AND DOWNHILL GRADES

Uphill and downhill grades are more trouble than they're worth in terms of realism. You can make the edge of the

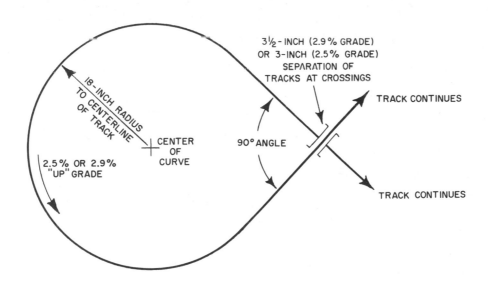

Fig. 3-8. The shortest route to create an overpass for HO scale layouts.

table slope up or down (like it does for the river-crossing on the 9 x 9-foot Burlington Northern layout and the 7 x 8-foot Burlington Route layout in Chapter 20) in order to give the effect of uphill or downhill railroading. It's hard enough to keep the tracks level without trying to build in a slope. The most difficult problems to overcome are those that result from too sudden a change at the top or the bottom of any hill. The diagram in Figure 3-8 shows the percentage of grade that is needed for the bridge and trestle kits in the train sets to elevate the tracks about 3 inches above one another at the crossing. If you are using a plywood and Homasote roadbed (see Chapter 5) for a bridge inside a tunnel, you will need to have at least 3-1/2 inches of clearance below the Homasote at the bridge. That 2.5- to 2.9-percent grade is as steep as you'd want on your model railroad. The real trains seldom exceed 1 percent on

their climbs. That grade percentage is figured on so many units per hundred, so a 2.5-percent grade would be a rise of 2.5 units for every 100 units of track.

It is extremely difficult to apply scenery to the simple plastic trestle supports, except on a short industrial trestle. If you do use grades on your layout, then you should be capable of doing the carpentry work to build the open-grid type of benchwork shown in Chapter 5. Alternately, you can use the lightweight blue Styrofoam insulation construction methods with Woodland Scenic's Subterrain system of 2-percent or 4-percent grades made with flexible Inclines supports shown in Chapter 6 (Figure 6-27). Use the chart in Figure 3-9 to determine how steep any of the grades on your layout must be. The figures above 3 percent are there only for interest. You would be lucky to get a locomotive alone up a hill as steep as 10 percent.

Planning, Benchwork, Trackwork and Wiring

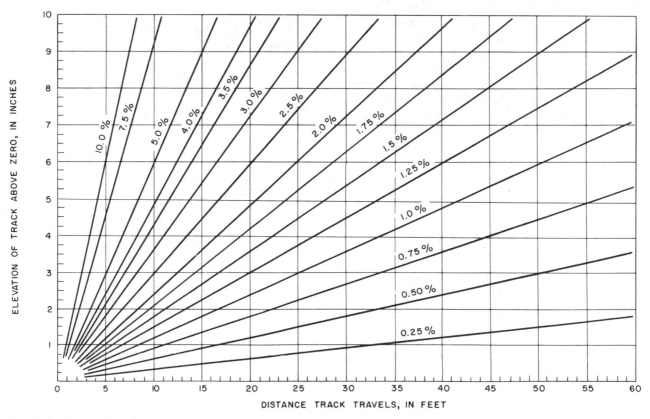

Fig. 3-9. Chart of grade percentages.

DO'S AND DON'TS FOR TRACK PLANNING

- Do design a trackplan, even if you use actual track sections, before nailing the track in place.
- Do build any layout on a shelf no wider than about 30 inches or on peninsulas no wider than 60 inches so you can reach the track and scenery at the rear of the layout.
- Do position yards, tracks and industrial sidings where you will want to couple and uncouple cars and operate turnouts, near the forward edges of the table for better accessibility and easier viewing.
- Do try to find space for an around-the-wall layout, built on a shelf 12 to 30 inches wide. The trains will really seem to be going someplace.
- Do keep most of the tracks at least 6 inches away from the forward edge of the table to leave room for some foreground scenery on at least half of the layout.

- Don't try to fill a 4 x 8-foot piece of plywood with a layout and shove the layout into a corner. You won't be able to reach anything along the back 18 inches of the layout.
- Don't build a 4 x 8-foot layout as your final layout unless you really are limited to that small an area.
- Don't place complicated trackage at the rear of the layout, even if it is only 30 inches away from the front of the table.
- Don't attempt to squeeze in tracks that don't match the track geometry, they'll create sudden lurches in the smooth path of the rails that will cause derailments.
- Don't try to cram track into every square inch of tabletop. There won't be room for credible scenery or structures.

CHAPTER 4

Movable Model Railroading

ONE OF THE JOYS of model rail-roading is designing a layout, building it, then redesigning and rebuilding it. That's difficult—but possible—with sectional track that's been nailed or glued to tabletop. The track sections that are included with most of today's HO scale train sets make it quite easy to create and recreate your own track layout designs. The new track systems have built-in plastic roadbed and ballast and snap-together alignment, like Bachmann's E-Z Track and Life-Like's Power-Loc track. With these new systems it is no longer necessary to nail or glue the track to a tabletop. In fact, you can continue to operate your layout on the floor if you wish, because these new systems provide adequate isolation from the dust and lint on the floor. They also provide positive locking and between-track sections. You can certainly create a track plan or system to suit your fancy with any conventional sectional track, E-Z Track and Power-Loc. With these types of track you have the realism of built-in ballast shoulders and the lock-together feature that makes track alignment easy.

E-Z TRACK VS. POWER-LOC TRACK

The Bachmann E-Z Track system is the best-selling sectional track and ballast system, because Bachmann sells more train sets. Most hobby shops also sell Life-Like's Power-Loc system and it, too, is included in tens of thousands of train sets. Both E-Z Track and Power-Loc track are available with either steel alloy or nickel silver rails. The nickel silver is a bit

easier to keep clean (for electrical conductivity to decrease the chance of stalled trains) but there is no major advantage. Both brands offer gray roadbed with the nickel silver, but it's not much more realistic than the black roadbed furnished with the steel rail.

There are other systems, including Atlas' True Track©, Kato's Unitrack and Marklin's C-Track, that include interlocking, built-in ballast, nickel silver rail, and are even more realistic than E-Z Track or Power-Loc track. E-Z Track, Power-Loc track and Atlas' True-Track are interchangeable with the standard sectional track shown on all the drawings in this book at the ends of the rails. Unfortunately, none of these three brands are interchangeable with one another's roadbed interfaces, so you really cannot mix and match brands unless you nail or glue the track to a tabletop. Neither Kato nor

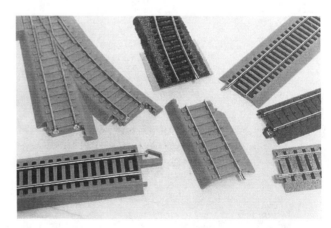

Fig. 4-1. The most common track with roadbed systems include (clockwise, from lower left): Bachmann E-Z Track, Life-Like Power-Loc track, cork roadbed with sectional track, Atlas True Track, Marklin C-Track, Kato Unitrack and (center) a Power-Loc 3-inch adapter track section.

Marklin offer track sizes that are interchangeable with the standard sectional track pieces. Their ballast interlocking systems are also not interchangeable with any other systems so, if you like the realism of Kato or Marklin, pick one and use only that brand. The rule: if you are going to operate on the floor or want to be able to rearrange the track on a tabletop, pick one brand and stick to it.

SELECTING THE BEST TRACK

If you are mounting your track on a tabletop, however, you can mix and match just about any brand including the conventional sectional track on cork roadbed. Life-Like offers a 3-inch-long Power-Loc adapter track with no ballast connection on one end that you can use to connect different brands. It's just about as simple, however, to cut off any protruding interlocking tabs from both track sections and simply join the rails with rail joiners as you would with conventional sectional track. To join conventional sectional track to any of these brands, mount the sectional track on cork roadbed and, if necessary, add a piece of cardboard or two to shim the rails level with the plastic ballast. Frankly, it's usually not worth the trouble to try to interchange brands or to salvage your old sectional track by mixing it with E-Z Track, Power-Loc track or True Track.

There are some disadvantages to the E-Z Track, Power-Loc track and True-Track sections, including the relatively sharp 18-inch radius of the turnouts. All three brands offer 22-inch radius curves (as well as 18-inch radius), but that does not solve the problem of the 18-inch radius at the turnouts. Diesel locomotives with twelve wheels, most medium-to-large-size steam locomotives and 86 to 89-foot-long passenger cars and freight cars will often derail over these turnouts. There's little you can do to adjust the turnout, the locomotive or the car to prevent the problem. Kato and Marklin offer large-radii turnouts with their systems. If you re-ally need to operate these larger locomotives, I would recommend that you consider using a minimum Number 4-size turnout and a minimum 24-inch radius curve. Both of these options will produce layouts that require larger spaces than those shown in this book. It would be possible, for example, to squeeze just a single-track oval on a 5 x 9-foot tabletop using Number 4 turnouts and a minimum 24-inch radius curves.

LAYOUTS ON THE FLOOR

E-Z Track and Power-Loc track have hefty plastic roadbed with sturdy aligning clips. E-Z Track still uses rail joiners, but their purpose is only to provide electrical flow. It's the plastic tabs and slots that provide alignment and strength. Power-Loc track has a more positive interlocking, with copper contact tabs on the interface to provide electrical flow and, thus, it needs no rail joiners. The Atlas True Track roadbed has aligning tabs, but it is really best used on tabletop layouts rather than on the floor. The Kato and Marklin systems have somewhat larger plastic and metal rail joiners but they, too, are best used on a tabletop rather than on the floor.

One of the most important lessons you can learn from this book is to mount sectional track firmly on a tabletop with nails or glue. The sectional track, with just ties and rails, uses the thin metal rail joiners to join both the rails and the track sections themselves. The joiners are just not strong enough to hold anything but the rails.

That lesson, however, does not apply if you are using the new track systems like E-Z Track and Power-Loc track with built-in roadbed and ballast that snaps together. These systems can be operated on the floor. There are still good reasons to build a table, if only to get the track and trains up to eye level where you can really see the details and achieve a more realistic view. Even if you opt for a tabletop layout, I'd suggest that you use the floor and the actual track sections to design a layout. Now, at least, you have the option of running the trains on the floor if you wish.

SCENERY FOR FLOOR-LEVEL LAYOUTS

You can lay E-Z Track or Power-Loc track right on the carpet, linoleum or bare wood floor and just run trains. If you use duct tape on the joints of Bachmann's E-Z Track, you can even lift a simple oval as a unit and store it on a wall. Power-Loc has joints firm enough that you don't need the duct tape. Moving entire layouts like this is risky, however, because the plastic material itself is not strong or flexible enough to withstand much bending. I would recommend that you disassemble any layouts into segments or sub-assemblies, with no more than six or eight track sections per segments. It only takes a few minutes to disassemble and to re-assemble and you won't risk breaking track sections.

You may, however, want to have something besides the bare floor and table or chair legs to surround the trains. There's a new system of covering the earth on a permanent layout in Chapter 7 that I call the Grass-That-Grows concept because the grass really does grow through real dirt. The basic material is felt from a fabric store. I would suggest that you use the same beige felt that's the basis for the Grass-That-Grows system, but spray the beige felt lightly with a Kelly Green paint so that only the upper fibers are colored and let it dry thoroughly. Skip the application of real dirt and the rest of the steps shown in Figures 17-8 through 17-16 in Chapter 17 so you don't have any loose material to make a mess of the floor, track and equipment. If you'd rather not paint the felt, just buy green felt like that shown in Figures 4-2, 4-3, 4-4 and 4-5. Wad-up some newspapers to form a mountain ridge and put them on the floor before covering it with a 4 x 8-foot piece of felt. The felt I purchased, incidentally, came only in 6-foot widths, so I tucked the

edges under. For trees and shrubs, use lichen and ready-made trees available from a hobby shop. For streams, use wrinkled-up aluminum foil or clear plastic wrap, with lichen bushes placed along the shores. You can make roads from cardboard. And all of this, the felt, the scenery and the buildings, is as portable as the track itself.

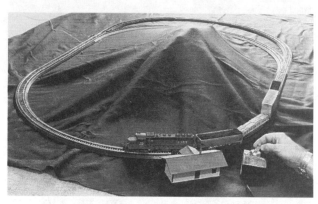

Fig. 4-2 For movable scenery, wad-up some newspapers and drape them with a 4 x 8-foot piece of green or beige felt. The 7 x 8-foot Burlington Route layout in Chapter 20 (Figure 20-5) began with this simple E-Z Track oval with an extra pair of turnouts and four pieces of 18-inch radius curved track.

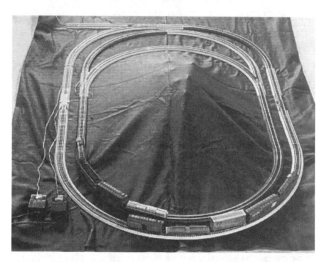

Fig.4-3. The simplest way to run two trains is to lay two unconnected ovals and use two power packs. Here, the outer oval has a 22-inch radius curve in the foreground, with an 18-inch radius curve (and two 3-inch straights plus a left-hand turnout) in the distance.

FROM AN OVAL TO THE BURLINGTON ROUTE ON THE FLOOR

I really did design the plan for the 7 x 8-foot Burlington Route on the floor. It's pictured on the cover of this book and shown as a track plan in Chapter

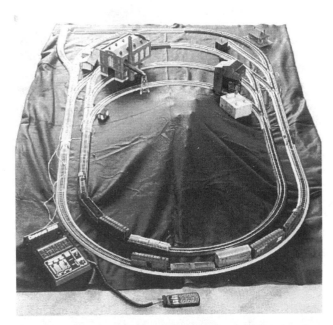

Fig. 4-4. This is the way the Burlington Route plan in Chapter 20 (Figure 20-5) would look if the layout was built without the 1 x 3-foot extension and the wye. Here, the two pairs of crossovers have been added to connect the inner and outer ovals. The power pack is an MRC Command 2000 Digital Command Control unit that allows you to run two trains on the same track without a second power pack and no extra wiring as described in Chapter 9.

20 (Figure 20-5). I started with a simple oval with a passing siding on one end as shown in Figure 4-2. I then added an outer oval with a second power pack and a 22-inch radius curve on the nearest end as shown in Figure 4-3. Note that there are no crossover pairs of turnouts between the inner and outer oval so each power pack controls its own independent track and train. There's a mixture of the E-Z Track with black roadbed and steel rails and E-Z Track with gray roadbed and nickel silver rails. There's no need to discard the steel-railed E-Z Track that came with the train set.

Finally, I moved track in and out of the plan and developed the layout in Figure 4-4. I added two pairs of turnouts to connect the inner and outer ovals. To avoid the need for any insulating gaps (as explained in Chapter 9), I replaced the two separate power packs with a single Model Rectifier (MRC) Command 2000 Digital Command Control power pack with a single locomotive

equipped with a DCC module. I also opted for the MRC Walkaround 2000 throttle so I could walk (crawl, actually) around the layout to follow the train without keeping my hand on the power pack's control. The two additional passing sidings inside the inner oval are for the Loads-In/Empties-Out operations between the mine and the power plant described in Chapter 19. The two stub-ended sidings in the upper left corner will lead to the 1 x 3-foot extension and form a wye as shown on the plan in Figure 20-5.

This movable layout allowed me to test the operations and to even determine that the power plant and the mine needed to be modified to clear the curved tracks. I could have done this same work on the tabletop but I wanted to be sure I could fit all these operations into a 4 x 8-foot space before I built the table. I had time to build some of the structures for the layout which gave me a chance to try them in different positions and to make some track rearrangements to provide better building sites.

MOVABLE TRACK ON A TABLETOP

If you decide to build a permanent layout on a tabletop I would recommend that you resist nailing or gluing the track or even starting on scenery for a few months. Test-run the track, build a few buildings and see where they fit and, in general, play with the layout until you see where you might want to make changes. It's easy enough to change before the track is in place. It is, of course, possible to pry up the track (particularly if you use latex caulking to install it) and relocate it, then repair the scenery, but it is messy.

I discovered that there were several possible track arrangements for the industrial area at Abbott on the Burlington Route layout shown in Chapter 20 (Figure 20-5). At first, I thought it would be interesting to have a siding inside the wye parallel to the wall, but I discovered

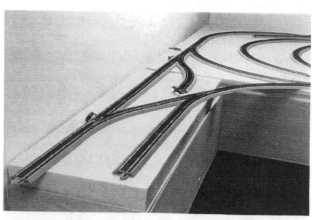

Fig. 4-5. When you use the track with built-in road-bed, you can just let it rest on either the floor or the tabletop so you can rearrange it to obtain the best possible track layout. This was my first attempt at locating the siding for the freight station at Abbott on the Burlington Route, using a right-hand turnout.

Fig. 4-6. The freight station siding at Abbott has been relocated for easier switching by using a left-hand turnout, but the space around the actual model building was too cramped.

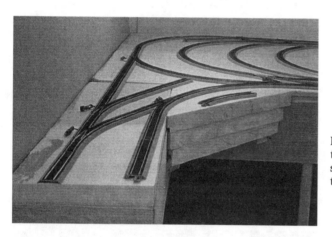

Fig. 4-7. My third try at finding just the right combination of space for the building and ease of switching the spur that serves the Abbott freight house resulted in this right-hand turnout with a diagonal siding.

Fig. 4-8. This combination rif track sections worked best for locating the freight house at Abbott using the same configuration as in Figure 4-7 but with a 3-inch straight inserted between the two turnouts.

that it was too difficult to move cars in and out of that siding with the limited length of track on the point end of the turnout (Figure 4-5). I then replaced the right-hand turnout with a left-hand, and tried the track in the configuration shown in Figure 4-6, but there was not enough room for the buildings. Next, I reverted to the original right-hand turnout, but with the track angled to match the straight leg of the wye (Figure 4-7). Again, there was not room for the buildings and it was just as difficult to switch cars as with the first attempt (Figure 4-5). It all worked well when I added a piece of 3-inch straight track between the two turnouts to achieve the final scheme shown in Figure 4-8 with the buildings in place.

E-Z TRACK TURNOUTS

ADDING TURNOUTS IN PLACE OF CURVED-TRACK SECTIONS

The turnouts used in the Bachmann E-Z Track system and those in the Atlas True Track system have a built-in full-length curved track as shown in Figure 4-9. However, there is an extra 1-1/2 inches of straight track added to that curved route. When you install an E-Z Track or True Track (or a conventional sectional track) turnout in place of a curved track, you must add a matching turnout on the opposite side of the curve (180 degrees around the circle or f track) to compensate for the added 1-1/2 inches. The Life-Like Power-Loc turnouts do not have this extra 1-1/2 inches so they can be substituted (in layouts built for Power-Loc track) for curved track sections without the need to compensate for added track sections.

MODIFYING E-Z TRACK TURNOUTS TO MATCH SECTIONAL TRACK

Sectional track turnouts (shown at the top of Figure 4-9) include a separate 1/3-length of curved track. With that 1/3-curve installed as shown, the standard sectional track turnout and the E-Z Track or True Track turnouts occupy the same space. That built-in 1/3-circle does, however, make it im-

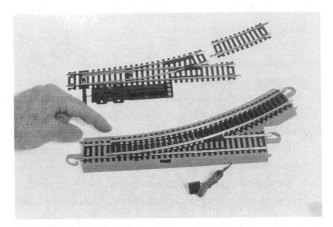

Fig. 4-9. The Bachmann E-Z Track turnout (bottom) with a standard 18-inch radius curve laid over the track reveals that the curved route through the turnout is about 1-1/2 inches longer than the standard 18-inch radius curve. Nearly all the sectional track turnouts (top) have the same geometry.

Fig. 4-10. The Bachmann E-Z Track (shown), Life-Like Power Loc track and Atlas True Track turnouts have the 1/3-curve permanently attached to the roadbed. To allow these turnouts to be used with sectional track plans, like Figures 3-4 and 3-5 and 20-3 and 20-6, this part of the turnout must be removed with a razor or a saw.

possible to use an E-Z Track turnout in most plans designed for conventional sectional track.

It is possible to remove a 1/3-curve from the E-Z Track (or Power-Loc or True Track) turnouts using a razor saw but I would not recommend the process (unless you are going to nail or glue the track to a tabletop) because you lose the strength and aligning features of the clips on the end of the roadbed. The modified turnout and 1/3-curve track section's joints are no stronger than with conventional sectional track. First, find a standard 1/3-curve as a pattern so you know exactly where to cut the E-Z Track

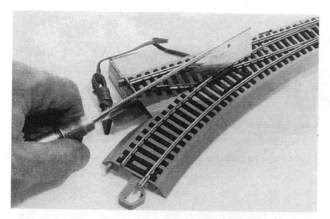

Fig. 4-11. To remove the 1/3-curve from an E-Z Track turnout, cut across the rails, down through the ties and roadbed, then cut along the straight track's ties to free the 1/3-curve.

Fig. 4-12. A triangular-shaped piece of the roadbed must be removed from the 1/3-curve so the piece of track can be turned 180 degrees to fit against the turnout.

turnout. Support the turnout on a plywood block and saw through the rails and the roadbed as shown in Figure 4-10. Make a second cut along the edges of the ties on the straight route of the turnout as shown in Figure 4-11. You now have a separate 1/3-curve piece of E-Z Track with a connector slip on just one end. When you rotate this piece 180 degrees, you'll discover that the edges of the roadbed prevent the rails from touching. Use the razor saw again to trim off the offending strip of roadbed as shown in Figure 4-12. You'll want to modify two turnouts to obtain two of those 1/3-curves. If you need additional 1/3-curves they can be cut from E-Z Track 18-inch radius curves. You will need two additional rail joiners for each cut and those are available at most hobby stores.

The two pieces of 1/3-curve allow you to make sidings and other compact turnout arrangements to match those possible with sectional track as shown on the track plans in Chapter 20 (Figures 20-3 and 20-6) and to make yards using the planning templates in Chapter 3 (Figure 3-6). The modified E-Z Track turnouts can also be used to make crossovers between parallel tracks as shown in Figure 4-14. This type of crossover is featured in the track plans in Figure 3-4 and 20-6. If more than two or three such modified turnouts are needed, I would suggest you use sectional track turnouts with cork roadbed or Homosote, and the track-

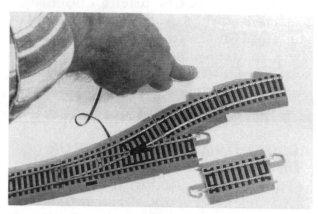

Fig. 4-13. Two turnouts must be cut to produce two 1/3-curves for a Bachmann E-Z Track turnout to be useful for the track plans for sectional track. Note that the two curves produce an odd length that cannot be compensated for with the 3-inch E-Z Track straight section. Combinations of turnouts are shown in the cutout track-planning templates in Chapter 3 (Figure 3-6).

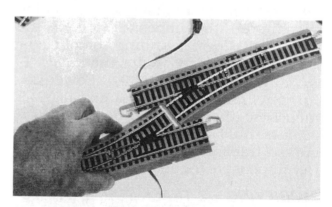

Fig. 4-14. When the 1/3-curves are cut from the E-Z Track (shown), Power-Loc track or True Track turnouts, the turnouts can be used to create the same type of compact crossovers that are possible with sectional track.

laying system described in Chapter 5 and used for the 9 x 9-foot Burlington Northern layout Chapter 20 (Figures 20-3 and 20-4).

CHAPTER 5

Bridges and Benchwork

THE VARIOUS BRIDGES on a real railroad serve a purpose that is somewhat similar to the benchwork on a model railroad. Both support the tracks that carry the trains. The benchwork has to come before the bridges on a model railroad, but the two supports should be planned together for the best effect. A model of a bridge cannot look even remotely realistic unless the track that bridge carries is elevated above the surrounding terrain. The over-and-under type of bridge and trestle sets are fine for toy trains, but they add very little to the realism of a miniature of a real railroad. You can certainly use the parts from the over-and-under sets as they have been on the Burlington Northern layout in Chapter 20. The concept of using only trestle bents to elevate a track is best limited to industrial sidings, such as the Alliance Coal & Fuel and the Coke Ovens at Emmett on the Burlington Northern layout. You must do some planning in order to build benchwork that allows the scenery to fall away from beneath the tracks, which makes a bridge just as necessary as it is on a real railroad.

TWO CHOICES FOR BENCHWORK

There are two different types of benchwork in this book: the conventional wood open-grid-style benchwork with wood supports for the roadbed benchwork and the blue Dow-Corning extruded-Styrofoam insulation board with thin plywood shadowbox benchwork in Chapter 6. The open-grid style has been traditional with model railroaders for more than fifty years. The blue extruded-Styrofoam is a relatively new development that provides somewhat lighter construction and provides for valleys and water-crossing beneath the layout. Look at both methods and decide what one best suits you.

OPEN-GRID BENCHWORK

The open-grid-style benchwork for your model railroad is in about the same construction category as the framework for your house, and it's made of many of the same materials. The benchwork will eventually be hidden by scenery on the top side and by Masonite or plywood panels along the sides so that only the legs will show.

Use only the best grades of 1 x 3 fir or pine with no knots for your benchwork. You don't want warped wood and other track-distorting problems, and quality wood will help to avoid them. Use 2 x 4s for the legs. I strongly suggest that you

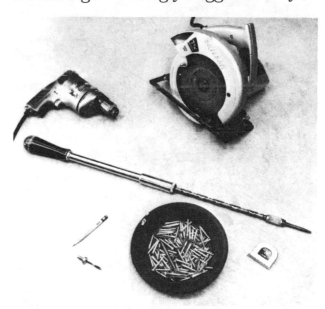

Fig. 5-1. An electric drill, Number 8 x 1-1/2-inch pilot bits and a Yankee screwdriver (or a powerful electric screwdriver) will make benchwork construction easy.

raise the top of the track to at least the level of your chest so you will have a more true-to-life (model-size life) view of the railroad. If you want to feel like Gulliver, then stand on a stool (the stool can also be used to reach more easily during some of the construction stages).

Divide your layout into subassemblies or modules that are no more than 30 x 60 inches. A 4 x 8-foot area can, for example, be divided conveniently into four 2 x 4-foot subassemblies. A pattern for dividing a 5 x 9-foot area is shown in Chapter 20 (Figure 20-1). Make a box with overall dimensions to match each of these subassemblies, with the 1 x 3s placed on edge. Add enough crossbrac-

Fig 5-4. Five separate subassemblies, each with open-grid construction, are used to make the L-shaped 9 x 9-foot Burlington Route layout.

Fig. 5-2. Two styles of Number 8 pilot bits. Either one will make assembling benchwork with wood screws as easy as using nails.

Fig. 5-3. Temporarily lay out the plywood and Homasote tabletop on the floor to locate the exact positions of the track and turnouts. Mark these locations with a felt-tip pen.

es so there is no open area wider than 15 inches (three crossbraces are needed for each of the 2 x 4-foot subassemblies). Secure each of the joints with two No. 8 x 1-1/2-inch wood screws. Drill a pilot hole for each of these screws with an electric drill and a Number 8 x 1-1/2-inch pilot bit, which you can buy at any hardware store.

You can make quick work of driving the screws by buying or renting either

Fig. 5-5. Vise-grip clamping pliers, such as these, or conventional C-clamps can be used to hold the subassemblies while the assembly bolt holes are drilled and the bolts installed.

a Yankee screwdriver (see Figures 5-1 and 5-3), where you just push the handle down to drive the screw, or a screwdriver attachment for an electric drill with variable speed. Touch each of the screws with a dab of soap to make it even easier. Bolt the subassemblies together with 2 x 1/4-inch stove bolts, washers, and nuts. Attach the legs with two 2-1/2-inch-long x 1/4-inch stove bolts or hex-head bolts with flat washers and nuts. Attach one leg to the table with a single screw, and clamp the others with C-clamps or vise-grip clamps while you adjust the legs to see that the benchwork top surface is level. Don't trust the floor to be level. Use one of the carpenter's spirit or bubble levels. When the legs are in the correct position, drill them and attach each leg with two of the 2-1/2-inch stove bolts. This completes the open-grid portion of the benchwork.

The top of the benchwork should be 1/2-inch plywood (inexpensive C-C grade is fine) with 1/2-inch Homasote wallboard between the plywood and the sectional track. If you are using Bachmann's E-Z Track, Life-Like's Power-Loc track, Atlas' True Track or any other track with built-in roadbed, you will not need the Homasote. The Homasote is one of the best materials to support sectional track with just rails and ties or

Fig. 5.6. Five of the subassemblies for the open-grid benchwork were clamped and bolted together to build the Burlington Northern layout in Chapter 20.

Fig. 5-7. A utility knife, guided with a steel ruler, is all that is needed to cut the 1/2-inch Homasote. Make four or five more heavy passes with the knife in order to slice clear through the Homasote.

flexible track because it is soft enough to carve ballast shoulders with a utility knife and soft enough to be sound-deadening, but firm enough to hold track nails or spikes. It must, however, be supported by plywood or it will sag. There is no equally suitable substitute for the Homasote, so call the lumber yards until you find one willing to order as many 4 x 8-foot sheets as you'll need. I suggest a simple flat tabletop for your first model railroad. If you're working on your second layout and you're certain the track plan you are using is perfect, then you can cut both the plywood and the Homasote about an inch on each side of the track's center line. You can use a utility knife, guided by a steel ruler, to cut the Homasote. Most tool supply firms also sell knife blades for saber saws like the Sears' Craftsman 2873 or the Vermont American 30022 that can be used to cut the Homasote quickly and easily and with nearly no mess.

The plywood and Homasote can then be elevated about 3 inches above the top of the 1 x 3 benchwork, with short lengths of 1 x 3s placed vertically and attached to the plywood and the benchwork with number 8 x 1-1/2-inch wood screws. You can add a stream at a later date using the technique in the 9 x 9-foot Burlington Northern layout. Most of the scenery on the Burlington Northern layout was to be above the track, so the plywood was just attached directly to the edges of the benchwork with screws.

Many modelers even hide the benchwork's legs and the other under-the-table debris with drapes made from inexpensive materials. If you do decide on drapes, avoid the mistake of selecting those bright railroad-style patterns; they are a major distraction from what is on top of the table. A nice dark green or blue or brown, which will make the underside of the benchwork seem to disappear, is the shade to select.

BRIDGES

Small streams or lakes can be created by slicing through the Homasote with a utility knife to lower the earth to the level of the plywood's surface. That's how the lake near the Lumber Supply Co. was formed. The complete subassembly in the river section of the Burlington Northern, between the towns of Alliance and Emmett was dropped about 6 inches below the benchwork (Figs. 5-9, 5-10, and 5-11). Two-inch wide strips of the 2-inch plywood and 2-inch Homasote were placed beneath the track and supported by additional 1 x 3 scraps. The plastic trestle bents from a Model Power 490-79 Trestle Bridge Set were spaced about 2 inches apart for the approach to one bridge. The steel-girder bridge was cut from the span of the Atlas 150-855 bridge with abutments (vertical-end supports) from the Model Power 490-79 set. White glue—and lots of it—was used to attach the plastic to the benchwork and tube-type plastic cement holds the track to the bridges. Notice that an earth fill leads all the way to the abutment on the steel girder bridge, while the steel truss bridge is approached by track supported on a trestle. The earth fill is far more common on modern railroads, and, in fact, some of the earth fills you'll see are actually wood trestles that were buried with dirt to become fills as soon as the railroad could find the time.

Fig. 5-9. In this view from below the benchwork, the 2 x 4 is one of the bolted-on legs. The river section leads out to the far left. It is attached by bolts so the layout can be disassembled for any later relocating.

The benchwork for the center subassembly on the Burlington Northern was not built, because the plan indicated that that area would be nothing more than the interior of a mountain. You may be able to find similar areas of many large layouts where no benchwork at all is required. The 1 x 2 wood

Fig. 5-8. This 18 x 48-inch open-grid benchwork subassembly was lowered 6 inches below the rest of the Burlington Northern layout in order to create a space for a river.

Fig. 5-10. An under-the-table view of the opposite end of the lowered river section. The small triangle (top) is part of the 2 x 4-foot extension of the L-shaped layout.

Fig. 5-11. The tracks across the river area are supported on narrow strips of 1/2-inch plywood and 1/2-inch Homasote by vertical 1x3 boards.

Fig. 5-12. The completed river scene on the Burlington Northern layout. A steel girder bridge, supported by a fill and a pair of wood trestle bents, and a deck truss bridge span the river.

supports for the center of the mountain were cantilevered from the other portions of the benchwork.

You can finish off the edges of the benchwork with profile boards of 1/8-inch tempered Masonite or plywood cut to match the proposed hills and valleys. I suggest you delay cutting those supports until you have mocked up the shape of the hills with wadded-up newspapers, as described in Chapter 12. A lot of construction time is needed between the completion of the benchwork and the initial scenery work; all the track-laying and wiring should be completed and the structure sites selected (even if the structures themselves have not been purchased) before scenery is started.

DO'S AND DON'TS FOR BENCHWORK

- Do consider building the benchwork so the track is at about the level of your chest or shoulders and you can view the model trains from the same angle you view real trains.
- Do use screws to assemble every joint in the benchwork and install those screws from below the table so they will be accessible even when the layout is completed. You will be able, then, to alter or move the track without destroying the entire layout.
- Do use only well-seasoned or aged wood that has been stored in the same area as the layout for a year, if possible, to avoid any radical changes in the benchwork caused by the lumber warping and bending. For this same reason, it's also wise to seal all wood with at least one coat of paint.
- Do build the benchwork in modules or sections no larger than 30 x 60 inches and bolt the sections together so you can unbolt them if you ever need to move the layout. The 30 x 60-inch sections will fit through most standard doorways.
- Do raise the roadbed and track (or lower some of those segments of the benchwork) so the track can be elevated above the earth on embankments or fills and to provide spaces, below track level, for rivers and streams.

- Don't build a layout at waist or hip level unless you want it to be visible or accessible for very small children. From that high viewing angle even the most realistic models look like toys.
- Don't use nails or glue to assemble the benchwork. If you do want to make any changes, later, the terrific force needed to separate the joints will destroy most of the layout.
- Don't use green, freshly cut wood for benchwork. It's better, in most cases, to find old used wood that has already warped or bent as much as it is likely to before it becomes part of your model railroad.
- Don't build a room-filling layout with 8-foot or longer boards that can only be moved by tearing the layout completely apart.
- Don't build the entire layout on a flat piece of plywood or Homasote unless you are creating just an industrial yard or city scene.

CHAPTER 6

Lightweight Benchwork and Bridges

The real excitement of model railroading begins when you get your eyes close enough to the models so your viewpoint is similar to that of when you look at real railroads. You can get that view by lying your head on the floor and watching the models roll by. It's easier, to be sure, if those models are elevated so you can look at them with that real life viewpoint. Model railroading really is more enjoyable when the trains are on a tabletop.

Model railroaders call the table that supports the trains "benchwork" because it may not have a tabletop at all. In fact, the benchwork for the 9 x 9-foot Burlington Northern layout in Chapter 5 has an open grid design with tabletop only beneath the tracks. Conversely, the benchwork for the 7 x 8-foot Burlington Route layout in this chapter and in Chapter 7 (the plan is shown in Figure 20-5 in Chapter 20) really does have a tabletop, one made from a stack of three layers of 2-inch thick, Dow-Corning blue extruded-Styrofoam insulation boards as shown in this chapter. Dow-Corning makes their extruded-Styrofoam insulation board with a blue color. Other brands use other colors, but be sure the insulation board is extruded polyfoam. The white insulation boards (sometimes called beadboard) are expanded Styrofoam or expanded polyfoam and are much too soft and fragile for this application. Also, do not use the urethane boards because they are brittle and far more difficult to work with for this type of project.

STYROFOAM BENCHWORK

I've developed a lightweight system to support this blue extruded-Styrofoam

tabletop that's shown on these pages, but you can simply add legs to a 4 x 8-piece of 1/2-inch plywood or even build an open grid support as shown in Chapter 5 to provide support for the blue Styrofoam. You can even support the whole lot on a couple of folding card tables, hinge it from the wall with a pair of fold-down legs or hang it by cables from the ceiling of an unfinished basement or garage. I used nine 2 x 2 legs for the 7 x 8-foot layout in this chapter. When we're done, we'll have a 4 x 8-foot flat surface of blue Styrofoam like that in Figure 6-1.

You can decide if you want to leave this flat tabletop surface as-is and use the portable scenery shown in Chapter 4 so you never need to attach the track permanently to the tabletop. With the E-Z Track and Power-Loc track you do have the option of allowing the track to simply rest on this flat tabletop with no nails or glue. You also have the option of building the Lightweight Scenery shown in Chapter 16. Read and

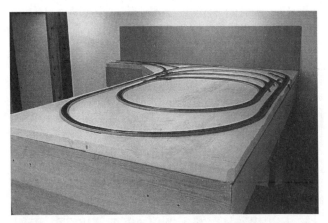

Fig. 6-1. The lightweight blue Dow-Corning extruded-Styrofoam insulation board provides the tabletop with much of the strength possible with this method of benchwork construction.

understand that chapter before you build the benchwork because you may want to have a stack of three (or more) 2-inch-thick layers of blue Styrofoam so you can elevate the track above valleys. Or, you may simply want a flat surface and, if so, a single 2-inch layer of blue extruded Styrofoam is all that's needed.

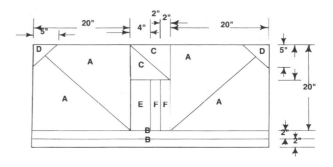

Fig. 6-2. Plan to cut the braces for the 7 x 8-foot Burlington Route layout from a single 2 x 4-foot sheet of 1/2-inch plywood.

THE SHADOWBOX FRAME FOR THE BENCHWORK

I built a shadowbox from 1/8-inch Cherry veneer plywood to protect the edges of the blue extruded-Styrofoam. A 4 x 8-foot panel costs no more than a sheet of conventional 1/2-inch A-C grade plywood. I paid the dealer to cut it into 9-inch-wide strips and I had those strips cut into two 8-foot, four 4-foot, two 3-foot, and two 1-foot pieces. The 8-foot pieces and two of the 4-foot pieces form the sides of the Shadowbox for the main layout. The 1 x 3-foot extension of the benchwork is a second shadowbox made from the two 3-foot and two 1-foot pieces. The remaining two 4-foot pieces were used to brace the legs on the 4 x 8-foot portion of the layout.

The shadowbox alone is flimsy but has a tough surface, while the blue extruded Styrofoam has tremendous strength to resist bending forces. This design combines the best strengths of the thin plywood with the best strengths of the Styrofoam. When the edges of the three 2-inch layers of blue extruded Styrofoam are glued to the 1/8-inch plywood shadowbox, the finished structure becomes what aircraft engineers call a monocoque. It's far stronger than a single sheet of even 3/4-inch plywood and even stronger than an open-grid design made from 1 x 4 boards like those in Chapter 5. And, the entire layout, scenery an all, weighs less than a single sheet of 3/4-inch plywood!

The legs will require a firm support because the Styrofoam has no surface strength. I cut four 20-inch triangles

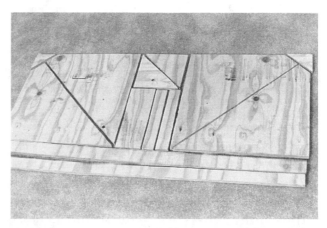

Fig. 6-3. Use a circular saw to cut the wood shadowbox and to support the legs for the 7 x 8-foot Burlington Route. Refer to the drawing (Figure 6-2) to mark the lines to cut.

and other supporting wood from a single 2 x 4-foot sheet of 1/2-inch plywood (lumber yards usually sell plywood in sheets that small). I made the cuts as shown in Figure 6-2 using a circular saw. The triangles marked A in Figure 6-2 support the legs for the 4 x 8-foot portion of the layout. Pairs of triangles C and D support the legs and corners of the 1 x 3-foot extension of the layout. The 2-inch strips B brace across the 4 x 8-foot layout and support the slide-out drawer for the power pack. The pieces marked F are used to provide extra strength where the 1 x 3 extension attaches to the 4 x 8-foot layout. Piece E provides a brace for the two legs on the 1 x 3-foot extension.

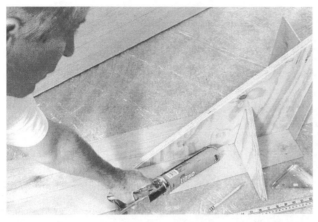

Fig. 6-4. Use construction-grade caulking to assemble the plywood pieces. Cement just one triangle A to each of the 1/8-inch plywood 9 x 48-inch shadowbox sides and to each of the 9 x 48-inch shadowbox ends to make two 48 x 96-inch L-shaped pieces. Assemble the two C triangles, one each to the 9 x 36-inch and 9 x 12-inch extension table sides and ends to make two 12 x 36-inch, L-shaped pieces. These four L-shaped pieces will be assembled to make the 4 x 8-foot and the 1 x 3-foot shadowboxes for the 7 x 8-foot Burlington Route layout.

ASSEMBLING THE SHADOWBOX FRAME FOR THE TABLETOP

I assembled the 1/8-inch plywood shadowbox so the three layers of 2-inch thick blue extruded-Styrofoam were protected by the plywood with 1-1/2 inches of the uppermost layer exposed above the edges of the plywood. The triangles A will actually support the corners of the Styrofoam, so position them 6 inches from the top edge of the 8-foot x 9-inch pieces of 1/8-inch plywood. Use construction-grade Liquid Nails, yellow resin glue or similar glue at each joint. Use the remaining triangles as braces while the glue dries. When the glue dries, add one of the 4-foot x 9-inch pieces to make a 4 x 8-foot L-shaped piece. Make two of these, then use triangles C and D and the two 3-foot x 9-inch and two 1-foot x 9-inch pieces of 1/8-inch plywood to make two more L-shaped pieces. Let these four L-shaped pieces dry for at least a day.

THE STYROFOAM TABLETOP

The blue extruded Styrofoam seems to be the most readily available material of its type. This is a dense extruded-polystyrene material, far stronger than

the expanded-foam beadboard that is also available at lumber dealers. Woodland Scenics offers small sheets of the white expanded foam for their SubTerrain system shown later in this chapter. I used that material for the road surfaces and building bases, but it lacks the strength for a layout surface. There are other brands of extruded-polystyrene insulation, offered in other colors, so check with your local lumberyard. The blue extruded-Styrofoam seems to be commonly available in 2 x 8-foot sheets, 2 inches thick. The 8-foot edges have a tongue-and-groove design to interlock the panels. Use a latex cement to attach the Styrofoam to itself and to the plywood. Liquid Nails makes a latex-based compound for a caulking gun called Projects and Foamboard cement that works well. Test any cement on the Styrofoam, because some will dissolve the Styrofoam.

You can cut the Styrofoam with a variety of tools including a hacksaw blade, a serrated kitchen knife or special hot wire cutters. The hacksaw blade and knife produce dust and shavings that are difficult to clean up. The hot wire produces fumes that can be toxic, especially to anyone with allergies. If you use a hot wire cutter, work outdoors. If you use a hacksaw blade, you can hold it in your hand (Figure 6-5) or buy one of the holders that allow about half of the length of the blade to protrude. I would recommend a serrated knife (Figure 6-6) only for smaller cuts and for shaping finished scenery.

CUTTING STYROFOAM WITH A HOT WIRE

I used a hot wire cutter made by Avalon Concepts to cut the foam for the Burlington Route 7 x 8-foot layout. It is a relatively expensive tool but it works quickly, and the only mess, even when sculpting scenery shapes (Chapter 16) are potato-chip-size flakes. The Avalon Concepts hot wire Foam Sculpting Detail Station set includes a transformer to reduce the 110-volt current to a usable

Fig. 6-5. The blue extruded-Styrofoam insulation board is easily cut with a hacksaw blade.

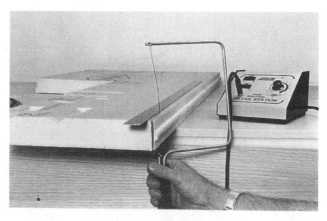

Fig. 6-8. The Avalon Concepts' Shaper tool works like a jig saw to quickly melt its way through the blue extruded-Styrofoam. Guide it with a ruler for straight cuts like removing the tongue from one edge of the 2 x 8-foot panels.

Fig. 6-6. You can use a serrated kitchen knife for small cuts and for carving the blue extruded-Styrofoam insulation board.

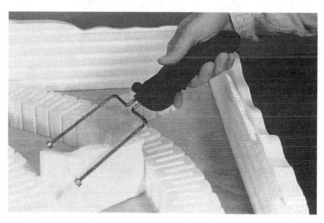

Fig. 6-9. Woodland Scenics Hot Wire Foam Cutter has adjustable temperature controls and can be used for cutting either white or blue Styrofoam including the Woodland Scenics Profile boards shown later in this chapter.

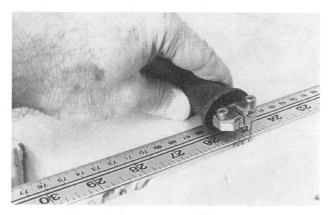

Fig. 6-7. The Avalon Concepts Detail Wand with a piece of their Wand Wire bent into a 3-inch U-shape and bent again at a 90-degree angle as shown in Chapter 16 (Figure 16-4, top). Adjust the wire so the tool makes a perfect 90-degree cut, then keep that cut straight by guiding the tool with a ruler as it melts its way through the blue extruded-Styrofoam.

level. The heated wire is still potentially dangerous, however, because it is very hot—it can become as hot as an electric stove—and the melted plastic that can drip off the wire is hotter than melted candle wax, so burns are possible. I'd suggest you wear cloth gloves and long sleeves so no skin is exposed. The fumes that the melted Styrofoam produces can also be harmful, so always work outdoors when using any type of hot wire cutter on any type of Styrofoam. Caution: do not try to use a hot wire cutter with the urethane foams because the fumes produced can be toxic.

I bent a piece of Avalon Concepts wire to form a 2-1/2-inch-long x 1/2-inch-wide U-shape with a 90-degree bend (see Figure 16-4 in Chapter 16). It can be clamped into Avalon Concept's Detail Wand (that is included in the Foam Sculpting Detail Station set). The tool can then be laid flat on the Styrofoam (Figure 6-7) and it will automatically produce a clean 90-degree cut. Experiment with the edge of one of the pieces of blue Styrofoam to be sure the cutter really is producing that right angle cut and make any bending adjustments that are needed to the wire. Use a ruler to guide the tool for perfectly straight cuts while the 90-degree bend in the hot wire helps make the cut a right angle. Follow Avalon Concepts' instructions and clamp the wire securely with at least a 1/2 inch between the wires so, even when hot, the wires won't touch one another. If they do, it forms red-hot wire sections that can blow the fuse in the Avalon Concepts' Detail Station transformer.

Adjust the controls on the Avalon Concepts Detail Station so the wire is just hot enough to cut—as fast as you can saw—through 1/4-inch plywood with a hand-held jigsaw. You'll hear a popping sound as the hot wire breaks the countless air bubbles that are trapped in the Styrofoam and wisps of white smoke will emit from the cut. The blade should float through the material with little or no drag. Do not force the wire through the cut or you'll bend the wires which will make the cut uneven and can force the two wires together. If you are producing lots of hair-like wisps of plastic, you are pushing the hot wire too rapidly through the Styrofoam.

Avalon Concepts also makes a jigsaw-like hot wire Shaper. You can use it to make relatively shallow cuts for slicing off the tongue from the Styrofoam (Figure 6-8). Use a ruler to guide the hot wire for a straight cut. Woodland Scenics makes a similar hot wire cutter called a Foam Cutter. These jigsaw-like tools are fine for cutting strips, but they cannot reach down into the Styrofoam like the Detail Wand hot wire cutter or even a hacksaw blade.

ASSEMBLING THE MONOCOQUE TABLETOP

Test fit the L-shaped shadowbox pieces around two sheets of the 2 x 8-foot x 2-inch thick blue extruded-Styrofoam. I found that I needed to shave about 1/8 inch from the 8-foot edge of the Styrofoam, in addition to removing the tongue, so the Styrofoam would fit snugly inside the 1/8-inch plywood shadowbox. Pile the three layers (or however many you choose) of Styrofoam on the floor and position the L-shaped edges of the 1/8-inch plywood shadow-

Fig. 6-10. Stack six pieces of the 2 x 8-foot, 2-inch thick blue extruded-Styrofoam panels to make a 4 x 8-foot x 6-inch stack and place the two 4 x 8-foot L-shaped shadowbox pieces around them. Assemble a stack of three 1 x 3-foot blue foam panels and assemble the two 1 x 3-foot L-shaped pieces around them. Shim the two still-loose corners so the blue foam protrudes equally all around the bottom edges of the plywood, apply cement liberally, and tape the still-loose corners together tightly with masking tape.

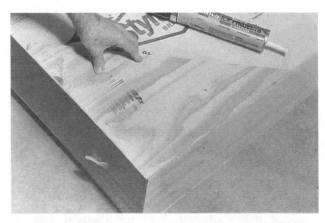

Fig. 6-11. Cement the two remaining A triangles inside the just-assembled corners of the 4 x 8-foot shadowbox and its 6-inch stack of blue foam and cement the two D triangles inside the 1 x 3-foot shadowbox and its 6-inch stack of blue foam.

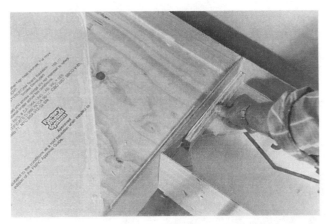

Fig. 6-12. Position the 1 x 3-foot extension of the Burlington Route layout in its proper place (remember, you're working upside down) next to the 4 x 8-foot box. Cement the two 2 x 12-inch pieces of 1/2-inch plywood F where the bolts that clamp the two boxes together will be located so the 1/2-inch plywood can reinforce the 1/8-inch plywood shadowbox.

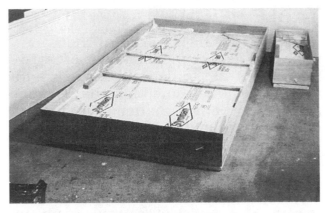

Fig. 6-13. Finish the 4 x 8-foot Shadowbox with a pair of 2 x 2 x 48-inch braces laid along the 8-foot sides and rest the two 2 x 48-inch pieces of 1/2-inch plywood B on the 2 x 2s to support a slide-out computer keyboard shelf.

Fig. 6-14. The slide-out shelf is intended to mount a computer keyboard beneath a tabletop but it will work fine for a control panel location on the Burlington Route layout. Position the braces B to fit the mounting diagram furnished with the slide-out shelf.

box over the foam. Support the corners with some scraps of wood and tape the still-unglued corners together with masking tape (Figure 6-10). Use liberal amounts of the latex glue to attach the edges of the top layer of Styrofoam to the plywood sides and to the plywood triangles. Do not, however, glue the two layers of the 2-inch Styrofoam together because you may want to be remove those top two layers when you work with the scenery. I used six full tubes of the Liquid Nails Projects and Foamboard glue for this purpose. Check all the edges to be sure that each layer of the foam really contacts the plywood and that every corner is square and even. Repeat the process to build the sides for the 1 x 3-foot extension.

I added the two 2-inch x 1-foot long pieces of 1/2-inch plywood F at the places where the 1 x 3-foot extension attaches to the 4 x 8-foot main layout to provide reinforcement for the bolts, nuts and washers that will clamp the extension to the main table. Connect the two with 1/4 x 2-inch bolts, fender washers and nuts (but remove the bolts and nuts after the glue dries). I reinforced the 4 x 8-foot layout with two 4-foot lengths of 2 x 2 along the 8-foot edges and installed the two 2-inch x 4-foot pieces of 1/2-inch plywood B as shown in Figure 6-13. I spaced the two

B pieces to attach a slide-out computer keyboard drawer that I purchased at an office supply store (Figure 6-14). The drawer will be used to hold the power pack, operation cards and a few freight cars or locomotives that might be removed from the layout as shown in Chapter 19 (Figure 19-7). There's very little ventilation space around the joints for the latex glue to dry and it is important that the assembly be completely dry to achieve maximum strength, so let the glue set for at least a week! When the glue is dry, reinforce the joints between the 1/2-inch plywood triangles and the 2 x 2 braces with drywall screws driven from outside the shadowbox, then remove the masking tape from the corners.

TABLE HEIGHT

Decide how high you want the layout to be and deduct the thickness of Styrofoam from that to determine the length of the legs. Just how high that a table top should be is a matter of individual opinion. Personally, I like the trains to be at about shoulder level. I'm 5'11" and that puts the highest rails at about 56 inches from the ground. Others prefer them waist-high or somewhere in between. You may, of course, want to place the trains at the shoulder level of the shortest member of your family so no one has to stand on a box to view the trains in action. It's your choice.

I used thick steel Corner Brackets, one 4-inch and one 3-inch, for each leg. I assembled the legs and the corner brackets while the tabletop was drying in its upside-down position, using a level to be sure the 2 x 2 legs were straight. Use construction-grade Liquid Nails to cement the steel brackets to the plywood. Attach the legs (and clamp the brackets in place) with 1/4 x

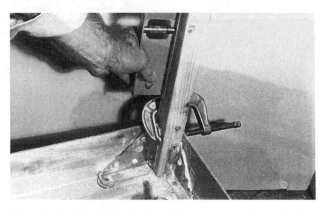

Fig. 6-15. A 3-inch and a 4-inch pair of tough steel corner braces support each 2 x 2 wood leg. Clamp the leg and the 4-inch brace to the 1/8-inch plywood and use a level to adjust the leg so it is perfectly vertical. Glue the steel braces to the wood with construction-grade caulking and use the screws supplied with the braces to attach them to the 1/2-inch plywood triangle corner braces. Drill 1/4-inch holes to fit the bolts to attach the legs and install those bolts, with fender washers on the outside of the 1/8-inch plywood. Tighten the nuts onto those bolts and repeat the process with the other legs. I used four legs down one 8-foot side of the 4 x 8 layout and three legs down the opposite side, with just two legs on the extreme end of the 1 x 3-foot extension. Brace the legs on the 4-foot ends of the table with the leftover pair of 9 x 48-inch pieces of 1/8-inch plywood, and brace the legs on the 1 x 3-foot extension with the 3 x 12-inch piece of 1/2-inch plywood E.

2-inch slotted-head bolts, fender washers and nuts. The bolts will be removed to remove the legs when the tabletop is turned over and to move the layout. The offset in the holes for the 4-inch and 3-inch brackets allows you to use two attaching screws per leg at 90-degrees to one another.

Fig. 6-16. Let the glue and caulking dry for at least a week, remove the legs, stand the two shadowboxes upright and replace the legs. Remove the top two layers of 2-inch blue foam and check to be sure the bottom layer is glued firmly to the 1/8-inch plywood. This edge, on my layout, needed a 1/4-inch filler strip and almost half a tube of caulking to form a complete bond.

FINISHING THE LIGHTWEIGHT MONOCOQUE TABLETOP

After the glue has dried for that week or more, remove the legs, turn the tabletop right side up and reattach the legs. Bolt on the 1 x 3 extension and its legs. The 1/8-inch x 9-inch x 4-foot braces can now be attached to the 2 x 2 legs with drywall screws. Attach the 1-inch x 1-foot, 1/2-inch plywood brace E to the two 2 x 2 legs on the 1 x 3-foot extension.

Try to remove the top one or two layers of Styrofoam to test the grip of the glue. If you can remove the layers (I was able to easily pry out the top two layers), fill in any gaps between the plywood and the edges of the Styrofoam with Styrofoam scraps leftover from trimming the Styrofoam and use plenty of Liquid Nails latex glue (Figure 6-16). Let the first layer dry for a few days before replacing the top two layers of 2-inch Styrofoam.

Fig. 6-17. Make a triangular piece of the roadbed with two 16-inch sides (to support the curved track of the wye that swings out from the 4 x 8-foot table to the 1 x 3-foot extension). Use 2 x 2 braces to support this triangular table addition.

Fig. 6-18. Cement the 16 x 16-inch triangle of three layers of 2-inch blue foam only to the 1 x 3-foot extension table so you can remove the extension with the triangular piece of the roadbed attached.

I added a 16 x 16-inch triangle of three layers of the 2-inch Styrofoam between the 1 x 3-foot extension and the main 4 x 8-foot layout to support the curved track of the wye. I cut pieces of 2 x 2 to support the triangle (Figure 6-17) and glued the three layers together and to the side of the 1 x 3-foot piece (Figure 6-18). Do not, though, glue the triangle to the side of the 4 x 8-foot layout. Let the triangle rest on the 2 x 2 so it can be removed with the 1 x 3-foot extension if the layout needs to be moved.

The sky backdrop for the Burlington Route layout is Aluminum Valley roof-flashing material that comes in 20-inch widths in 10 or 20-foot rolls, I cut a 10-

Fig. 6-19. Make a sky backdrop from a 20-inch x 10-foot piece of aluminum roofing Valley flashing. Fit it in 2-inch deep notches cut into the 1/8-inch plywood and attach it with just one or two drywall screws from the outside edge of the table. Paint the aluminum sky blue.

foot roll to fit the 7-foot back edge of the Burlington Route layout and cut 2-inch deep notches in the edges of the plywood so the aluminum could slide into the notches to form the backdrop between the layout and the wall. You could also install an aluminum sky backdrop to separate the layout into two 2 x 8-foot scenes like the layout in the color pages that was built, step-by-step, in the Bachmann NICKEL SILVER E-Z TRACK, Volume II. Paint the sky with Sherwin Williams SW17832 Bold Blue or an equivalent sky blue color from another paint maker.

LAYING INSTANT TRACK

Once you've snapped the E-Z Track or Power-Loc track together it is, effectively, laid. If you are going to apply ballast and other ground covers, however, you will want to anchor the track firmly to the tabletop. Use gray latex caulking and apply about a 1/8-inch bead just where the edges of the roadbed contact the tabletop. If some of the track wants to move into an incorrect position, anchor it with number 18-gauge x 1-inch nails. Use a modeler's pin vise with a 1/16-inch drill bit to enlarge the holes in the plastic ties and push the nails into place (Figure 6-20). Do not glue the track where it crosses the joint between

Fig. 6-20. Use a pin vise with a 1/16-inch drill bit to enlarge the holes in the E-Z Track or Power-Loc track roadbed to fit number 18 x 1-inch nails. Nail the track only where it does not want to stay in alignment. Use gray latex bathtub caulking to attach the roadbed, with a bead placed where the edges of the roadbed meet the tabletop.

Fig. 6-21. Raise the level of the earth to the height of the track for all building sites and for roads where they cross the track. Cement strips of 1/8-inch balsa wood to the table top and the areas between and beside the tracks.

the 1 x 3-foot extension and the 4 x 8-foot main layout. A 4-1/4-inch special-cut track section is needed (at F on the plan in Figure 20-5) and the joint between that track section and the adjacent 3-inch track can be placed right at the joint between the main layout and the extension. Cut the locking tabs from the bottoms of any track sections where they cross that joint so you can easily remove the 1 x 3-foot extension to disassemble the layout when you want to move it.

BUILDING SITES

One of the drawbacks to using E-Z Track, Power-Loc track, True Track or any of the systems with roadbed is that the track is higher than the foundations of any buildings and higher than any roads or highways. To elevate the building sites and roads, use 1/4-inch thick white Styrofoam (Woodland Sce-

nics sells it in 12 x 24-inch sheets) supported with 1/8-inch balsa wood strips (Figures 6-21 an 6-22) or the 1/8-inch thick Foamcore board sold by art supply shops, supported with 1/4-inch balsa strips. The Foamcore is made from a layer of white Styrofoam sandwiched between a top and bottom layer of plastic-coated cardboard. The 1/4-inch thick plain white Styrofoam is about as easy to cut as the 1/8-inch Foamcore. Hold the Styrofoam or Foamcore over the track and press it firmly onto the rails so the rails will make an imprint into the board. Turn the board over and cut 1/4-inch away from those lines with a hobby or utility knife. Mark the outlines of the buildings on the Styrofoam or Foamcore and leave room for roads and walkways around the buildings. Cut the excess Styrofoam or Foamcore away and mark the outlines of the building sites on the tabletop. Glue the 1/8 or 1/4-inch strips of balsa wood around the edges of these outlines with Liquid Nails latex glue or carpenter's glue. Glue the previously-cut 1/4-inch Styrofoam or 1/8-inch Foamcore in place on top the balsa wood strips.

Fig. 6-22. The entire 1 x 3-foot extension and most of the 16 x 16 inch triangular addition are covered with building sites, elevated to just below the level of the rails.

Fig 6-23. The Woodland Scenics' 1/4-inch white Styrofoam Sheets can also be used for roads. E-Z Track terminal tracks are designed to represent highway crossings, so the terminal tracks were positioned where I wanted the road to cross the tracks on both sides of the 4 x 8-foot layout. Use 1/8-inch balsa strips to elevate the white Styrofoam to the height of the rails.

ROADS AND HIGHWAYS

Use the Building Site system to elevate roads and highways above the tabletop to near track level. Modern two-lane roads are about 20 feet wide, which reduces to about 2-3/4 inches in HO scale. Cut the roads from the Styrofoam or Foamcore with a hobby or utility

knife. The roads can rest directly on the tabletop except where they are elevated with the balsa wood supports to reach rail level. Cut the roads so they are about 1/4 inch from the rails. Fill in the 1/4-inch gap with a 3/32-inch square wood or styrene strip, or butt the roads against the combination highway crossing/rerailer/terminal track sections from the E-Z Track (Figure 6-23) or Power-Loc track systems. Connect any roads that are necessary to the building sites and the layout is ready for final scenery shapes and textures (Figure 6-24).

THE WOODLAND SCENICS LIGHTWEIGHT SUBTERRAIN SYSTEM

Woodland Scenics is producing white expanded Styrofoam components, with a redesigned foam that is somewhat stronger than conventional white Styrofoam, for an alternate method of lightweight layout construction. Their system begins with a plywood or blue

Fig. 6-24. The 7 x 8-foot Burlington Route layout with the track glued down, the building sites and roads installed, and trains being test-run to be sure everything works as it should.

Fig. 6-25. The Woodland Scenics SubTerrain system's Risers can be used with cork or flexible roadbed and sectional track or with E-Z Track.

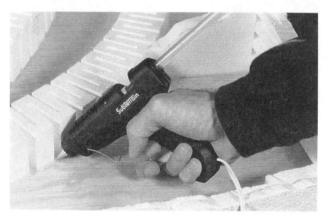

Fig. 6-26. The Woodland Scenics Low Temp Foam Gun and Foam Glue Sticks are designed to be used with either white or blue Styrofoam for a quick and sturdy bond.

Styrofoam flat tabletop. The track is elevated on 2-inch flexible Risers (Figure 6-25) placed beneath the track all around the layout. This elevation provides space for rivers and streams below track level. If you want deeper riverbeds, Woodland Scenics offers 4-inch flexible Riser. Woodland Scenics also has a Low Temp Foam Gun (Figure 6-26) that can be used to attach their Risers and Inclines to the tabletop and

to one another. The glue is cool enough so it can be used with the blue Styrofoam as well.

Woodland sells 12 x 24-inch sheets of white expanded-Styrofoam in 1/4-inch and 1/2-inch thicknesses to allow you to build lightweight building sites, towns and roads at track level. Woodland Scenics also sells 12 x 24-inch sheets of white expanded-Styrofoam in 1-inch, 2-inch, 3-inch and 4-inch thicknesses if you want to support buildings or roads on solid blocks of Styrofoam.

BUILDING ROADBED UPGRADES

The major drawback of using blue extruded-Styrofoam tabletop construction is that there is no simple way of providing for upgrades short of tilting the Styrofoam itself. You can, however, combine the blue extruded-Styrofoam system with the Woodland Scenics system. Woodland Scenics has white Styrofoam flexible Inclines to create either 2-percent or 4-percent grades. The Inclines come in sets that elevate the track in 2-inch increments—just the thickness of the blue extruded Styrofoam—so you can use stair steps of the 2-inch thick material for up or down grades (Figure 5-2). Frankly, I do not recommend using grades on layouts as small as 4 x 8 or 5 x 9 feet because there just isn't enough room to gain elevation and maintain realism. You can achieve the same effect by cutting away the edges of the table as was done on the Burlington Route layout that is visible in overall views of the layout in the color section and in Chapter 17 (Figure 17-16).

FINISHING THE SUBTERRAIN SYSTEM

Woodland Scenics also has some grooved sheets of 1/2-inch white Styrofoam called Profile Boards that interlock to form the edges of the layout and supports for the profiles of the scenery. These can be cut with a hacksaw blade, a serrated kitchen knife or a hot wire as shown earlier in this chapter. Shape the scenery with wadded-up newspapers as described in Chapter 15 (Figures 15-3 and 15-4). When you are satisfied with the shapes, cut the profile board around the edges of the layout to match, then drape plaster-soaked paper towels or plaster-soaked gauze over the newspaper and the edges of the profile boards. The techniques in that chapter utilize

Fig. 6-28. The Plaster Cloth can be wrapped over the Woodland Scenics Risers and the wadded-up newspaper scenery shapes.

Fig. 6-27. The Woodland Scenics Incline system can be used to stair-step uphill grades from one layer of 2-inch thick blue Styrofoam to a layer 2 inches higher.

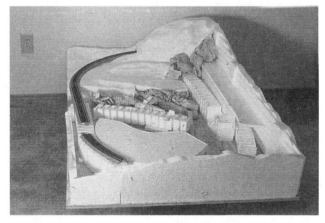

Fig. 6-29. A small layout showing the Woodland Scenics SubTerrain systems, including the Profile Boards around the edge of the layout and the Risers supporting the track, with Plaster Cloth hills in the background.

industrial grade paper towels dipped in Hydrocal plaster. Woodland Scenics recommends using their Plaster Cloth. This is a gauze material, with dry Hydrocal impregnated into the fiber, much like that used to make casts for broken arms or legs. Activa's Rigid Warpand Faller's Plaster Cloth are similar materials.

You can choose to remove the track before applying the plaster-soaked gauze or paper towels, or simply push the plaster material up to the edge of the roadbed as shown in Chapter 15 (Figure 15-11). Woodland Scenics recommends that you remove the track so the plaster-soaked gauze can better bond their Risers and Inclines to the Profile Boards and the plywood or blue extruded Styrofoam baseboard for greater strength (Figure 6-28). If you opt to remove the track, you must smooth the surface of the hardening plaster with sandpaper to provide a perfectly level sub base for the cork roadbed or for the E-Z Track, Power-Loc track or similar plastic roadbed. There will be a bit more noise from the trains with the plaster sub-roadbed technique than there will be if you mount the roadbed directly to the Styrofoam or Riser or Inclines. Finish the layout using the surface texturing techniques in Chapter 17.

CHAPTER 7

Trackwork

LAYING MODEL RAILROAD TRACK, with the track that has built-in road-bed and ballast like Bachmann's E-Z Track, Life-Like's Power-Loc track and Atlas' True Track, is one of the easiest aspects of creating a real railroad in miniature. The E-Z Track and Power-Loc track joints are strong enough so you can build and operate layouts on the bare floor with reliable and trouble-free operation. The sectional track, with only ties and rails like that in the cut-out track planning template in Chapter 3 (Figure 3-6), does not have strong enough joints to hold the track in alignment. It really should be nailed or glued to a tabletop to maintain the alignment you carefully work into it as you arrange the track plan. Atlas True Track has some built-in alignment features but it, too, should be nailed or glued to a tabletop.

CONNECTING DIFFERENT BRANDS OF TRACK

The only adapter to connect different brands of track with roadbed is the 3-

Fig. 7-2. The Power-Loc adapter track (top) can also be used to adapt this track to sectional track with cork roadbed (bottom).

inch straight Power-Loc adapter track. This piece of track has the Power-Loc interface on one end and the opposite end is just hollow plastic. You can connect the other brand using only rail joiners (Figure 7-1). I would suggest that, when connecting Power-Loc track to E-Z Track, you use a 3-inch piece of E-Z Track and that you glue the two pieces together firmly with Testor's Model Master Liquid Cement for Plastics and reinforce the joint with a 4-inch piece of duct tape pressed beneath the roadbed. If you are building a layout with both E-Z Track and Power-Loc track you will need two of these adapter tracks. Once the glue has set, the adapter tracks should be strong enough to use even for a layout built on the floor.

You can also use the Power-Loc adapter track to connect to sectional track with cork roadbed or to Atlas True Track with its plastic roadbed. The resulting joints will not be strong

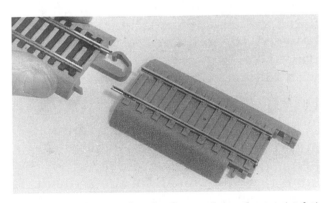

Fig. 7-1. Use the Life-Like Power-Loc adapter (right) to connect Power-Loc track to E-Z Track (left).

enough to use on the floor and, in fact, all the track should be nailed or glued to the tabletop if you use sectional track with cork roadbed or Atlas True Track. The Atlas True Track and the newest Kato Unitrack have smaller rails (called code 83, because it is about .083 inches high) than E-Z Track, Power-Loc Track or most brands of sectional track (which have code 100 rail, which is about .100 inch high). Atlas makes special rail joiners to join the code 83 rail to code 100 rail. The E-Z Track or Power-Loc roadbed is about 1/32 inch thicker than the cork or Atlas True Track, so a cardboard shim will be needed beneath the cork (Figure 7-2) or True Track. If you want to connect E-Z Track to cork (or to Atlas True Track), simply cut the interlocking tabs from the ends of the E-Z Track and connect the rails with rail joiners.

CUSTOM-FITTING E-Z TRACK

On some layouts, one or more pieces of track must be cut to fit to maintain perfect alignment at all the track joints. The straight portion of the wye at Abbott, on the Burlington Northern layout in Chapter 20 (Figure 20-5) will require a 4-1/4-inch piece of E-Z Track (Figure 7-3). Use a razor saw to cut the rails of the track first, then the ties and roadbed. I used several 3-inch straight tracks in this area so that one of the joints would

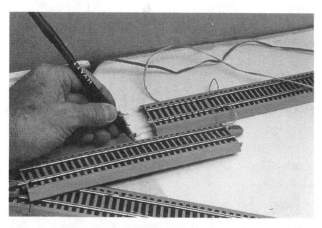

Fig. 7-3. To cut custom-length pieces of E-Z Track, mark the length needed, then use a razor saw to cut through the rails, then the ties and roadbed. Remove any burrs from the cut rails with a hobby knife.

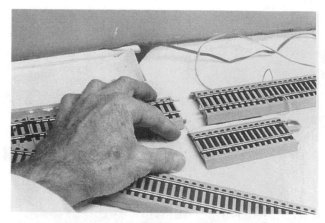

Fig. 7-4. For a tabletop layout, the cut piece of track does not need alignment tabs. Here, the piece is being used to complete the wye at Abbott on the Burlington Route layout in Chapter 20 (Figure 20-5).

fall over joint between the main 4 x 8-foot table and the 1 x 3-foot extension. This is where I placed that 4-1/4-inch straight (Figure 7-4). I also cut the interface locking tabs from the adjoining piece of E-Z Track so only the rail joiners would hold the two pieces of track across this joint between the two tables. I did the same with the locking tabs on the turnout near the joint between the 4 x 8-foot and 1 x 3-foot tables.

The Power-Loc turnouts have a slightly different geometry than the E-Z Track turnouts, as explained in Chapter 3. If you are building this layout with Power-Loc track you will need a 6-1/2-inch piece of track. You will need to remove 2-1/2 inches from the middle of a 9-inch piece of Power-Loc track so you will have the proper interfaces at each end of that finished 6-1/2-inch piece of track. I would suggest you try to make the joint between the 4 x 8-foot and 1 x 3-foot tables fall near this joint between the cut pieces of Power-Loc track so the tracks can be joined only with rail joiners.

LAYING SECTIONAL TRACK

The sectional track, with only ties and rail, slides together easily with rail joiners. In fact, it's almost too easy; the snap-together feature of the individual track sections makes it seem that that's all there is to laying track. But if you've operated a train set on the floor before, you know that it's not quite that simple. The tracks do snap together easily, but they snap apart almost as easily. And sharp dips and bends in the track are the rule rather than exception. The primary method, and in fact, the only way of ending the battle with track joints is to attach the track to a roadbed or ballast board with nails. In this way, the track will be secure and won't move about. In the various pieces of track are holes that fit a Number 19 x 9-inch nail just fine. The trap here, however, is that you won't solve all the track-caused derailments and train startlings by simply nailing it down, particularly if you haven't been extremely careful. With some care and the application of the experience of other model railroaders, though, you can virtually eliminate derailments and other track problems.

THE SURVEYOR'S TASK

No brand of sectional model railroad track is self-aligning. Even if you manage to get every single rail joint to fit tightly, other problems can occur. Slight variations in the length of the individual pieces of rail, slight warpage in a few plastic ties, and a few other minor misalignment problems can add to one another to create a major problem. In fact, just moving the track a fraction of an inch can disturb the alignment. Once you do get sectional track aligned, so the joints are perfect fits, nail it (at least temporarily) to the cork or Homasote roadbed as quickly as possible When it is aligned, then squeeze the track joiners tight (Figure 7-5).

TRACK ALIGNMENT

I suggest you purchase a 3-foot-long steel or aluminum ruler or, at least, a perfectly straight 2 or 3-foot 1 x 4 board. The board will keep the straight track sections truly straight when two or more of them are snapped together. An extra piece of curved track can be used as an alignment gauge for curve-to-curve joints (Figure 7-6). That leaves

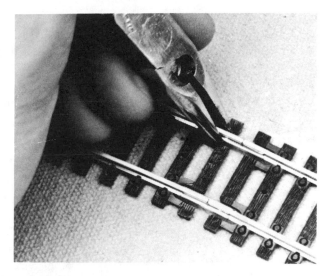

Fig. 7-5. Squeeze any loose rail joiners with needlenose pliers to ensure tight track joints.

only one problem, the places where a curved section joins a straight section must be aligned so the geometry will be almost perfect. Any sudden lurch to the left or right at the beginning of a curve is too toylike, and, worse, it can be the cause of unpredictable derailments. Use a pair of right and left conventional turnouts to help you eyeball that curve-to-straight alignment. The r-t-r turnouts are perfect combinations of straights and curves. By placing the turnout upside down over the curve-to-straight transition, you can see that the rails are all in alignment.

RAILROAD GRADES

I cannot recommend upgrades or downgrades for anything but industrial sidings. If you're an experienced carpenter and like to build benchwork, you may not have too much trouble. The plastic supports for over-and-under Figure-8 shaped layouts are nice toys, but they are neither substantial enough nor realistic enough for a model railroad. The transitions between the level and the bottom and the tops of any grade are very difficult to make. An abrupt change isn't that much of a problem when you're just pushing a single car or two into a siding on a hill. Pulling or pushing long trains up or downgrade, however, will

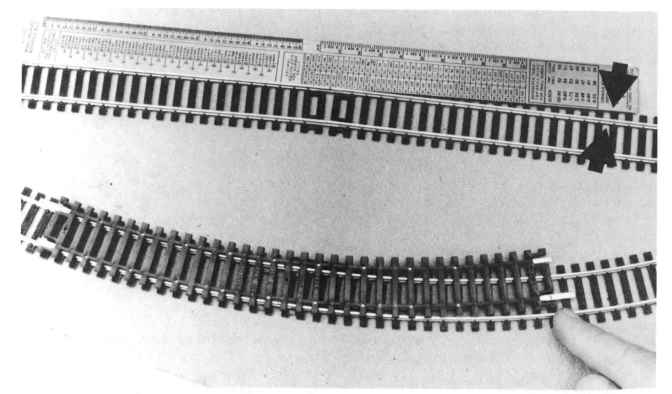

Fig. 7-6. Use a straightedge to help locate out-of-alignment straight track (arrows), and a spare piece of curved track to check the curve track for alignment.

cause derailments, and that can take a lot of the pleasure out of the hobby.

Try it this way: When you've built a layout as complete as the 7 x 8-foot, 9 x 9-foot, or 10 x 10-foot empires in Chapter 20 and you have a smooth operation with few derailments, then you can advance to your third layout and experiment with all kinds of up and downgrades. The charts for figuring grades appear in Chapter 3 (Figure 3-9) for advanced modelers. Spend your track-laying time on that first layout or two, and get the track to align properly in the two dimensions of a level layout before complicating things with the third dimension of up or downgrades.

TRACK-LAYING SIMPLICITY

The real railroads and even a few model railroads have a spiked track, with four spikes per tie. You will be able to lay hundreds of spikes at a time thanks to the prefabrication of sectional track. You will discover, however, that most layouts require the use of

short 1-inch, 2-inch, or 3-inch sections of track. And some sidings will require pieces even smaller than that. Dealers usually carry an assortment of 1, 2, and 3-inch straight track sections, or you can cut your own to ft. A razor saw and hobby knife are the only tools you

Fig. 7-7. The track may be slightly out of line even when the rails touch (center). However, the tracks at the left are fine despite the slight rail gap (arrow).

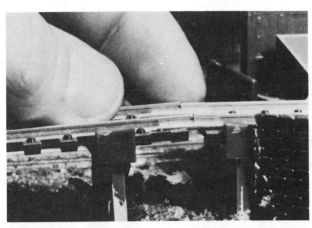

Fig. 7-8. The track must be bent slightly at the tops and bottoms of grades to eliminate sudden changes like this one.

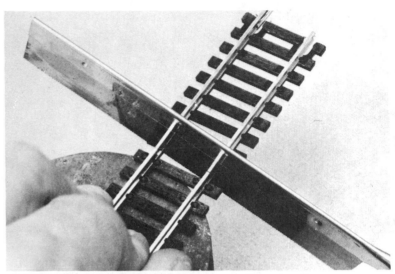

Fig. 7-9. Hold the track in a vise or other sturdy clamp while you cut through it with a razor saw. Be sure the cut is perfectly straight.

will need. Just be sure to follow all of the steps shown in the photographs so the custom-cut track pieces will fit as well as the other track sections.

FLEXIBLE TRACK

You may want to consider using the 3-foot sections of flexible track in place of several shorter pieces of sectional track. The flexible track can make the transition from curve to straight even gentler because the transition point can extend for an inch or two into the curve.

Flexible track is also useful when there are 3-foot and longer stretches of just straight track because the flexible track comes in straight pieces. You must bend the flexible track into a curve by carefully working apart ties on the outside of the curve. First, though, be sure to keep a section of sectional curved track to use as a guide for the radius of any curves you may bend with flexible track. This way you're sure to have a smooth radius all the way through the curve. You'll find that one of the rails will wind up being longer than the other with any flexible track curve. Cut that rail with a razor saw and trim away any burrs with a hobby knife. The sections of flexible track must be pre-fitted, just like any other piece of track, before nailing the track in place.

The secret to perfect trackwork with flexible track is to see that the entire portion of your layout is in perfect

Fig. 7-10. The flush-cut diagonal cutters make a cut with a flush surface (top) on one side and a severe edge on the other (bottom).

alignment before you permanently drive any nails to secure the track. Do, however, use a few nails, driven so the heads are 1/16-inch or so above the ties (for easy removal) to help hold the track you have already aligned in place. Try to work with a complete oval or the

Fig. 7-11. Shave the plastic from beneath the rails with the razor saw to make room for the rail joiners on the tops of the ties.

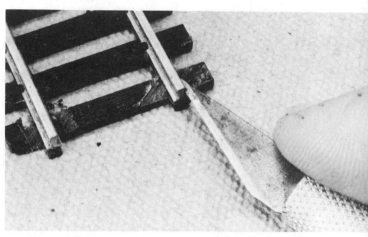

Fig. 7-12. Scrape the corners of the cut rails with a hobby knife to remove any burrs before installing the rail joiners.

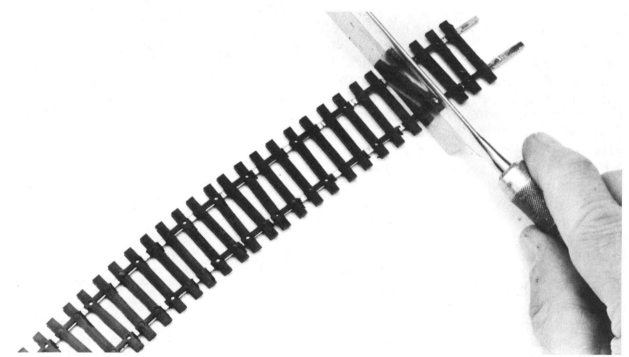

Fig. 7-13. Cut through every other tie, on opposite sides of the bottom of track sections, to make your own flexible track.

entire passing siding so you can align every inch of the track with every other inch. When you're sure that portion of the layout is perfect, mark the edges and each track joint with a pencil. Then you'll know if any section shifts while you're nailing down the rest. Be very patient and pull as many nails as you must to realign any of the track that has shifted out of alignment.

THE ROADBED

Remember, there is no equally useful substitute for Homasote-brand cardboard wall panels as a roadbed for a model railroad. The thinner Upsom board is similar but has a skin on one side and it must be glued firmly to the plywood subroadbed or it will warp. Ordinary plywood is too hard; you'll snap plastic ties (and your temper) trying to get the track laid and the trains will sound like toys when you're done. Other types of wall board, such as Celotex, are too soft, and plaster board is too brittle and crumbly. You can use cork, but the nails must be long enough to penetrate through the cork and into the plywood

and it is difficult to get both cork and track aligned with one another. Atlas has several books that describe the process. The Homasote can be cut with a hardware store's utility or carton-cutting knife, and then you can shape the edges into ballast shoulders with any hobby knife. The Homasote is just hard enough to hold the track nails securely, but it's soft enough so you can drive the nails into place with a pair of needlenose pliers. Be sure to support the Homasote with at least 2-inch thick plywood. (The benchwork to support the plywood is described in Chapter 5.)

NAILING SECTIONAL TRACK

Use Number 19 x 1/2-inch common nails to hold the track sections. Push the nails through the holes in the center of some of the ties in each piece of sectional track with the needlenose pliers. The head of the nail should not actually touch the top of the tie or it will likely pull the tie downward to distort the tie and alter the track gauge (rail spacing). I cut a V-shaped notch in the end of a plain index card (Figure 7-15). I hold the

Fig. 7-14. The 1/2-inch thick Homasote can be cut with heavy pressure on a hardware or utility knife. Trim the edges to simulate ballast shoulders.

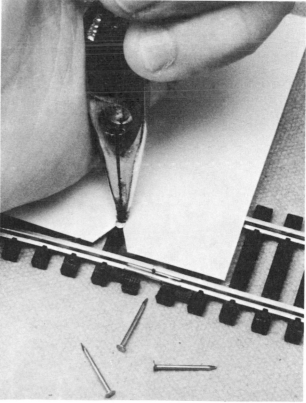

Fig. 7-15. Cut an index card to use as a gauge so you won't push the track nails too far into the Homasote.

index card next to the shank of the nail and push the nail head down with the tip of the pliers until I can just feel it touch the index card. I then remove the index card. That leaves just the right amount of clearance between the head of the nail and the top of the plastic tie.

BALLASTING THE TRACK

The E-Z Track, Power-Loc track, True Track, Unitrak and C-Track all include ballast. The ballast on the Unitrak and C-Track is realistic enough to use as-is. I would suggest, however, that you add loose ballast (later held firm with Matte Medium) for E-Z Track, Power-Loc track and True Track. You will, of course, want to use loose ballast with cork or Homasote roadbed.

The very first step when applying ballast to track laid on Homasote or cork roadbed is to seal the area beneath the track with a coat of latex paint. This is a job that's really best done when you first glue and nail the Homasote to the plywood, but it can also be done by using a small paint brush (size 1 or 2) to apply the paint between the ties. It won't hurt if you get some of the paint on the ties; the ballast and the weathering you add later will disguise the paint smears. The paint seals the Ho-

masote, so the Matte Medium won't soak into the Homasote before it has a chance to glue the ballast.

I suggest that you wait until the scenery is almost complete to do this. You may find that you want to relocate the track or add additional turnouts during the interim, and those changes are a lot easier if you don't have to worry about the ballast and the track at the same time. Also, the real railroads add ballast last, so some of its spills over the surrounding terrain and you can be capture that effect by applying ballast as one of the final steps in creating scenery.

You can use common dirt or sand for ballast or buy one of he many brands of prepared ballast. Pick a color that corresponds to the type of ballast used on your favorite real railroad. You can even pulverize chunks of real ballast by putting them in a thick cloth bag and hitting it with a hammer. Sift the ballast through a kitchen strainer. The mesh in the strainer should be the same size as door screen, or use a scrap piece of door screen for the sieve. Use only the finer portion of the material that passes through the screen for your ballast or, if you buy ready-made ballast, buy a size that would sift through a door screen. With some brands, you may want Fine or even N Scale ballast. For extra realism, use a gray or brown color for the main-line tracks' ballast and a beige color for the sidings. Later, in the weathering phase of track-laying, you can spray on a wash of black acrylic paint and water to give the ballast the dirty look it has on the real railroads. Always check for iron particles in any dirt you use by passing a small magnet over the loose dirt. If any particles cling to the magnet, find another source of dirt.

Buy a plastic mustard or ketchup dispenser with a pointed tip and use this to apply the Artist's Matte Medium or white glue to bond the ballast. I prefer to use Artist Matte Medium to glue ballast and other loose scenic textures. The Matte Medium is used for mixing acrylic paints and it's available at any

Fig. 7-16. Spread the ballast with a paintbrush and remove any excess from turnouts and crossings.

good artists' supply store. It looks and feels almost exactly like plain white glue. However, it's slightly more flexible to keep the trackwork from amplifying sounds, and it's a bit easier to pry the trackwork loose when you want to relocate it or add a turnout to the layout. The Matte Medium also dries with little or no gloss.

Apply a bead of Artist's Matte Medium along the edges of the ballast, just missing the ends of the ties. Apply a drop of oil that is marked as being harmless to plastics to the moving switch tie bar and to any visible moving parts of the turnout.

Cover the turnout's moving switch points with small strips of masking tape so the spray cannot reach them to carry the dilute Matte Medium into the working parts of every turnout.

The ballast can now be sprinkled over the track. Apply more than you feel you might need and spread it around with another brush. Use the brush to carefully sweep away any ballast from around the switch points or between the second (guard) rail at every turnout frog and crossing frog (the places where the rails cross) so there will be no places where the ballast could hit the wheel flanges. Finally, spray the ballasted track with water. This will allow the dilute Matte Medium to work its way around each grain of ballast through a general diluting action. Mix nine parts water with one part Matte Medium and add a drop of dishwashing detergent to help reduce the surface extension so the mixture will not puddle so easily. You can also use Woodland Scenic's Scenic Cement or Champ Decal Company's Resinbond Spray fluid as described in Chapter 17. Next, spray the track and the ballast with mist of the dilute Matte Medium from a plastic pump-type spray bottle or a plant atomizer. Let the ballast dry for at least a day and vacuum away the excess. Remove the masking tape from the turnout's moving switch points.

Be sure to keep both the ballast and the Matte Medium well away from the working parts of all the track turnouts

Fig. 7-17. Spray the ballast with the dilute Matte Medium using a pump hair spray bottle, a plant atomizer or Woodland Scenics Scenic Sprayer.

including the moving switch points. Simply paint the area around the switch points in a color to match the ballast. (No one will ever notice that there aren't any of those loose-looking rocks in that area.) The ballast itself can jam the switch points, and the Matte Medium will obviously render the switch worthless. I cannot provide a suitable method of removing glue-stuck turnout points, except to remove the turnout, try to free its mechanism from below and if that fails, replace the turnout.

No doubt some granules of the ballast will have been glued to the sides and the tops of the rails. Go over the track with an old hobby knife blade to scrape away both dried Matte Medium and ballast from the tops and the inside edges of the rails. Push a gondola or flat car over the track with a bit of downward pressure so you can feel if the wheels encounter any Matte Medium or ballast on the running surfaces of the rails, between the guard rails, or on the sides of the rails that you might have missed. If you decide to weather the track (a step I feel is as important as the ballast itself), then you might as well save this track-cleaning until that step is completed.

Fig. 7-18. Paint both sides of the rails with Box Car Red paint to simulate rust, then scrape the tops and inside corners of the rails to allow electrical contact.

Fig. 7-20. You can remove plastic ties and cut the tabs with a razor to make end bumpers (top left). Small Hayes Wheel stops (top right) are available from Tomar Industries and Selley and similar wheel-stops are available from Sequoia Scale Models. The bumping post (bottom) is available from Tomar Industries, Sequoia Scale Models and Creative Model Associates.

Fig. 7-19. The varying colors of the ties and the rust on the rails can be simulated with Box Car Red paint and dilute black paint on a model railroad.

WEATHERING THE TRACK

The track on a real railroad is constantly exposed to weather, and that is why the cars and locomotives look so well used. Few modelers realize that their layouts have this major flaw. Clean track simply doesn't look like the real thing.

In weathering track, first spray all the trackwork with a wash of ninety-five parts water to five parts black acrylic paint, concentrating a bit more of the spray down the center of the track where oil and grease would drip from passing trains. The sides of the rails can then be painted with reddish brown using model railroad Box Car Red paint. A few dribbles of paint on the simulated plastic spikes or on the ties will probably look just like rusted ties or tie plates, so don't worry about them. Then, spray the entire area with a wash that matches the color of the dirt on the surrounding hills. This means everything, including the buildings. The entire layout should have a very light hint of that earth tint. Now you can scrape the rail tops and check for any paint or ballast that might stop the flow of electricity between the rails and wheels or cause a derailment.

DO'S AND DON'TS FOR TRACK AND TURNOUTS

- Do cut track sections to fit precisely into any odd-length gaps so the track and rails flow smoothly with no kinks.
- Do squeeze each rail joiner with pliers, along the base or web of the rail, to be certain it fits tightly.
- Do be certain the track is in perfect alignment across each rail joint, then nail or glue the track in place.
- Do place at least one 9-inch section of straight track between any S-bend so the trains will not lurch from left to right as they travel through the S-bend. The lurch is not realistic and it can cause derailments.
- Do try to place a larger-radius transition curve at the beginning and end of every curve. Use, for example, one length of 22-inch radius track at each extreme end of every 18-inch radius curve.
- Do use only a hard rubber eraser like those sold by Life-Like, Model Power and Bright Boy to clean the tops of all rails.

- Don't try to bend the track to fill any gaps.
- Don't rely on the fit of rail joiners as they are furnished by the factory.
- Don't rely on the rail joiners to hold or push the track into alignment.
- Don't connect any radius right curve to a left curve without that transition section of straight track.
- Don't join tight curves (18 or 15-inch radius) directly to straight track sections except in yards or industrial areas.
- Don't use a file, emery paper or sandpaper to clean the rails. The surface of the rail will be scratched and the scratches will make it easier for dirt to collect and oxides to re-form.

CHAPTER 8

Remote-Control Turnouts

FEW MODEL RAILROADERS will admit it, but the sight of a miniature train following a path they have selected for it by remote control is one of the most exciting aspects of the hobby. The movement of the turnout's moving points, which change the direction of the train, is so slight compared to the bulk of the train that the whole process almost seems miraculous. The track turnouts allow two trains to pass and cars to switch in and out of trains. They also allow complete trains or locomotives to make reversing movements, and trains can be made up however you want. Most importantly, turnouts allow for the multiple routes that make the track plans in chapters 3 and 20 so versatile. If you have to choose between buying another locomotive and buying another pair of turnouts, pick the turnouts. Through them, you'll get a hundred times more enjoyment out of all the model railroad equipment you already have.

TURNOUT POSITIONING

There are good and bad places to put turnouts. In some places, you should use remote-controlled turnouts, and in other places it's better to use manual turnouts.

The diagrams and data in Chapter 3 will explain where curves and turnouts can and cannot be mixed in order to minimize the chances for track misalignment and the resulting derailments. In brief, the standard straight/curve turnouts should be used only in place of straight track sections or at the beginning of curves. The curved/curved switches should be used only in place of a piece of curved track. Wye turnouts

should be used only in stub-ended wyes, such as those in Chapter 9.

If a turnout is placed more than 2-1/2 feet from the edge of the table, or in a tunnel, it should definitely be a remote-control turnout. Try to avoid placing turnouts in tunnels, and, if you must, make a portion of the mountain above the turnout removable so you can work on the turnout or rerail any wrecks. Turnouts that are within 2-1/2 feet of your control panels might just as well be the manual type, which are thrown by moving the pin directly at the turnout. The remote-control turnouts add three more wires for each turnout to what is already complicated wiring. The fewer turnouts you use, the easier your layout will be to maintain. If you have to walk up to the control panel to work a remote-control button or turnout lever for a turnout that's as easy to reach as the panel itself, you are adding unnecessary complication to the layout. You might notice, by the way, that every turnout on the 9 x 9-foot Burlington Northern layout in Chapter 20 (Figure 20-3) is a remote-control type, while on the 7 x 8-foot Burlington Route (Figure 20-5) only one turnout (the one against wall between Abbott and Chester) is a remote-control turnout. The remote-control turnouts can still be operated by moving the pin beside the turnout, however.

WIRING FUNDAMENTALS

Working with the wires from a remote-control turnout may very well be the first bit of complicated wiring you will have to do on your layout. The actual track wiring is seldom complicated by the addition of a turnout because the r-t-r firms have a system of routing electrical power through the turnout regardless of what direction it is thrown. The only time you must add additional track wiring is when the addition of a turnout creates a wye or a reversing loop as part of the track plan. Wiring for wyes and loops are shown in Chapter 9; there are reversing loops in two of the Figure-8 plans in Chapter 3; and there are wyes in the 7 x 8-foot, 9 x 9-foot and 10 x 10-foot plans are in Chapter 20.

Each of the remote-controlled turnouts has three wires of its own, and these must be connected to the turnout controller on your control panel and to the AC terminals-2 on your power pack. On a complicated layout, which might have dozens of turnouts, it's a good idea to purchase a separate power pack for the turnouts and use another one to operate the accessories. The use of a turnout or an accessory can affect the speed of a train at a critical moment. For most 4 x 8-foot first-time layouts, a single power pack for all three trains, turnouts, and accessories is sufficient.

It is not necessary to solder any of the connections on your model railroad. Each of the r-t-r turnouts and most accessories have screws to attach the wires. However, there are right and

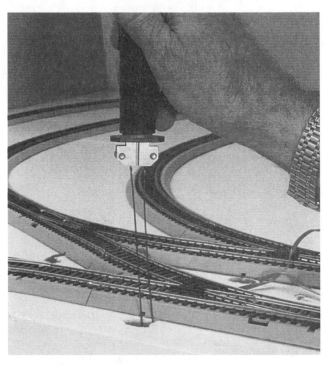

Fig. 8-2. If you have built a lightweight layout of blue foam insulation board as described in Chapter 6, you can drill holes for the switch machine wires and for the track connector wires using the heated wire in the Avalon Concepts Detail Wand to melt a hole 4 inches deep through two layers of insulation board.

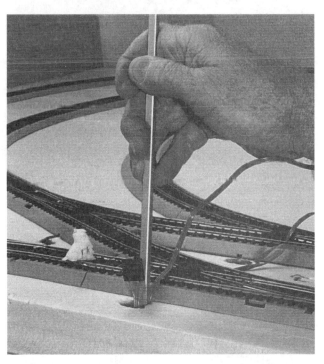

Fig. 8-3. Finish the hole through the third layer of blue Styrofoam by simply punching it out with a long screwdriver. Save the cone-shaped punches to use as plugs (left) to fill the area around the wires. When the hole is punched through, loop the wire over the end of the screwdriver (shown) and push the wire through the tabletop.

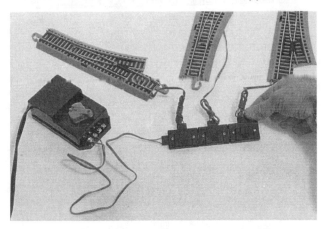

Fig. 8-1. The turnouts in the E-Z Track (shown) and Power-Loc track systems have simple plug-in wiring that is pre-soldered to the turnout. The three-wire plug is plugged into the switch controller (left).The two wires from the AC side of the power pack (bottom, left) also have a plug that is connected to the side of the switch controller. Two, three, or a dozen switch controllers can be plugged together, side-by-side, like these.

Fig 8-4. If you have a plywood and Homasote table-top, use an electric drill to cut a 1/4-inch hole for the wires from switch machines or track connecting wires.

Fig. 8-5. Push the wires down through the hole in the plywood and Homasote and paint the exposed ends of the wires beside the turnout or track connectors to match the ballast.

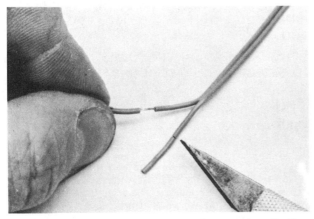

Fig. 8-6. Careful use of a sharp hobby knife will allow you to strip the insulation from wires without cutting the wire itself.

Fig. 8-7. Twist the ends of the wires, then bend them into backward-question-mark shapes before attaching them to the terminal screws.

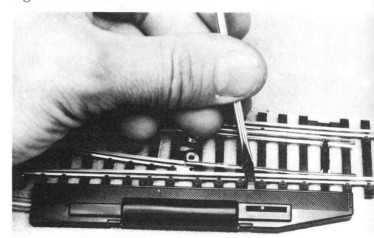

Fig. 8-8. Pry outward and upward to snap the tabs of the switch machine cover clear for access to the switch machine.

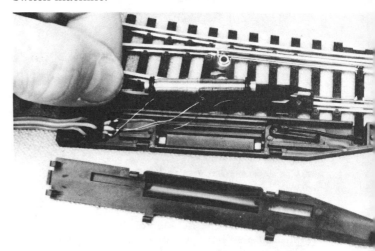

Fig. 8-9. Remove the cover of the switch machine and clean any dirt or dried Matte Medium from inside.

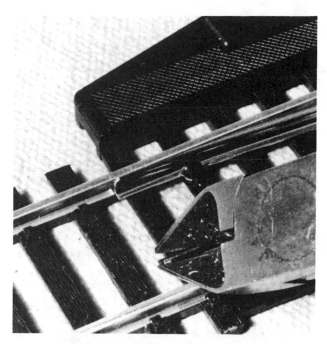

Fig. 8-10. Trim the ends of the any troublesome turnout points to a slight 45-degree angle to help eliminate derailments.

wrong ways to perform that seemingly simple task. I suggest that you use a sharp hobby knife to cut through the insulation on the wires, rather than using a conventional wire stripper. You can feel the point when you reach the wire with the hobby knife, so you can avoid even nicking the delicate hair-like strands of wire (Figure 8-6). It takes some practice to get the feel of cutting just the insulation and not the wire, but it's a technique that will always work once you learn it.

You'll need to remove only about 1/4 inch of insulation. If you remove much more, you'll have an excess of wire, and it might touch a nearby terminal screw and cause a short circuit. If you remove too little insulation, it will be difficult to get the terminal screw to grip the wire. When the insulation is off, twist the wire strands together immediately by rolling the exposed end of the wire between your fingers. Watch those ends carefully until you get each terminal screw tightened; re-twist the wire if the individual strands start to wander about.

Each of the wire strands must be captured under the head of the terminal screws. If you leave a few of the hair-like strands free, they'll eventually find their

way to the next terminal screw for that hard-to-locate short circuit. The twisted ends of the wires must be bent in a backward question-mark shape (Figure 8-7), with the loop just 1/32 inch or so larger than the diameter of the screw threads and about that much smaller than the diameter of the screw head. The reverse question mark- shape loops the wire around the Shank of the screen, so the action of the tightening screw head will tend to pull the wire around the screw for an even tighter joint. Any other bend or even straight-in installation of the wire on the screw terminal will result in several of those individual wire strands popping out from beneath the screw head. This may all sound like a lot of bother, but, really, it's just as easy to do it the right way once you learn how.

There will undoubtedly be times when you need a wire longer than that supplied with the turnouts. Save any leftover wires for just that purpose, or buy some additional hook-up wire from an electronics hobby store. (The technique for splicing wires is illustrated in Chapter 9.) Do try to match the color of the two wires you slice so you can trace any short circuits or loose connections by wire color. Be sure you have at least 3 inches of slack in the wire between the turnout and the controller and/or the power pack. You might have to lift the turnout slightly to adjust or relocate it or move the turnout controller. The extra length of wire will give you enough room to make such changes. The extra length may also be needed, someday, if you build a master control panel and need to splice in extra wire length to reach the new control panel.

THE TRAIN THAT NEVER DERAILS

There will never be such a thing as a train, real or model, that never derails. However, you can come very close if you pay careful attention to the alignment of your track and to the operation of your turnouts.

Fig. 8-11. Derailments and Track Troubleshooting.

Trouble	Probable Cause of Trouble	Solution
Train derails frequently at one particular place.	1. Offset rails at joiners.	1. Align rails and rail joiners with steel ruler and needlenose pliers.
	2. Excess plastic "flash" or wisps from ties on inside edges of the rails.	2. Trim "flash" with a hobby knife.
	3. Plaster, glue, or some foreign object stuck to track.	3. Remove it.
	4. Ends of rails burred or rough.	4. Smooth the tops and inside edges of the rails with number 400 sandpaper.
Train derails at turnout.	1. Switch points not throwing far enough to make firm contact with "through" rails.	1. Remove any foreign matter from area around points and check the action of switch lever inside the switch machine.
	2. Turnout twisted or bent, so all rails do not align in both "main" and "siding" turnout positions.	2. Bend the turnout into perfect alignment.
	3. Coupler pins hitting switch rails or frog.	3. Cut pins to proper length, as outlined in Chapter 14.
	4. Any of four problem areas for "regular" track.	4. Correct, as outlined above.
Train derails everywhere.	1. Running the train too fast.	1. Run it slower.
Turnouts do not throw.	1. Turnout buttons on remote-control unit wired incorrectly.	1. Be sure wires are connected exactly as shown on the turnout's package and to "AC" terminals on the power pack.
	2. Button on turnout control not depressed when it is moved into position.	2. Simple operator error. Remember to *both* slide and push the button to actuate remote-control turnouts.
	3. "AC" portion of power pack not functioning.	3. Touch the wires from an r-t-r street light (test light) to just the "AC" terminals of the power pack. If light does not glow, have your dealer check the power pack.
	4. Turnout control is faulty, or contacts inside are dirty.	4. Touch the street-light wires to screws number 1 and 2 (the center screw) while you move the switch lever to the left and to the right and press it down. The light should glow. Touch the street-light wires to screws number 2 and 3 while you slide the switch lever to the right and push it down. The light should glow. If the light does not glow with the button to the right *or* left and depressed, replace the switch controller.
	5. Mechanical portion of the turnout and switch points may be bent or clogged.	5. Remove any debris from points and from switch machine and align switch parts.
	6. Hair-size wire inside remote-control switch machine broken.	6. Have wire soldered together at an electronics store.

The ends of the turnout's moving switch points are just sharp enough to sometimes cause derailments. The flanges of the cars and locomotives tend to pick at the sharp corners of the switch points and derail. If you have a turnout that causes persistent derailments, you may want to trim just 1/32 inch off the corner of the turnout points (Figure 8-10). Do not trim any more than that or you'll make the point-picking problem even worse. Don't tempt fate either; if your other turnouts are working without causing derailments, then leave them and their points alone!

Many model railroaders place a hat pin or a map pin into the layout at every place a derailment has occurred. The pin reminds them where to look for trouble (see the Derailment Troubleshooting Chart in Figure 8-11) when it comes time for an evening of maintenance. Cars or locomotives that are persistent derailers are placed on a shelf for attention at the same time. If you follow this kind of maintenance, you will soon locate and eliminate all of the troublesome spots on your layout.

VANISHING SWITCH MACHINES

Nothing on a real railroad even resembles the switch machine beside a model railroad's turnouts. The switch machines on the E-Z Track and Power-Loc track turnouts are hidden beneath the roadbed, with just a small pin visible to manually control the turnout. Other brands, however, and all types of sectional track have bulky switch machines beside the turnout. You'll increase the realism of your layout considerably, then, by hiding those switch machines. Do not try to cover up the switch machines with the plaster scenery. The switch machines are so close to the track that the steps of some locomotives and the sides of others actually rub the switch machine for a moment, so there is no room for the added thickness of scenery on the rail side of the switch machine. The best trick is to paint the switch machine with the basic brown earth color I suggested for the Homasote beneath the track. When you mask the switch points during the ballasting, keep the switch machine clear so that it will receive some of the wash of flat black and earth colors used to weather the rest of the track. You'll be amazed at how well the switch machines blend into the layout when their colors match the scenery. It's not so obvious in the photographs because the switch machine's shape is still visible, but the camouflage-with-paint technique does work.

You can go a step further with some of your switch machines, and hide the portion that is away from the track with bits of ground foam-rubber leaves to simulate weeds and bushes. A few scraps of balsa wood or some old brass rail can be cut and piled on the back side of switch machine's where there are no adjacent tracks. The switch machine will then become just part of the pile of wood or rail. Be careful, when working with glue around the switch machine, that no glue finds its way inside the switch machine or anywhere near the switch points.

Fig. 8-12. Disguise switch machines and terminal track connections with paint or with ground foam weeds.

CHAPTER 9

Control Panels and Wiring

YOU CAN BUILD a complete model railroad with dozens of turnouts, and wire it with just a train set power pack and only two wires clipped to a single terminal track if you want to operate only one train and you do not include any reversing loops or wyes in the track plan. The design of most snap-together HO scale turnouts (Atlas, Bachmann, IHC, Life-Like, Model Power, Peco, and Roco) and crossings route the track power directly through the switch or

Fig. 9-1. The DCC systems, like MRC's Command 2000, are available with walk-around controllers. This one, on the 7 x 8-foot Burlington Route layout, and the power pack are mounted on a slide-out shelf.

crossing, so many of the gaps you may have heard about are unnecessary.

If you are willing to invest in a Digital Command Control (DCC) system instead of a second conventional power pack, you can operate two (or more) trains with just two wires. You will still need to have additional wires, four electrical insulation gaps in the rails and a reversing switch, however.

The common rail wiring system for two-train operation is another wiring shortcut that allows you to use an additional power pack for each train, but with just one additional wire (and one rail gap) for each electrically isolated block. The wiring for your railroad in miniature should be only as complicated as you want it to be.

WALK-AROUND CONTROL

Walk-around control can make your entire railroad seem more realistic without any real expense or labor. Walk-around control is the process of placing the throttle (speed control and reversing switch) on a tether or extension cord so you can walk around your layout to follow your train. It was developed about twenty years ago for large, shelf-style, around-the-room layouts, such as the 10 x 10-foot track plan in Chapter 20 (Figure 20-6). With it, the operator has the ability to run the railroad from a single control panel in the manner of a real railroad dispatcher or towerman, and it also offers him the chance to be an engineer.

Walk-around control will have a far greater effect on your attitude toward your models than you could imagine. Even a simple model will seem many

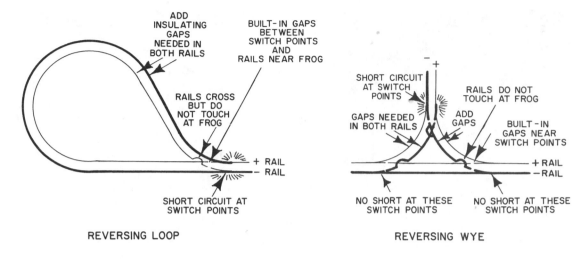

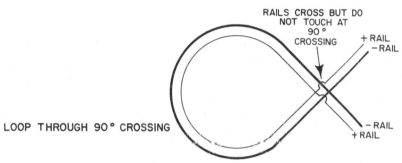

Fig. 9-2. Short circuits will occur at wyes and loops unless gaps are cut through both rails.

times more true to life when you are moving along beside it with the throttle and reversing control in your hands. The controls for the turnouts and the blocks (for two-train operation) are still located on control panels, but those panels are located near the yards or towns or other concentrations of complex trackwork. On basement-filling layouts, the turnout and block controls are strung out all along the edge of the benchwork just in front of the tracks they control.

The mechanics of walk-around control are simple enough: an additional throttle and reversing switch are built into a box small enough to be held in one hand. That box is generally referred to simply as the throttle.

Each brand of throttle has its own specific wiring instructions, but most can be connected with four long (10 to 20-foot) wires to the four terminals on the back of most power packs. Those four wires are the tether cable for the walk-around

throttle. You will be able to walk along beside your train for the length of that cable. Position the power pack near the center of the edge of the layout. The best places to have a connection of the tether of a walk-around control would be on the end of the Burlington Route layout near the steel viaduct (Figure 1-2, in Chapter 1), near Emmett on the Burlington Northern layout (Figure 20-3, in Chapter 20), or near the circled letter I on the Around-The-Wall layout (Figure 20-6). If you use a 12-foot long set of four 16-gauge insulated wires, you will be able to have just a single connection for the walk-around throttle's tether cable. The 12-foot tether cable will allow you to walk beside the train anywhere on those three layouts.

For larger layouts you will need to provide sockets, located around the edges of the layout about every 10 linear feet, as shown in that figure and in Figures 9-15 and 9-16. Some of the walk-around throttles use a standard telephone jack

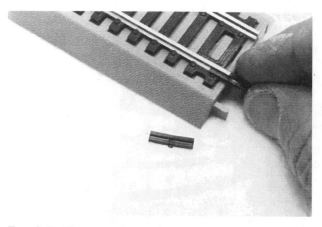

Fig. 9-3. Plastic rail joiners can be used to replace the metal rail joiners to provide insulating gaps at reversing sections or blocks.

and are pre-wired to their own plug, so you need only install the telephone-style socket on the edge of the layout.

Your dealer can order walk-around throttles for you. The least expensive ones will have only the throttle and reversing switch, but some also have a pulse control on-off switch for better slow-speed control for momentum so the train feels like it really weighs thousands of tons.

All of the walk-around throttles are designed to be held in one hand with the throttle knob or switch operated by a thumb or forefinger of that same hand. That leaves your second hand free to operate the block switches or to uncouple the cars from the train as shown in Chapter 18.

TWO-RAIL WIRING BASICS

It's to the credit of the engineering efforts of the model railroad manufacturers that they have managed to make the electrical system of their trains look so much like the tracks of the real railroads. The rails of the tracks on your model railroad lead a double life. They guide and support the flanged wheels of the locomotives and rolling stock just like real railroad rails. The rails of a model railroad, however, also function as exposed wires, which are part of the electrical circuit that carries the power to the electric motor in the locomotive. One of the rails is positive and the other negative, and these carry the current to and from the locomotive. If the positive rail ever touches the negative rail, it will cause a short circuit. The plus and minus rails would appear to cross at every turnout or every 30-degree or 90-degree crossing track. The r-t-r turnouts and crossings, however, are designed so that the plus rail passes beneath the minus rail at the frog (the plastic center of the turnout where the rails cross). A thin piece of plastic molded into that plastic frog insulates the two rails. An insulating gap has been placed between the turnout's moving switch points and the rest of the rail, so no short circuit can occur there.

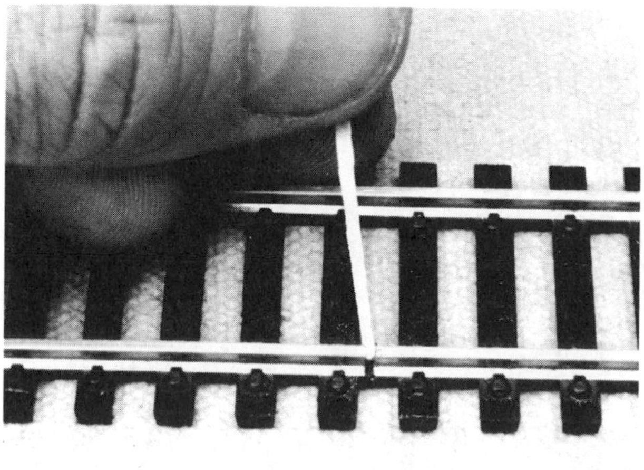

Fig. 9-4. After a gap has been cut through the rail with a razor saw, the gap should be filled with epoxy so it cannot close.

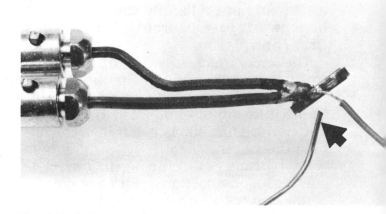

Fig. 9-5. Solder (arrow) can be used to attach track wires to metal rail joiners where space does not permit a terminal track. Atlas and Kato both offer rail joiners with the wires already attached.

Fig. 9-6. Locomotive and Electrical Troubleshooting.

Trouble	Probable Cause of Trouble	Solution
Locomotive does not run (and headlight does not glow).	1. Power pack not plugged in, or the outlet is faulty.	1. Plug in the power pack or check an appliance in the outlet.
	2. Track wires may be attached to the "AC" terminals of the power pack.	2. Connect the track wires to the two "DC" terminals.
	3. Wires may be improperly connected to the track terminals.	3. Check the "rules" and diagrams in Chapter 7.
	4. Insulated rail joiners may not be in correct positions.	4. Check the "rules" and diagrams in Chapter 7.
	5. Locomotive may be off the track.	5. Rerail the locomotive.
	6. Wheels or track rails may be dirty.	6. Clean the tracks.
	7. Nails, wires, tinsel, or other metals may be causing a short circuit by laying on the track.	7. Remove the material.
	8. Locomotive may be sitting on the plastic frog of a switch or crossing; on an insulated rail joiner; on a track with an operating-signal man or operating crossing gates.	8. Move the locomotive.
Locomotive does not run (but headlight does glow).	1. Check all of the above probable causes. Number 2 is the most likely.	1. Be sure to turn the power pack off immediately while you search for and correct the problem.
Locomotive does not run, and none of the above 8 checks solves the problem.	1. Use an operating light or 12-volt lamp bulb as a "test light." Touch the two wires to the "DC" terminals of the power pack with the "throttle" on. If the light glows, the pack is fine.	1. If the light does not glow with the power pack plugged into a working outlet and with the throttle full on, have the pack checked by your dealer's service department.
	2. Touch the test-light wires to the terminals on each of the terminal tracks with the throttle full on and the "Blocking Switch" (if any) for each block turned on. If the light glows, the problem is likely in the locomotive. If the light does not glow, there is a break in one or both of the wires from the power pack to the terminal.	2. Replace the wires.
	3. Place the locomotive on the terminal track that you just checked and found to be working. If the locomotive runs, then the problem is a loose or missing rail joiner or incorrect wiring.	3. Check every track joint and see that any complex wiring is correct according to the "rules" and diagrams in Chapter 7.
	4. If the locomotive does not run on a terminal track you know is getting power, and you have performed every other troubleshooting check, the problem is likely to be the locomotive. Try another locomotive as a double-check; if it does run, the fault lies in the first locomotive.	4. Have locomotive checked by your dealer's service department.
Locomotive runs but in a series of jerks and stops.	1. Dirty track or locomotive wheels, or, on some steam locomotives, dirty truck-pivot area.	1. Clean everything as outlined in this chapter.
	2. Loose wire connections or loose rail joiners.	2. Check EVERY one in the areas behind and in front of places where the locomotive stalls, and check the terminal track and the power pack wires.
	3. Lack of lubrication on the locomotive (but this is highly unlikely).	3. Lubricate as outlined in this chapter.
	4. Worn motor brushes.	4. Replace as shown in Figures 10–26, 10–27, and 10–28.

FROG SYSTEMS

The r-t-r design is called the insulated frog system, and its greatest advantage is that it allows you to connect the track wiring on either side of the turnout and to mix in any quantity of turnouts and still have power (but no short circuits) anywhere on the track system. If you try to use another brand of turnout that has a live frog design with an r-t-r turnout, you may create a short circuit in your layout. The live frog turnouts must receive electrical power from the point (or single-track) side of the turnout. If you do have other brands of turnouts, it's best to use them for stub-ended industrial sidings or yards. In these places, the turnout can be at the end of the track.

WYES AND REVERSING LOOPS

The r-t-r turnout and crossing design contains one problem that can't be eliminated. A short circuit is created whenever the track is arranged to form a reversing loop or a wye, such as those in this chapter. The reversing loop or wye is designed to allow you to turn a train around without removing it from the tracks. If you think about the logic of reversing a complete train or even a single locomotive, you'll realize (the diagrams will help) that the positive rail must touch the negative rail and vice

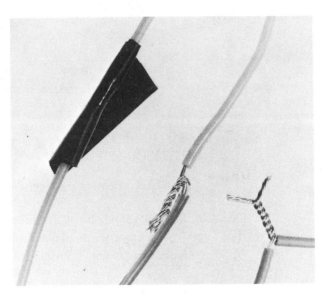

Fig. 9-8. Twist the wires to be joined together (right), bend the ends back (center), and wrap them with plastic electrical tape to leave a tab (right).

versa. You may accidentally include a reversing loop or wye in a free-lance track plan; a diagonal track across an oval layout, with turnouts on both ends of the diagonal, will create a reversing loop like that in Figure 9-12. A similar, but less obvious, reversing loop is part of the Figure-8 track plans in Chapter 3 (Figures 3-3 and 3-5). Wyes are included in the 7 x 8-foot, 9 x 9-foot and 10 x 10-foot track plans in Chapter 20 (Figures 20-3, 20-5 and 20-6). Generally, you will want to include a wye or reversing loop on the layout just to add the variety of clockwise and counterclockwise operation without hand-carrying the trains.

A wye or reversing loop must have a section of track that is used for the actual reversing action. The diagonal track on the typical reversing loop and, sometimes, the stub end of a wye (as in Figure 9-10 and the track plan in Figure 20-6) are the obvious portions of the track that will be used mainly during the time when the train is being reversed. A connection between a main line and a branch line, such as that in Figure 9-11, is a third example of where a reversing section might be located—this is the type of wiring that would be used with the wyes in Figures 3-3, 3-5, 20-3 and 20-5. In every case,

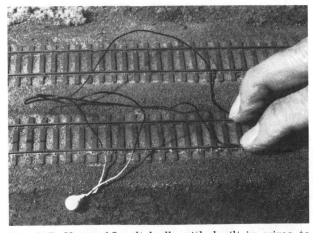

Fig. 9-7. Use a 12-volt bulb with built-in wires to check for electrical current flow to the rails.

Control Panels and Wiring

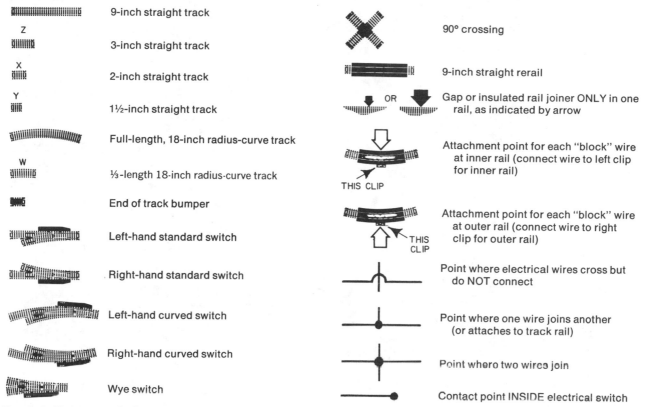

Fig. 9-9. Key to symbols on track plans and wiring diagrams.

the reversing section must be isolated electrically from the rest of the layout by cutting right through both rails on both ends of the reversing section.

You can substitute the insulated plastic rail joiners for metal rail joiners rather than cutting the rails if you wish. The rail joint created with plastic rail joiners is not quite as rigid as that done with metal rail joiners, so I recommend that you actually cut the rails whenever there is room. Sometimes it may be necessary to place a gap between turnouts if there is space for only an insulated rail joiner. In that case, cut the gap with a razor saw and apply a dab of 5-minute epoxy or household cement (but not plastic cement) into the gap. This will prevent the rails from moving back into contact with one another.

The reversing section must be fed with electrical power, but an electrical reversing switch must be placed in the circuit between the wires from the power pack and the connections at the track (Figures 9-10, 9-11, and 9-12). If you are using

one of the DCC (digital command control) systems, you can purchase a device that allows the DCC-equipped locomotives to automatically activate the power in reverse loops or WTES so no switches are needed on the control panel.

Use a toggle or slide-type DPDT switch as a reversing switch by crossing the wires on the back as shown in (Figures 9-10, 9-11, 9-12, and 9-22). Atlas makes a pair of prewired DPDT slide-type switches, the Twin (Figures 9-20 and 9-23). Any of the three can be used to control the operation of trains through the reversing sections of the track. When the train enters the reversing section, it will either stop or proceed, depending on how the reversing switch on the power pack is set in relation to the DPDT switch that controls the reversing section. If the train stops, then you must flip the DPDT switch that controls the reversing section until the train is just about to exit the reversing section. While the train is in that reversing section, the direction switch on the power pack must

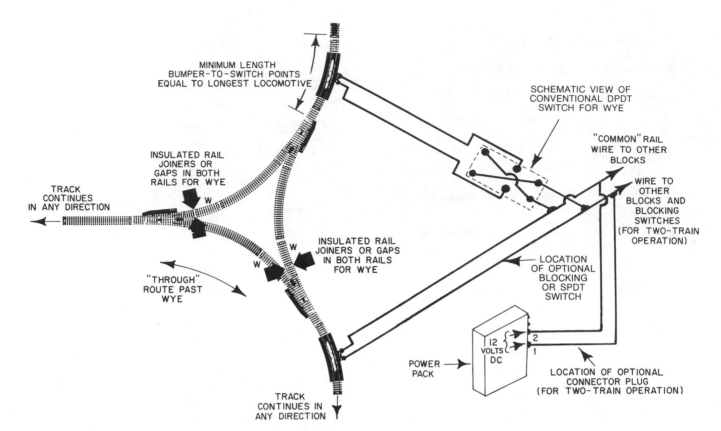

Fig. 9-10. Wiring diagram for stub-end reversing-wye trackage.

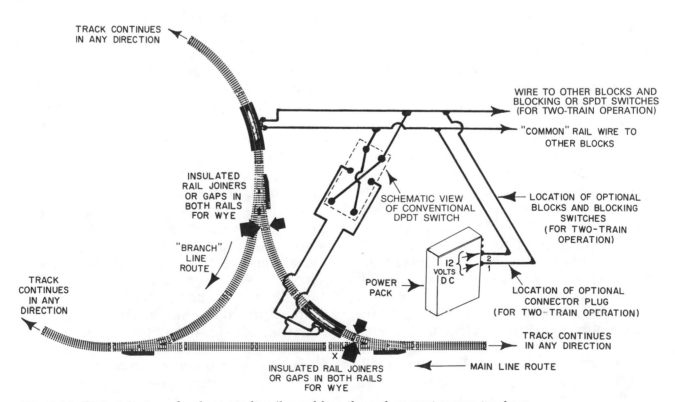

Fig. 9-11. Wiring diagram for the main line/branchline through reversing-wye trackage.

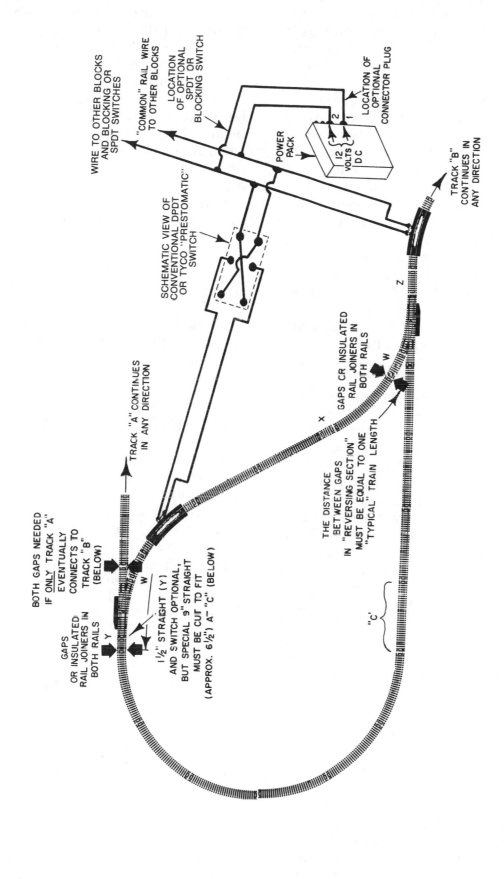

Fig. 9-12. Wiring diagram for reversing loop trackage.

be flipped to the opposite direction. When the train leaves the reversing section, it will proceed onto the mainline. You must, of course, change the turnouts to route the train so it won't derail as it moves through the reversing loop or wye to reverse direction.

If the train proceeds through the reversing section, then you do not have to flip the switch. The DPDT (direction or reversing) switch on -1the power pack must, however, be flipped each time the train leaves the reversing section.

The short length of the reversing section may not allow you to use one of the terminal track sections to connect the wires to the track. In that case, an electronics hobby or television repair shop may solder a few feet of wire onto two metal rail joiners so the rail joiners can serve as a terminal track anywhere you need them (some hobby shops also sell pre-wired rail joiner connectors). You could have a half-dozen sets made in case you need them later for two-train wiring. It is not necessary, incidentally, to solder simple wire-to-wire connections if you carefully twist both the individual wire strands and the ends of the two wires together, as shown in Figure 9-8. Be sure to twist both of the wires so you will not have just one straight wire with the other curled around it. Bend the twisted ends back over the insulated part of the wire and wrap the joint with about an inch of plastic electrical tape. Bend the last 1/8 inch of the tape back onto itself (sticky side to sticky side) to form a tab. The tab looks sloppy but you'll be glad to have it when it comes time to unwrap the tape to make a wiring change or repair.

TROUBLESHOOTING

For your first layout, I suggest a relatively simple track plan with no more than six or eight turnouts and a single train and a single power pack. Try as many aspects of the hobby that you feel might interest you, from track-laying to waybill operations. Once

you've completed the wide range of projects possible, you'll know if you want to attempt the more complicated wiring required for two-train operations and other more advanced model railroading possibilities.

Even with a simple layout, however, there is the chance for operating problems. Locomotive and electrical Troubleshooting (Figure 9-6) includes several solutions to problems that can be related to track wiring. You can use one of the 12-volt bulbs (with built-in wires) sold by hobby stores to illuminate buildings or passenger cars as a test light. Touch the bare wire ends from the bulb to the rails, as shown in Figure 9-7, and the bulb should glow if the power pack, throttle and on-off switches are all turned on. The same bulb can be used to see if the power is reaching the terminals of the walk-around throttle and the terminals on the power pack.

TWO-TRAIN CONTROL

The least expensive way to control two trains is to use two power packs and to divide the layout into electrically isolated blocks, as shown later in this chapter. You can, however, avoid the need for all those blocks and for a second power pack by purchasing one of the Digital Command Control (DCC) power packs and a second locomotive equipped with a decoder or receiver. Most of these DCC systems allow you to run any one of your non-DCC-equipped locomotives on the same track with that second locomotive that is equipped with the DCC decoder.

The DCC systems truly do provide two-train control and, like a real railroad, you can have head-on or tail-end collisions. It's also far more realistic to skip the need to turn a toggle switch on or off every time you want your train to move a few feet around the layout. Once you've operated a layout with two or more trains running at the same time under DCC control, you'll never want to go back to the conventional block system (Figure 9-13) again. Remember, though, you will still need to have the electrically isolated blocks for reverse loops and wyes (Figures 9-10, 9-11 and 9-12). If you have a really large layout, say twice the size of anything in this book, you may want to divide the layout into two or more blocks to make it easier to isolate any short circuits that might occur. Also, even with these smaller layouts, it's wise to connect additional booster wires so that there is a connection for approximately every 30 feet of mainline track. I'd suggest connecting to both the inner and outer ovals of the track plans in this book.

You can purchase the less expensive DCC systems, like MRC's Command 2000 (Figure 9-1) for about the price of three or four medium-priced locomotives, and the system includes a locomotive with the decoder already installed so you really do need to connect just two wires. The system needs a 14-volt AC power supply, but you already have that available with your train set's power pack. The system includes a push-button set of encoding commands that are explained in the instructions. For about the price of another locomotive, you can purchase the MRC Walkaround 2000 controller for the MRC Command 2000 system so you have both walk-around control and DCC.

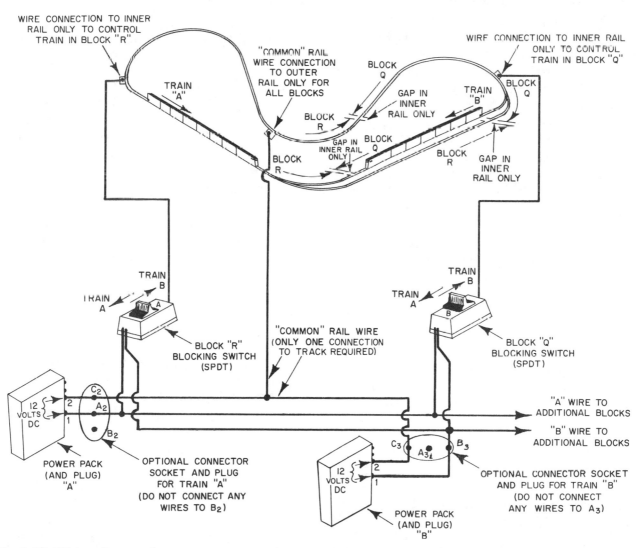

Fig. 9-13. Wiring diagram for two-train control with conventional power packs.

The MRC Command 2000 has controls for three locomotives built into the power pack. You will need a third locomotive with a second decoder installed. You can buy additional locomotives from MRC with decoders installed and you can buy plug-in decoders for about the price of a toy locomotive. Most of the better HO scale Life-Like Proto 2000, Athearn Genesis, Bachmann Spectrum, Atlas, Kato, E&C Shops, and some Walthers diesels have sockets wired to the locomotive's circuit board that allow you to plug the DCC decoder in without connecting a single wire inside the locomotive. The MRC Command 2000 also has sockets to allow you to plug in one of the Walkaround 2000 controllers and that controller will operate two locomotives. You could be operating up to five locomotives at a time, each under completely independent control. Further, each of those locomotives will have its own code and the system allows you to encode five more, for a total of ten locomotives. There's a memory function, so you can set up to five of those locomotives running and use the same throttles for independent control of five more. You can use this system to double-head two or more locomotives, with each one's decoder adjusted so it runs exactly the same speed as every other locomotive. The MRC system, then, allows you to operate up to ten locomotives and MRC offers an accessory that you can use to encode up to 117 more locomotives (assuming each has a decoder installed) that can rest anywhere on the layout awaiting their call to operate.

Remember, you can get started in this DCC system with any conventional locomotive and just the one DCC decoder-equipped locomotive. You can then expand to control as many additional locomotives as you wish to equip with DCC decoders. You can also park any locomotive not fitted with a DCC decoder, using the insulation gaps and push buttons described later in this chapter, while you operate just one other non-equipped locomotive (plus up to nine more decoder-equipped lo-comotives) with the MRC Command 2000 DCC system.

There are more expensive systems that will allow you to operate up to 200 locomotives and that can provide sound systems that are controllable through a walk-around throttle. Some of the more expensive systems even have remote-controlled walk-around throttles with no tether wires. Your hobby dealer should be able to suggest systems that are popular in your area, or you can consult the ads in the model railroad magazines to find different brands of DCC systems. Most of these systems use the same decoder technology, so you can operate your locomotives that are equipped with MRC decoders on another model railroad with another system and locomotives from that layout can operate on your system.

CONVENTIONAL TWO-TRAIN CONTROL

Two trains can be operated on the same layout by simply dividing the track into three or more blocks in a manner similar to that used for reversing loops or wyes. The two-train wiring and rail-gapping is much simpler, though, than that required for reversing sections if you use the common rail wiring system. Most model railroad books and magazines suggest the use of a single power pack with two throttles for two-train operation. That system dates back to the days when a power pack cost as much as 50 dollars or more. Today, it's just about as inexpensive to buy two complete power packs as it is to buy or add on that second throttle. You'll save countless hours of wiring and even more time troubleshooting any short circuits with the double power pack common rail wiring system shown here.

COMMON RAIL WIRING SYSTEMS

With the common rail wiring system you designate one rail as the common and connect a single wire to that rail through the usual terminal track. The only secret to the application of the system is to be absolutely and positively certain to always remember what rail is common regardless of how the track twists or turns. If you have a complex layout, I suggest you tear off some short strips of masking tape and place them temporarily on top of the common rail every few feet until all of the wiring is complete and the layout is operating with no short circuits.

Notice that a power pack with two throttles will NOT work as the only power pack for common rail wiring. You must purchase an additional power pack for operating that second train with this system.

BLOCKING THE TRACK

You will need to cut additional insulating gaps in the rail opposite the one you have designated as common to divide the track into blocks for independent control of two trains. Cutting gaps in just one rail means that just one wire needs to be connected to supply power to each of the blocks of track between the gaps. Even on a medium-size layout, that can mean almost a 50 percent savings in wire and in complexity. Each of those blocks needs to receive power; the SPDT or Blocking Switch, wired as shown in Figure 9-13 will do the job. The Atlas Connector switch (Figure 9-23) has three SPDT slide switches in one box. The Atlas Selector (Figure 9-23) has four SPDT slide switches, each

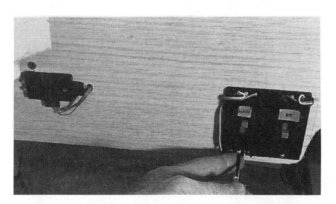

Fig. 9-14. The 7 x 8-foot Burlington Route layout (Figure 20-5) has only two controls: a single button for the one remote-controlled turnout (left) and this Atlas Twin switch used for the wye at Abbott.

with a center-off position. Similar SPDT slide switches are available from Model Power, Peco and Roco. Electronics stores, such as Radio Shack, sell SPDT and DPDT switches (Figure 9-23).

BLOCKING SWITCHES

There's somewhat more logic in having the Blocking Switch decide what train, rather than what track block, you will operate. If you reverse the wiring direction of the switch, so the one wire connects to the block, one each of the two wires can connect to the two power packs. This is the system used in Figure 9-13. You will need almost twice as many SPDT or blocking switches, but the layout wiring will actually be simpler this way once you add a third, fourth, or fifth block. This system also avoids any possible chance of your trying to switch both power packs into the same track, because the blocking switch can only be turned to one power pack at a time. All of the wiring connections you'll see in this book are based on the possible use of both this type of block-selection system and on common rail wiring.

The wiring diagram in Figure 9-13 is somewhat more complex than it needs to be for just two power packs and two blocks because it includes the wires you'll want for any number of additional blocks; for example, A and B connect to future blocks S, T, U, and so forth exactly the same way the two wires from either Q or R blocking switches connect. The diagram also includes the locations for wiring the optional connector plugs and sockets for plug-in power pack connections to make walk-around control easier. The actual wire connections for the connector sockets (and plugs) are shown in Figure 9-16. Figure 9-15 shows the origins of the wires. Notice that block A must have a different connection to socket A than the connection to block and socket B. The plugs, which connect to those sockets, are attached to the walk-around throttles through 8- to 20-foot-long tether wires. Those plugs are wired in the same way so that either walk-around throttle can be plugged into either socket A or socket B. The wiring to the sockets makes A different from B. You can add additional pairs of A and B sockets along the layout (so you don't have to have such long tether wires on the throttles) by extending all three wires, A, B, and C, on and around the edges of the layout to sockets wired like A and B, as shown in Figure 9-16. You can install any number of additional pairs of sockets or any number of additional blocks with the use of these wiring diagrams. Note that these wiring diagrams are only for conventional power packs and blocking system; the DCC systems will have different connections for their walk-around throttles that are in their instructions.

REVERSING SECTIONS

The reversing sections of the reversing loop or wye track arrangements should have both an SPDT blocking switch—to allow use by either train (or

throttle) A or B—and the DPDT (reversing) switch. The arrows in the wiring diagrams in Figures 9-10, 9-11, and 9-12 show where the SPDT (blocking) switches should be installed. Briefly, another C (common-rail) wire connection is needed for each reversing section. The two end wires on a slide-type DPDT switch (Fig. 9-22, right) will connect to the C wire and to the block wire from the blocking (SPDT) switch; the two upper wires will connect to the two terminals (track rails) on the track.

If you find the whole concept of wiring the reversing wyes or reversing loops too complicated to understand at this point, just cut the gaps in the rails (there's no way around that!) and buy another power pack to operate only the electrically isolated reversing section of your layout. You would simply turn control of any train (A or B) over to the reversing section power pack during that portion of the train-reversing moves. This second power pack system

Fig. 9-15. You can include plug-in walk-around control by installing either these older-style telephone sockets or the conventional telephone jacks sockets at several locations around the edges of the layout.

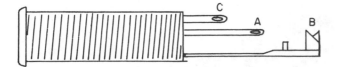

CONNECT WIRES: C_2, C_3, ETC., TO C TERMINAL
A_2, A_3, ETC., TO A TERMINAL <u>ONLY</u>
FOR POWER PACK "A" SOCKETS
B_2, B_3, ETC., TO B TERMINAL <u>ONLY</u>
FOR POWER PACK "B" SOCKETS

Fig. 9-16. Wiring diagram for older-style telephone sockets and plugs for walk-around control. Note: socket only is shown. For plug wiring, connect either one of the walk-around throttle's wires to both A and B. Connect the second walk-around throttle's wires to C on plug.

for reverse loop wiring will only work if you are using conventional power packs, not the DCC systems.

CONTROL PANELS

The more complicated your layout becomes with additional turnouts, electrical block switches for two-train control, and animated accessories, the more you'll need a control panel. It's best to include a control panel in the layout design from the very beginning. If you make the control panel large enough, you'll have a ready place to mount the switch controls when you add additional switches. If, however, you make the wiring simple enough using a DCC control system and operating the turnouts manually, you may only need a walk-around controller and a slide-out shelf (Figure 9-20) to hold the DCC power pack and, perhaps, the Waybill cards described in Chapter 19.

I suggest you make a frame for the control panel from 1 x 2 lumber and the face from 1/4-inch plywood. You'll need so little material that it might actually be cheaper to have a cabinet shop make your control panel (or control panels)

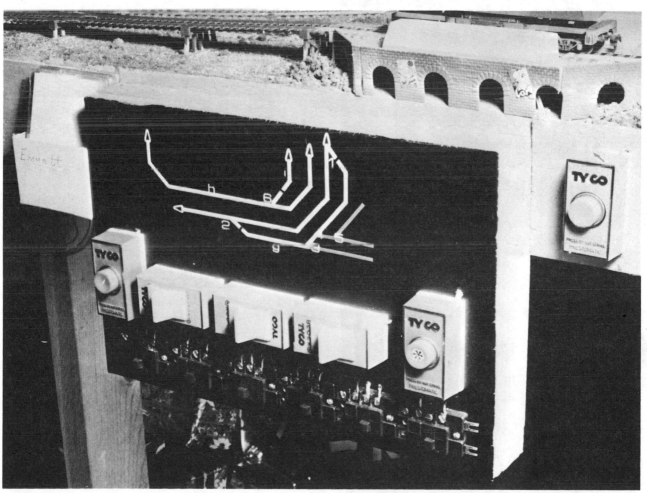

Fig. 9-17. One of the control panels (at Emmett) on the 9 x 9-foot Burlington Northern layout illustrated in Chapter 20 (Figure 20-4).

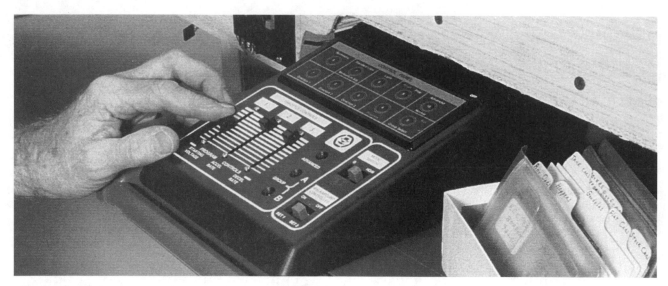

Fig. 9-20. The only control panel on the 7 x 8-foot Burlington Route layout is this slide-out drawer with an MRC Command 2000 DCC power pack. An Atlas Twin switch (left) attached to the side of the layout for the wye and a remote-control turnout push-button.

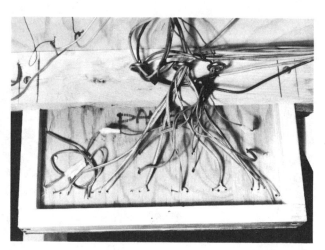

Fig. 9-18. The back side of the control panel at Emmett. Note the three screw hooks that gather the wires.

Fig. 9-19. The control panel at Duncan on the 9 x 9-foot Burlington Northern layout.

Fig. 9-21. The Alliance panel on the 9 x 9-foot Burlington Northern is the most complex because it controls more blocks and turnouts.

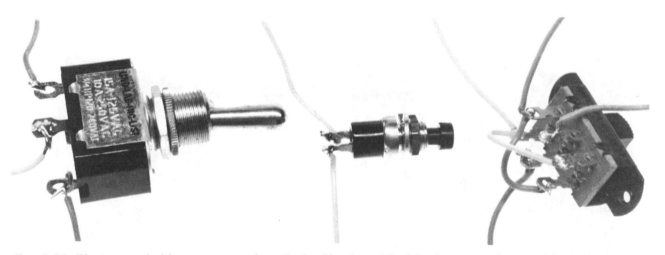

Fig. 9-22. Electronics hobby stores , such as Radio Shack or Allied Radio, carry these toggle-type switches: SPDT (left); push-button SPST (center—a simple on-off switch); and slide-type DPDT switches (right). You must solder the wires to them, as shown, before mounting them in holes bored into the control panel face.

than to do it yourself. Of course, you will have to drill the holes for the wires and screws that will connect the controls to the face of the panel. Paint the face of the panel flat black. Leave the top half of the panel clear so you can use draftsman's 1/8-inch-wide striping tape (or colored plastic hardware tape cut into 1/8-inch strips) to put a schematic diagram of your layout on the panel. Use decal or dry-transfer numbers and letters (available at most artists' supply stores) to designate the blocks and the track switches. Put matching letters and numbers right on the electrical switches themselves. You might also want to get some decal or dry-transfer arrows or other symbols to mark the panel and the electrical switches.

The control panel shown in Figures 9-17 and 9-18 is one of three panels used to operate the 9 x 9-foot Burlington Northern layout in Chapter 20. This particular panel has the block switches for blocks g, h, and i, the switch controllers for the six switches in the towns of Bedford and Emmett, which are nearest the panel, a push-button SPDT switch (far left) to kill the power in hidden track i, and a push-button SPDT switch (marked with an asterisk) wired according to the instructions furnished with it to work as a remote-control uncoupler. The card-file box to the left of all three control panels holds the envelopes for the Way-bills, described in Chapter 19. The push-button SPDT button to the far right of the panel is the one furnished with the original Tyco Dump Car set, which is immediately above the button. Most of the current action cars are operated manually, so these buttons are no longer necessary. The control panel is mounted on the layout so the portion with no wires (the track diagram) is against the 1 x 4 table side, and the lower backside of the panel is accessible for checking the wiring or adding additional controls.

HOLDING TRACKS

The wiring system described here has no provision for shutting the power off in any block. It only turns off the power pack itself. This is fine if you have only two locomotives and the two power packs to run them. When you add a third locomotive, however, you need some place to park it when the other two are in operation. The blocks a and b in the engine terminal of the 9 x 9-foot Burlington Northern layout in Chapter 20 are there to hold locomotives; blocks j, f, and i are long enough to hold a locomotive and a complete train. A SPST push-button style switch (Figure 9-22, center) is inserted into the wire leading from the blocking

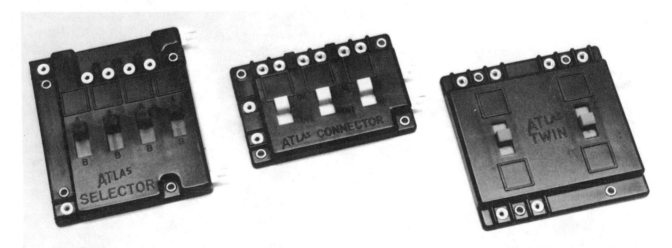

Fig. 9-23. Hobby shops carry pre-wired Atlas electrical switches, including the bank of four center-off SPDT switches (left) called the Selector, the trio of SPDT switches (center) called the Connector, and the pair of center-off DPDT switches (right) called the Twin. Each switch includes wiring instructions and mounting screws.

switch for those blocks to the track. The button will then be used to control the flow of power to that isolated block so that the locomotive runs only while the button is being pressed. Install an insulated rail joiner in the rail opposite the common rail (Figure 9-12) to isolate each of these locomotive-holding blocks to be controlled by the push-button SPST switch. With this system, you can park a locomotive in one of these electrically isolated blocks and forget about it until you want it; the locomotive will only leave that block when you hold down the button controlling that block.

DO'S AND DON'TS FOR CONTROL PANELS AND WIRING

- Do use extreme care in cutting the insulation from wires so that the delicate individual wire strands are not broken. Twist the strands together as soon as the insulation is pulled free.
- Do purchase a separate power pack to control switch (turnout) machines and lighting as well as a separate power pack for each additional train (when you want to operate two or more trains at once).
- Do at least consider the advantages of a separate throttle for walk around control so you can walk along beside your train with its controls in your hand.
- Do drill holes in the tabletop or roadbed so all wiring can be routed beneath the table and so it will be accessible even after all the scenery is in place.
- Do consider purchasing one of the DCC systems for operating two or more trains at once, rather than wiring with blocks for two or more conventional power packs.

- Don't attempt to use one power pack for more than one function. Some of the power packs, however, do have provisions for separate control of two trains. A third power pack will still be needed for switch machines and lighting.

- Don't attempt to make your own walk-around control. The available units are simple enough to attach with four wires to the back of most power packs, using the wiring diagram supplied with the walk around control.

- Don't run wires on top of the table or beside the tracks.

- Don't attempt to run two trains with two conventional power packs without making at least three electrically isolated blocks so you can park one train while the second goes to the next available block.

PART III: Tools and Techniques

CHAPTER 10

The Workbench

YOU CAN BUILD a model railroad with nothing more than a hammer, a screwdriver and a knife. A lumberyard will pre-cut the legs for sawhorse table supports and supply sheets of 1/2-inch-thick, 4 x 8-foot plywood and Homosote, or Dow-Corning blue extruded-Styrofoam insulation boards and plywood. Ready-to-run structures are available as well as ready-to-run locomotives and cars, so all you really need to do is install, attach the wires, position the buildings and drape some green-painted beige felt here and there for hills with sifted-on ground cover, such as those described in Chapter 16. The 4 x 8-foot plans in Chapter 3, particularly the Figure-8-shaped plan, will provide plenty of operating action, and you will hardly have to build anything. Most model railroaders, however, find the hobby fascinating because it does offer endless opportunities to build things. It's just nice to know that the hobby is versatile enough so you do have the choice.

Roughly three categories of tools are used for model railroading: the basic assortment for laying track and painting ready-to-run equipment; tools for advanced structure or locomotive conversions involving the actual cutting, fitting, and assembly of plastic parts; and the array of woodworking tools needed to assemble open-grid-style benchwork. (The tools for building benchwork aren't really model-building tools at all, however, so these are discussed separately in Chapter 5 in the explanations of how to build benchwork.) There are some very basic modeling techniques and some specific tools you'll need to use on your real railroad in miniature.

THE BASIC TOOLS

The tools that are the most important are the ones that are necessary to lay the track, assemble plastic building kits, and perform any necessary maintenance or adjustments on the rolling stock, locomotives, and track. You may already have many of the tools around the house, but it would be better to get a specific set for the exclusive use of building and maintaining your model railroad. You can make some minor substitutions for the tools I suggest in terms of sizes; a 5-inch pair of needle-nose pliers will do just as well as a 7-inch pair. However, do not try to second guess the list. Don't, for instance, substitute common pliers for needlenose pliers or a pocket knife for an X-Acto hobby knife.

One final bit of experience garnered from more than 30 years of similar mistakes; spend the extra few dollars to get the very best tools at a hobby or hardware store rather than picking up dollar bargains. The better tools will probably last a lifetime, so their cost on a per-year basis is only pennies:

Basic Model Railroading Tools
- Pointed tweezers
- Small standard screwdriver
- Small Phillips-head screwdriver
- Flush-cut diagonal cutters (small)
- Flush-cut diagonal cutters (to cut rail:optional)
- Small needlenose pliers
- Scissors

•Kadee Number 205
    coupler-height gauge
•X-Acto Number 1 hobby-knife
    handle with extra
    Number 11 blades
•X-Acto Number 5 hobby-
    knife handle
•X-Acto Number 235 razor-
    saw blade

The use and purpose for most of these tools will be obvious to anyone who has assembled a train set. Some of them, though, are intended for rather obscure purposes. The flush-cut diagonal cutters are sold by many hobby, hardware and electronics supply stores. Like most diagonal cutters, they are designed to cut wire by virtually squeezing through it to produce a cut that has a 45-degree bevel on both sides. The flush-cut diagonal cutters have angled cutting surfaces on their jaws, so that the angle is on just one side of the cut; one side produces a perfectly flush or vertical cut. Do not attempt to use them for cutting the track rails. This will dull the cutting surfaces. Some hobby shops also sell larger flush-cut diagonal cutters that are designed to cut brass or nickel silver rail (as shown in Chapter 7, Figure 7-9).

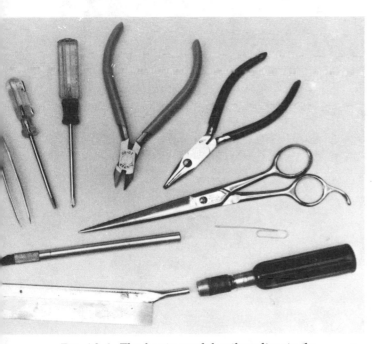

Fig. 10-1. The basic model railroading tools.

The small flush-cut diagonal cutters are intended to cut wires with a minimum of pulling and damage to the individual wire threads. Their most important use, for a model railroader, will be to cut the windows and other plastic parts for structure kits from the molding sprues, or trees, of scrap plastic. If you cannot find flush-cut diagonal cutters, buy regular diagonal cutters and use them for cutting wire.

The X-Acto Number 1 hobby-knife handle and Number 11 blades can be used to cut these structure parts from their sprues. Hobby shops also sell Sprue Cutters, which are smaller versions of the flush-cut diagonal cutters, for cutting plastic parts for their sprues. Do not attempt to pull or break the plastic parts away from their sprues; there's a good chance you'll break the part rather than the sprue. The Kadee number 205 gauge is useful for adjusting the height of the knuckle couplers on rolling stock or locomotives shown in Chapter 18.

The X-Acto Number 5 hobby-knife handle and the Number 235 razor-saw blade are the tools you need to cut the rails for custom-fitting snap-together track on some layouts, if you do not wish to purchase the second pair of large flush-cut diagonal cutters. Custom-fit track sections are necessary with some track plans, and a cut-to-fit end-of-track piece for a siding can often mean the difference between the siding holding one car or two. You can save money and have a smoother flow of track on your second model railroad layout by substituting 3-foot lengths of flexible track for long stretches of sectional track. The flexible track will seldom fit in any layout without at least one of the rails being cut to fit. It's somewhat tricky to get the flexible track shaped into smooth curves, so I suggest that you build at least one layout with the track with built-in ballast, like Bachmann's E-Z Track or Life-Like's Power-Loc track, before using sectional track and flexible track. You will probably use the razor saw most for cutting plastic walls and other structure parts for building conversions such as some of those discussed in Chapter 14.

SPECIAL PLASTIC-WORKING TOOLS

You may want to spend some time creating the special conversion structures, like those in Chapter 14, that will set your railroad in miniature apart from all others. The X-Acto razor saw is the basic cutting tool for these custom-built models, and the Number 1 knife and Number 11 blade can be used for final trimming and finishing. The pointed tweezers and tube-type as well as liquid cement for plastics needed to assemble box-stock kits will work just as well for any conversions involving the use of two or more models. The secret to success in making conversion models, however, lies in seeing that your modified parts fit at least as well as the stock-kit components, and that means you'll need a few more tools.

Plastic-Working Tools

- X-Acto Number 1 knife with Number 11 blades
- 12-inch-long steel ruler or straightedge
- Draftsman's plastic triangle
- Medium-cut large flat-mill file
- File card or brass-bristled suede shoe brush
- Bench vise (with adjustable head), such as a PanaVise
- Liquid and tube-type cement for plastics
- Tube of patching or spot automobile body putty

The steel straightedge or ruler and plastic triangle are necessary in order to guarantee that all of your cuts are straight and true. The mill file will help to keep the surfaces true as well, but

Fig. 10-2. Special plastic-working tools.

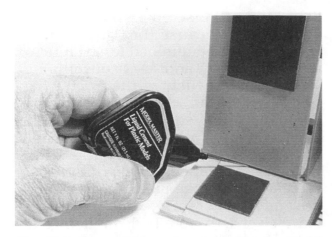

Fig. 10-3. Use a thickened cement, like the Model Master Liquid Cement for Plastic Models, to assemble plastic structure kits.

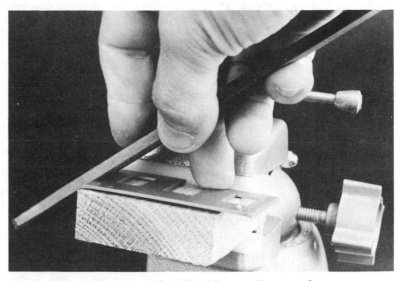

Fig. 10-5. File the edges of any building walls or roofs you have cut to a 45-degree bevel so they can be joined tightly to other walls.

Fig. 10-4. The PanaVise type of swivel-head vise allows you to position the sawing block for more comfortable working conditions.

it's most useful for filing 45-degree bevels on the mating corners of walls cut to length so they can be assembled in the same manner as those in a stock kit.

If you are going to work with structure-conversion projects, where you need to cut plastic parts, I recommend that you consider purchasing one of the bench vises with an adjustable head, such as the PanaVise. You can also use the vise for making more precise and safer cuts to shorten and fit track sections. The vise should not be used to actually clamp the plastic pieces but, rather, to clamp a short scrap of 1 x 3 or 1 x 4 wood. The wood serves as a stable backing for the part you are cutting, while your fingers serve as clamps to hold the plastic against the wood by squeezing the plastic part and the wood backing together. The vise keeps the wood stable and secure, and the adjustable (or swivel-style) head allows you to position the block comfortably, both for clamping by hand and for cutting or filing. You can use the same technique with a conventional bench vise, but you'll have to contort your body into some rather uncomfortable positions to clamp with one hand while cutting or filing with the other.

The nice thing about model railroading, particularly in HO scale, is that you don't need much more than a 2 x 3-foot workbench area. An old desk or table would be an ideal workbench for your modeling, or you could purchase a breadboard from a lumberyard and use it as your work surface with a shoebox to store your tools. You should have a sturdy table to back up the breadboard, so stay away from card tables, TV trays, and the like. If you don't have a strong, stable structure, your finished models will probably look as wobbly as your workbench.

LIGHTING FOR THE WORKBENCH

The most critical model building tool is proper lighting. Try to arrange your workbench area so you have at least two sources of light in order to avoid having to work in your own hands' shadows. It's best to have the same type of lighting for your workbench as you have for your layout area. This will guarantee that the colors and subtle weathering shades you apply at the workbench will look the same on the railroad itself. I prefer incandescent light bulbs (the screw-in kind) for layout lighting because they give a softer light and can be dimmed for evening or night effects by adding a conventional wall-dimmer switch in the circuit. It's best to have an electrician add that dimmer switch so you don't run the risks of injury or fire hazard possible with 115-volt house wiring. The disadvantages of incandescent lighting, however, are that it can make the work area uncomfortably warm, and it requires more electricity to equal the light output of fluorescent tubes.

CHAPTER 11

Rolling Stock

THE ORDINARY FREIGHT CAR is what real railroading in miniature is all about. Freight cars provide a living for the real railroads, and the simulation of the car and its movements is what makes model railroads come alive. I'll show you how you can operate freight cars in the same way the real railroads do it (but without any of the paperwork) in Chapters 18 and 19; there you will find all the information you need to get your fleet of freight cars into a shape that at least resembles a real railroad. It isn't possible to duplicate the thousands of freight cars that move in and through each town on a real railroad. Only a club layout is large enough to recreate the hundred-car trains of the prototype. But part of the art of model railroading is making just a relatively few freight cars look like many, and to make them at least appear to be carrying something somewhere.

Also, real railroads have hundreds, even thousands, of freight cars that look alike except for the car numbers and the degree of weathering. Model railroaders tend to pick as many different kinds and colors of cars as possible. Next time you buy a freight car, particularly one lettered for your favorite real railroad, buy as many of the same style, same color freight cars as you can afford, but this must be reversed when it comes to structures.

YOUR FREIGHT CAR FLEET

There is a nearly limitless choice of plastic freight cars in HO scale. The Walthers catalog devotes 100 pages to freight cars alone, and it doesn't show them all! You can certainly pick any car that you like. You may, however, want to focus your purchases on cars from a particular era in railroading history to make your layout more like the real world. Again, the choice is virtually limitless. You can easily assemble a 100-car train of freight cars that were common in the thirties, a similar train of fifties-era cars, cars of the sixties, or the modern era. But there's another option, especially if you have a limited layout space: buy cars from two or more eras and only operate those from a single era at any given time. You can, of course, match your locomotive choices to the eras of the rolling stock.

There are no car-by-car guides to help you determine what cars are appropriate for certain eras. You'll have to do some research, which means you'll have to look at lots of pictures of trains. That's probably what you like to do anyway, but now you have a reason to invest in those real railroad books you crave. Simply, wood freight cars were virtually the standard until about 1915, when steel cars began to take over. Similarly, 40-foot cars were common from the teens through the forties, when 50-foot cars began to take over. Each era also had its own particular paint schemes, as both railroads and private owners changed heralds and colors on their cars and the traffic patterns shifted on the railroads. Refrigerator cars (reefers) were rare until the twenties and they are rare today. Reefers were, however, a large part of the prototype freight cars fleet from about 1925 until 1955.

If you are going to operate your model railroad using the Waybill system in

Chapter 19, you will want to collect enough cars to serve the industries you have selected. You will not likely need auto rack cars, for example, and neither the 9 x 9-foot Burlington Northern nor the 7 x 8-foot Burlington Route layouts have any oil industries. You can certainly operate auto racks and tank cars on through freights that are traveling from imaginary points on either end of your railroad, and there is no real reason why you could not include an oil depot if you like to see tank cars in action.

ROLLING STOCK RELIABILITY

Real railroads are generally operated on nearly endless stretches of straight track with curves that would reduce to about a 144-inch radius in HO scale. The real railroads, then, don't have the

problems with tight curves that plague model railroaders. Almost any of the HO scale plastic cars or locomotives will make it around the 18-inch radius curves that are standard in train sets and in all the track plans in this book. Many of the longer freight and passenger cars and locomotives will, however, derail on the turnouts as they lurch from straight to curve and pick and click over the turnout points and rattle through the frogs of the turnouts. If you are going to build a layout as small as those in this book, I would recommend that you limit the length of your freight cars to 50 or 60 feet and passenger cars to 72 feet. I would also suggest that you avoid passenger and freight cars with six-wheel trucks because they, too, tend to derail on the turnouts. The alternate solution to the problem is to use larger Number 4 or

Fig. 11-1. Everything in this scene, from the locomotive to the freight cars to the vehicles, helps create the illusion of a late fifties setting on the 7 x 8-foot Burlington Route layout.

Number 6 turnouts and 24-inch radius curves, but you will only be able to squeeze a single-track oval layout into a 5 x 9-foot space and those larger-radius tracks won't fit on a 4 x 8-foot layout.

PICKING PASSENGER CARS

Note that locomotives with six-wheel trucks will also derail on these turnouts, but we'll discuss that in Chapter 13. Do notice, though, that the 85-foot passenger cars look very toy-like negotiating an 18-inch radius curve (Figure 11-2). Athearn, Bachmann, Life-Like, MDC, and Model Power produce 72-foot simulated-steel passenger cars from the era of steam locomotives. More modern streamlined cars are available from Athearn, Con-Cor, Life-Like Marklin and Model Power. So far, no one offers any of the modern Amtrak 85-foot Amfleet, Metroliner or Superliner cars in anything but their correct 85-foot lengths. It would, of course, be possible to cut down the longer models by removing a section near one end, but it would be a task for an experienced modeler. The Athearn 72-foot streamlined coach is only a bit shorter than the Walthers 85-foot Amfleet coach in Figure 11-3 but the trucks on the Amfleet car are mounted much further toward the ends of the car, which results in more overhang inside the 18-inch radius curves. You might be able to get by with relatively few derailments with the Amfleet cars, however, because they have four-wheel trucks rather than the six-wheel trucks of the heavyweight passenger cars of the fifties and earlier. Better to wait to run those longer cars for the day when you build a larger model railroad.

Fig 11-2. An E8A diesel with heavyweight steel passenger cars arrives at Chester on the Burlington Route layout. Again, all the equipment and vehicles help date the scene to the late fifties. For this size layout, it would be wise to use an F3A or F7A diesel with 4-wheel trucks rather than the E7A with its 6-wheel trucks. The larger trucks tend to derail on the 18-inch radius turnouts.

SELECTING FREIGHT CARS

Fortunately, there are relatively few prototype freight cars longer than 60 feet. Some examples are shown in Figure 11-3. The notable exceptions, of course, are the automobile rack cars that carry new automobiles and trucks, the intermodal flat cars that carry two 45-foot trailers or containers and some 86-foot auto parts box cars. There are models for all of these cars but there are also models of the shorter freight cars that carry similar loads. Atlas, for example has a 53-foot box car that has proportions similar to the 86-foot Athearn Auto Parts cars. A-Line, Con-Cor, Model Power and Walthers offer 50 or 60-foot intermodal well cars, both as individual cars and articulated sets, for carrying trailers and containers. The articulated sets are also derailment-prone on tight curves so pick the individual cars for these smaller layouts. If you want intermodal cars from the 1950-1970 era, Athearn, Con Cor, Walthers and Model Power all have 50-foot intermodal flat cars with one or two highway trailers.

FREIGHT CAR LOADS

I suggest that you add some type of load to all of your flat cars, but you should load only half of your fleet of hoppers or gondolas. Ways to simulate loads for hoppers and gondolas appear in the Loads-In/Empties-Out section of Chapter 19. The r-t-r action cars are the type that can be loaded and un-

Fig. 11-3. The long and short of it: Longer rolling stock does not look as realistic as shorter rolling stock on the 18-inch radius curves used in all the layouts in this book. The Athearn 86-foot auto parts box car (upper left) can be replaced with an Atlas 53-foot plug-door box car. The Athearn 86-foot piggyback or intermodal flat car (upper right) can be replaced with Walthers, Athearn or Con-Cor 50-foot well cars or with an Athearn, Model Power or Walthers 53-foot flat car with one or two trailers for the 1955-1960 era. The 85-foot Walthers Amfleet cars (lower left) are a bit too long for these layouts, too. The Athearn, MDC Con-Cor, Marklin or Model Power 72-foot passenger cars will look more realistic on the tight curves.

Fig. 11-4. Partially loaded flat cars lend more authenticity to your operations than empty or fully loaded ones.

loaded without your hands touching the cargo. The log-dumping cars are a typical example, but the dumping principle is also offered, by the r-t-r firms, in coal, ore and even box-dumping versions. You can decide if it's worth the bother to use real loads.

Coal is available in several sizes or grains from hobby stores, or you can powder real coal by putting it in a cloth bag and hitting it with a hammer. Cut a piece of cardboard to fill the car interior so only about 1/4 inch of coal is needed to fill it. Pour in the coal so the peaks of the piles are level with the car sides but no higher. Spray the loads with water from a plant atomizer or one of the lever-style plastic hair-spray bottles. Mix three parts water to one part Artist's Matte Medium and apply it to the water-wetted load with an eye dropper. You may need to add a few drops of liquid detergent to the Matte Medium and water to keep it from sitting on top of the coal loads.

Flat cars are more realistic in operation if they are partially loaded. This way, if you leave a Trailer Train type of flatcar at an unloading dock for a scale day, you can pick the unloaded car up again without anyone wondering much about it. A completely empty flatcar is far too obvious to serve as a loaded car unless, of course, you really do want to load and unload those cars with r-t-r action accessories.

Be sure to tie down any loads of lumber or other loose commodities. You can use 7-pound test nylon fishing line dyed black with common Rit dye. The nylon line can be woven through the various stake pockets along the sides of the flat cars and tied at just one place out of sight on the bottom of the car. Thread is too coarse and has too many hair-like strands to be realistic rope or cable in HO scale. Chapter 19 includes some ideas on using highway trailers and intermodal containers for flatcar loads.

ROLLING STOCK MAINTENANCE

Rolling stock must be free-rolling, not wobbling as it rolls down the track, with trucks that are free to swivel so the cars don't derail on curves or turnouts. All couplers must be the same height, with no low-hanging uncoupling pins. In addition, all rolling stock must be able to travel anywhere on the layout without derailing. The Derailment and Track Troubleshooting Chart (Figure 8-11 in Chapter 8) describes the problems that cause derailments. Most often, the problem will lie with the track rather than the rolling stock. Still, if a single car derails and no other cars have problems, inspect that car carefully for possible causes of derailments. The most frequent cause of derailments on rolling stock is coupler pins that hang down so far that they snag at turnouts or crossings. Chapter 18 includes information on how to be sure the couplers are mounted properly.

The second most common cause of derailments by freight cars is dirt, which usually is attracted to freight car

Fig. 11-6. Use a hobby knife and scrap of wood to slice about 1/64 inch from the truck pivot to eliminate side-to-side rocking.

wheels and bearings by oil. Virtually all of the HO scale freight car models and kits include plastic trucks made of a slippery plastic that should never require lubrication. Oil in the ends of the axles on freight cars merely attracts dust and dirt and turns it into a sticky substance. Excessive oil or grease on locomotives can also dribble onto the rails to be picked up by the wheels of the rolling stock. You can, then, avoid most dirt by simply not lubricating anything but the metal bearings and gears of the locomotives with the least amount of oil or grease possible.

If you find a sticky residue on the wheels, scrape it off very gently with a hobby knife or the blade of a small screwdriver. The wheels can be removed from most model railroad trucks by simply spreading the plastic sideframes apart between your fingers so the axle and wheel set falls out. With the wheels removed, the bearings for the pinpoint axle ends can be cleaned with a toothpick dipped in paint thinner. Work outdoors and avoid any fire or sparks when using any flammable fluids. Do not use a knife to scrape the bearings clean or you may scratch the bearings and reduce the free-rolling qualities of the trucks.

If you find that the cars rock from side to side as they roll down the

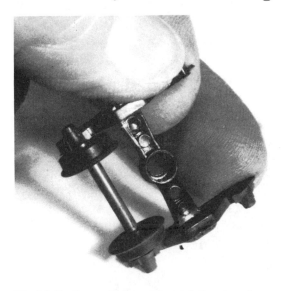

Fig. 11-5. Spread the sides of the truck apart between your second and third fingers to remove the wheels.

tracks, one of the truck pivots must be tightened. The lower-cost freight and passenger cars that have trucks with a split pin that snaps into the bolster in the floor are difficult to correct. Sometimes, you can spread the pin slightly but not enough so the truck cannot pivot freely. On models that have trucks mounted with a separate press-in pin or with a screw, the underframe often can be modified at the truck pivot (bolster). Use a hobby knife to slice about 1/64 inch from the truck pivot. With this material removed, the screw for that truck can be tightened enough so the truck will only pivot. Leave the opposite truck alone so it can wobble from side to side as well as pivot. The single pivoting (but not rocking) truck will keep the car level and the rocking truck will allow the trucks to follow uneven or rough trackwork without derailing the car.

Some of the least expensive cars may have thin wisps of plastic around the extreme outer edges (the flanges) of the wheels. This plastic is called flash and occurs during the manufacturing process. You can remove it with a sharp hobby knife. For really free-rolling freight or passenger cars, cars that have the sound of real railroad wheels, replace the wheel and axle sets on all your freight cars with metal wheels and axles. Hobby dealers can supply these wheelsets for any HO scale model.

CHAPTER 12

Painting, Lettering & Weathering

THERE ARE ENOUGH CHOICES IN ready-to-run locomotives, freight cars and passenger cars so you never really will need to paint or letter any model. You may, however, want to change the number on a car, especially if you have two or more identical cars. And you may discover a particular prototype that you wish to match with your model and the only way to do it is to paint and letter the model. Painting and lettering allows you to match the unique character of real railroad equipment.

You won't find one freight car in a thousand on a real railroad that's as bright and clean as those in a model train set. It only takes one night in the dew and one day of dust or rain to weather a real freight car, so their freshly painted look never lasts very long. When you learn to visualize what a real railroad looks like, you'll discover that many of the cars look identical, except for the amount of weathering and the car numbers. Brightly painted toy train cars will never look realistic unless you weather them.

It's far too obvious that you don't have enough cars on your layout when each one stands out from the rest. If you use similar weathering colors on a few cars with different factory paint colors, they will blend together in the same way the real ones do. However, don't be afraid to buy two or three identical cars rather than two or three different ones the next time you add to your rolling-stock fleet. You can apply slightly different weathering hues to them if you like and change at least one of their numbers by using decals. You'll increase the realism of your railroad far more than you can imagine simply by matching the mix of identical versus unusual cars on the real railroad.

REPAINTING TECHNIQUES

Most of the ready-to-run cars are painted to match the bright colors of real-life railroad cars. However, in a typical real-life railroad train or train yard, only a few of the cars are that bright. Most freight cars of the pre-1980 era are painted in the reddish-brown color which is so typical of the majority of real railroad cars. That reddish brown can vary from an almost chocolate brown to a cedar or redwood color, depending on the railroad and the year the car was painted. The color is so common because the paints used at the turn of the century could be colored for almost no cost by using powdered clay; and that's how the earthy colors came to be.

MATCHING COLORS

You can match a couple of the shades, Boxcar Red or Roof Brown, using spray cans of Testors or Pactra paints. Testors' Dark Brown will appear to be Roof Brown if the finished model is then sprayed with Testors' clear DullCote. The slightly redder Boxcar Red can be approximated by spraying the Dark Brown-painted finished model with Pactra's Clear Flat. The DullCote seems to darken most colors about one shade, while the Pactra Clear Flat does not change the color but adds a semi-matte finish. You can buy a bottle of any real railroad color from Floquil, Polly Scale, Modelflex,

SMP, or Scalecoat and apply it with a paint brush, but it's a lot easier and quicker to use spray paint. Floquil makes some aerosol railroad colors. You may find some other brands of clear flat finish that will give the same type of finish as Testors', but you must experiment by spraying them on a test surface with both the paint and the decals you use. Most brands of clear flat spray paint will cause decals to wrinkle or curl, and they might even do the same to the paint itself!

Hobby shops and some art supply stores sell an airbrush that is a miniature version of the spray guns used to paint automobiles. The airbrush, with its own air compressor, can be used to spray Floquil, Polly Scale, Modelflex, SMP, or Scalecoat bottled paints.

Repainting a model freight car or locomotive means that you must also apply new letters, heralds, and numbers to the model after the paint dries. You should also remove the original letters, heralds, and numbers, however, because they will show through the paint in the form of a raised outline all around the markings. Common rubbing alcohol and a cotton swab or tissue will remove most markings. Dip the swab or tissue in the alcohol and rub the lettering or numbers on the side of the car with it for a moment until the marking is erased. The inks used on most models are alcohol-based and can be removed quite easily with this technique. However, some inks may have to be removed with an abrasive like Number 600 sandpaper.

REMOVING THE ORIGINAL PAINT

The original paint on model railroad cars is very difficult to remove. You can try an oven cleaner, such as Easy-Off, or automobile brake fluid, but you could ruin the model rather than removing the paint. Several types of plastic are used on model railroad cars and on the locomotive bodies too. A paint remover that doesn't dissolve one body, though, might melt another.

You must apply a coat of primer to give the surface some tooth so you can keep the applications of that final color coat as thin as possible. I have found that the Magic brand of primer sold by Standard Brands and the Tempo primers sold by some hardware and automobile-parts stores work quite well. Some primers will attack paint or plastic, and most are so thick that they obscure most of the rivets and other fine details. You'll have to experiment with the primer you want to use (even if it's one of the two I've had good luck with) to be certain it won't attack the paint on your particular model. Test spraying on the inside of the body or near the bottom of one of the car ends will reveal whether or not the primer will cause the paint beneath it to curl or crinkle.

SPRAY PAINTING

There's a bit of an art to spray painting with an aerosol can. First, wash the models in detergent before any painting, rinse them, and allow them to air dry to remove all traces of grease and fingerprints. Then, you will need some

Fig. 12-1. Remove the trucks, couplers, and the underframe before painting any car or locomotive.

sort of a handle to hold the model so that you don't touch the paint. I use a wire coat hanger has been straightened

Fig. 12-2. Rub the lettering off with a cotton swab dipped in alcohol before painting.

and bent again to a small e shape so the inside of the car body is held under a spring tension by the wire. For smaller parts I attach masking tape, sticky side up, with smaller pieces of tape. The smaller parts can be placed on the tape, spray painted, and left there until the paint dries. I wear a disposable plastic work glove on one hand for holding the coat hanger and the scrap of wood, and I spray the car or parts with the aerosol can in my other hand.

To begin, hold the can under warm (never hot!) running water, and be sure to shake it vigorously for a count of at least 100. Practice your spray painting technique on some old cars until you can apply a thin and even coat of paint with no runs and no orange-peel textures. You'll find you can get a smoother coat if the model and the spray can are at room temperature (70 degrees F). Begin the spray just off the model and pass it evenly over the model before releasing the button. Starting or stopping

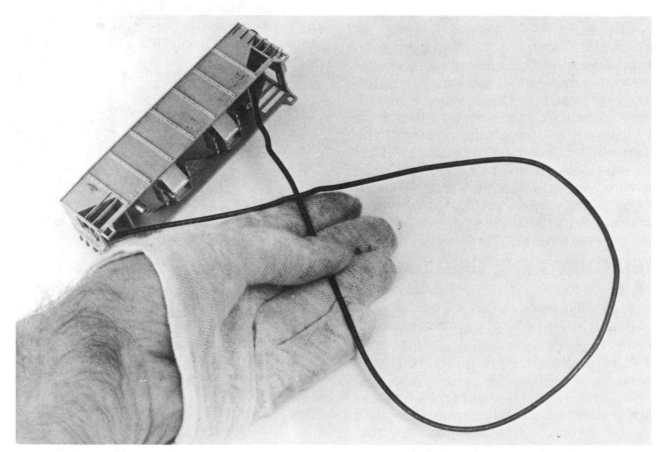

Fig. 12-3. Bend a coat hanger to this shape so it will have a spring-grip on the inside of the car. Protect your holding hand from paint overspray with a disposable rubber glove.

Fig. 12-4. Apply several light coats of primer from a distance of about 9 inches to get a smooth and even finish.

the spray directly on the model can produce splatters and runs. It's best to apply as many as a dozen very light coats rather than trying to do the job with just one; you'll almost always produce runs in the paint if you try to cover with just one or two coats. If you're finished with the spray can for an hour or more, invert the can so the nozzle is down and press in on the nozzle until just gas but no paint flows from the nozzle. The paint-pickup tube will be above the paint, with the can inverted, so this technique allows the can's own pressure to clean both the nozzle and the spray tube inside the can. Gloss paint makes a much better surface for the application of decals but you can achieve a glossy finish over flat-finish paints by spraying a final coat of clear gloss.

DECALS

A decal is nothing more than a number, name, herald, or other marking that is painted on a piece of glue-covered paper. The colored portion of the decal is then sprayed with several coats of clear paint. When you soak the glue-covered paper in water, the glue dissolves and allows the decal to be pushed from the paper and onto the model. Because the decal is too thick to snuggle in tightly around rivets, seams, and other details, decal manufacturers, such as Champion and Microscale, make decal-softening fluids that can be applied like so many drops of water. These fluids almost dissolve the decal back to its original paint state, so it really does look as though it's painted on.

The major decal manufacturers can handle direct-mail orders, and Champion, and Microscale offer catalogs for 6 dollars each. Walthers includes theirs with the 900-plus page HO SCALE MODEL RAILROAD CATALOG, but the catalog price varies from year to year so send a stamped, self-addressed envelope to Walthers for the current price of the catalog or ask your local hobby dealer to order a copy of the catalog. I suggest you obtain all four decal makers' catalogs so you'll know what choices you have for relettering rolling stock and locomotives. A few decals are made for station and industrial signs as well as names, and these can be used if you want to make up your own railroad names. Contact the decal firms directly:

Champion Decal Company

P.O. Box 1178
Minot, ND 58701

Microscale Industries

P.O. Box 11950
Costa Mesa, CA 92627

Wm. K. Walthers, Inc.

P.O. Box 18676
Milwaukee, WI 53218

HOW TO APPLY DECALS

The decal must first be cut close to the printed portion with scissors or a hobby knife to remove as much of the clear border as possible from Walthers and Champion decals. Microscale decals have a tapered edge to most of the clear decal films. This can be seen

if you hold the decal so that light reflects off the shiny clear part. Cut the Microscale decals apart near the outer edges of the clear portions. From this

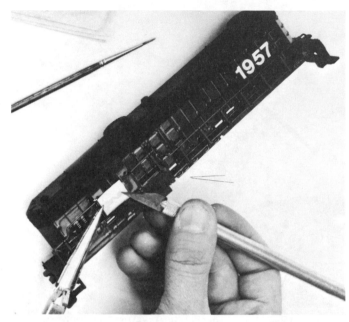

Fig. 12-6. Use tweezers to position the wet decal and its paper backing, then hold the decal with a knife tip while you slide the paper from beneath the decal with tweezers.

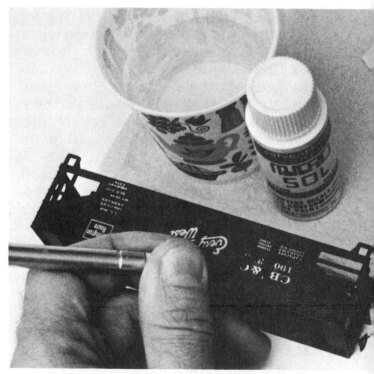

Fig. 12-7. Any trapped air bubbles can be punctured with a knife tip and the decal covered with a second applications of decal-softening fluid.

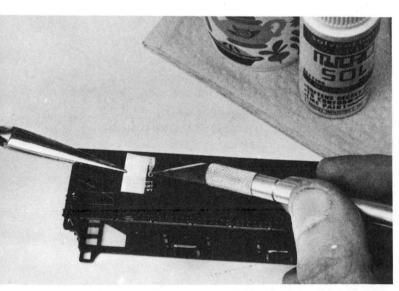

Fig. 12-5. Hold the decal in position with a hobby knife while removing its paper backing with tweezers.

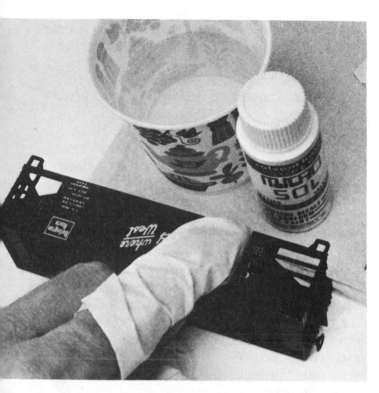

Fig. 12-8. Gently dab the decal immediately after it has been softened with Micro Sol, or with any decal-softening fluid, to force the decal down around the rivets and other details.

point on, the decal cannot be touched with a bare finger until the final protective coat of clear flat paint has dried. Use pointed tweezers to pick up the decal and dip it into warm water for just a moment. Set the decal on a blotter or on a paper towel for a few minutes while the glue dissolves.

When the decal can be moved on its paper backing, it is ready to be applied to the model. Hold both the decal and its paper backing exactly where you want the decal. Keep just the decal in place with the tip of the hobby-knife blade while you pull the paper backing from beneath it.

Apply a thin coat of Champion's Decal-Set or Microscale's Micro Sol to the decal with a Number O-size paint brush. If the area that is beneath the decal is textured with rivets or other details, it's wise to wet the area with the decal-softening fluid. Allow the fluid about 15 minutes to dry, and, if necessary, dab at the decal lightly with a finger wrapped with a dampened tissue to force the decal down over the surface.

Don't push too hard or the decal will grab the tissue; just dab at it. It might take as many as six applications of the decal-softening fluid, applied over a period of an hour or more, to get some decals to snuggle tightly around curved or highly detailed surfaces. When the decal-softening fluid has dried overnight, scrub the surface of the decal lightly with a cotton swab dipped in water to remove any traces of the decal-softening fluid or the decal glue. Let the model dry overnight again and apply a protective spray-on coat of Testors DullCote, Model Master Clear Flat, or some other spray-on flat finish clear paint that you have pre-tested to be sure it will not attack either the paint or the decals. The final coat of paint will match the finish or gloss (or lack of gloss) of the decal to the rest of the model, and it will help to disguise those clear edges of the decal so only an expert could tell it was a decal rather than painted-on lettering.

DRY TRANSFER MARKINGS

CDS, (P.O. Box 78003, Cityview Nepean, Ontario, Canada K2G 5W2), Clover House, P.O. Box 62, Sebastopol, CA 95473) and Woodland Scenics offer dry transfers (Figure 12-12). Dry transfers are somewhat easier to apply than decals but you must have the dry transfer in precisely the right spot because there is no way to move it like you can

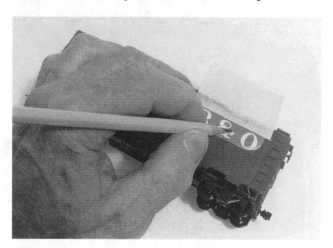

Fig. 12-12. Tape individual dry transfers to the model and the tape can act like a hinge so you can accurately reposition the transfer if you need to repeat the rub-on process.

with a decal. Cut each marking from the sheet, position the marking precisely where you want it, and tape its top to the model to act as hinge. Rub over the dry transfer firmly with a Number 2 pencil or one of the special decal burnishers sold by art supply stores. Gently lift the transfer on its hinge to see if all the transfer is stuck. If not, hinge the transfer back into perfect alignment and repeat the process.

THE LOCOMOTIVE PAINTSHOP

The same techniques described for painting rolling stock will work equally well on locomotives. On most diesel locomotives, however, the painting might become slightly more complicated because you may want to use a two-color paint scheme to match a particular prototype or for your own railroad.

MASKING AND PAINTING TWO COLORS

Use Scotch Magic Transparent Tape for masking. It's thinner than regular masking tape, and you can tell whether or not it's stuck by just looking to see if the part shows through the tape. Paint the lighter color first on most two-color paint schemes.

The black shades on the Burlington Northern diesels in this book are actually dark gray acrylic primer. This is a shortcut that saves the detail-hiding thickness of another coat of paint. You might be able to find a primer in a light gray or a light brown or even in white for the second color on other railroad paint schemes. Apply a strip of Scotch Magic tape all around the model, with one edge of the tape forming the color separation line between the existing color and the one you are about to spray on. If the color separation line has V or Z shapes, you may want to cover the whole area with the tape and cut through it to make the design; then you can remove the excess tape along the cut lines. You might also want to remove the end and side railings to make masking easier. I removed just the last posts from the side railings and the complete end railings to mask the end platforms so they would be black rather than green.

Spray on the second color and let it dry for at least a day. Use a new Num-

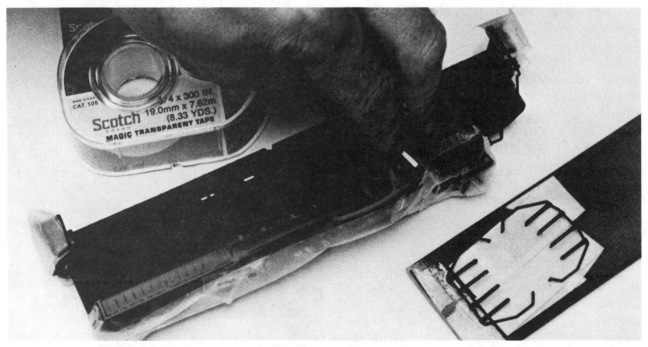

Fig. 12-9. Tape the end rails and other detail parts to a scrap of cardboard with masking tape doubled-over so the sticky side is up. Mask the body with Scotch Magic tape using a matchstick to force the tape to stick tightly into the corners of the body.

ber 11 blade in your X-Acto knife to slice carefully along the edge of the Magic tape so the second color won't stick to the tape. Do not rely on just the tape to make a clean color separation

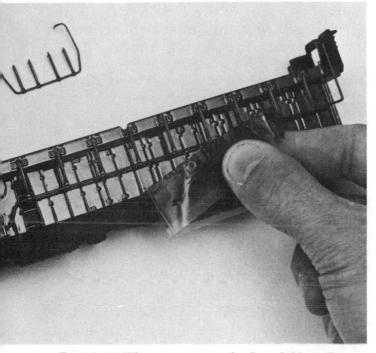

Fig. 12-11. When you remove the Scotch Magic Transparent Tape from a two-color paint job, pull the tape back over itself so it won't lift the first color with it.

edge because it will leave a ragged and rough line when it is removed. When you do pull the tape away, double it back over itself as shown in Figure 12-11 to minimize the chances of lifting the original color. If there are some zigs and zags in the paint separation line, touch them up with either (or both) colors applied with a Number O paint brush. When the paint is dry, the model can be decorated with decals. It will be necessary to use plenty of decal-softening fluid to get those decals to snuggle tightly around the louvers and rivets on any diesel body.

WEATHERING AND AGING TIPS

I cannot tell you how to weather a model car, locomotive, or structure. The only way you'll learn is to study the techniques. You'll have to go out into the real world to study how weathering really looks, and you'll have to practice the techniques I offer to learn how to use them properly.

Weathering is a term used to describe a final coat of very thin paint that is applied to the model to simulate

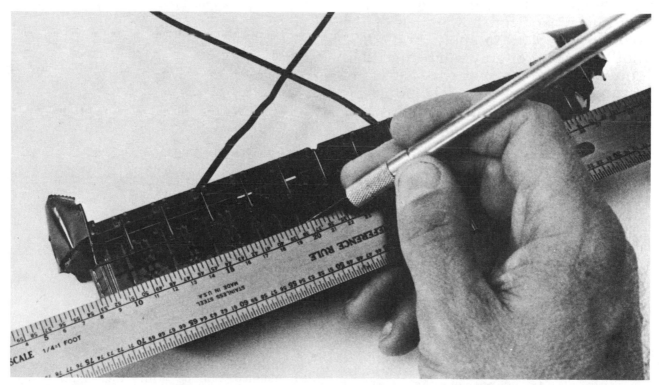

Fig. 12-10. Slice along the edge of the painted masking tape before peeling the tape back.

the effects of sun, wind, dirt, and rain. The paint can be just about anything from artists' water-base acrylics to artists' oil colors to artists' pastel chalks powdered on sandpaper and brushed onto the model. If you have access to an artist's airbrush (a miniature spray gun like those used to paint full-size automobiles usually priced from 80 to 300 dollars), you can use the incredible range of bottled model railroad paints. Excellent weathering effects can be achieved with oils, acrylics, or pastel chalks applied with a paint brush or a fine-pore sponge in a dabbing technique. The paint, however, must be thinned with about ninety-five parts water (for acrylics) or turpentine (for oil colors), so that the color will be barely visible.

SAND AND DUST

There are really only two secrets to the art of weathering a railroad miniature. First, keep the paint thin enough so that you can apply two or three coats without obscuring the lettering and numbers on the car or locomotive. Second, use photographs or very recent memories of the real thing as your guide to where and how much of the weathering colors to apply. You'll find that light beige or gray will be useful in simulating the sun-bleached effects of nature on any color car, locomotive, or structure. Those lighter shades can also be used on darker cars to simulate dust from desert areas, such as the Southwest. Many Southern Pacific cars, for instance, have a beige tint to their surfaces from traveling through the desert dust and from the effects of the hot Southwestern sun. Black or dark brown are the colors to use to simulate steam locomotive soot, diesel locomotive exhaust stains, and coal dust on your models. You'll see examples of all three different types of weathering in the color illustrations.

You should try to simulate as many different types of weathering as you can on your models, about half of them having weathering patterns common to the area you are modeling. Most of the cars you'll see in the coal-mining regions are stained with coal dust, and most of the cars that serve in limestone areas are streaked with gray, and the Southwestern cars are beige-tinted. Vary the degree of the weathering, from the barest trace that might collect on a new car to the years of grime that collect on an older car. If you apply too much weathering to a car or two, do as the real railroads do and paint over the number in the original car color and add a fresh decal number.

WOOD AND RUST EFFECTS

Weathering techniques can be used to weather track and to simulate wood flat-car floors or industrial loading platforms. Paint the wood surface a very light shade of beige, and then apply a wash of dark brown with a sponge, streaking the wash in the direction of the grain. Make every other board or tie or so a darker shade and just touch a few of them to leave mostly the faded-wood look of the light beige.

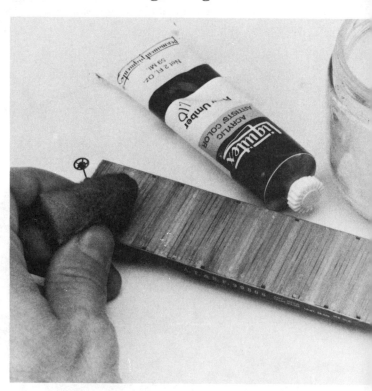

Fig. 12-13. Simulate wood grains by wiping over the beige-painted surface with water-thinned dark brown streaks.

Paint the track rails with dark red-brown to simulate rust, and add drops of rust to flat-car floors or loading docks to simulate rusted nails. Scrape just the tops of the rails gently with a knife blade to remove any paint from the electrical pickup surfaces, and do keep the rust-colored paint away from the moving parts of the switches. You can make your E-Z Track, Power-Loc track, True Track and sectional track look like it was laid on real wood ties with individual spikes by using these weathering techniques.

WEATHERING MODEL LOCOMOTIVES

Virtually all the three-dimensional details that appear on the real thing appear on the model. There are several ways, however, that you can make these locomotives seem even more like the real thing. A wash of ninety-five parts water and five parts black acrylic can be used to fill in the hollows of lou-vers and grills. This will make it appear as though there really could be engines inside the diesel bodies.

Every steam and diesel locomotive, even those at the head ends of passenger trains, have some degree of weathering such as that described in this chapter. Locomotives are even more likely to become dirty than rolling stock, but the patterns of the dirt will be different indeed. Again, photographs from railroad books and visits to real railroad yards will show you just where and how the real locomotives collect their dirt.

That black acrylic wash can also be applied to the trucks, ends and lower areas of the locomotives to simulate dirt and grime. You'll see an example of the light gray wash applied to one steam locomotive and three or four varieties of diesel weathering on the models in this book, but there are hundreds of other variations on the full-size locomotives.

CHAPTER 13

The Locomotive Factory

REPLICAS OF VIRTUALLY ANY FULL-SIZE DIESEL and many full-size steam locomotives are available as relatively inexpensive HO ready-to-run models. Many of those full-size locomotives, particularly passenger diesels and modern heavy freight diesels, are very long locomotives, often fitted with six-wheel trucks. Unfortunately, many diesels with six-wheel trucks will derail on the turnouts used with sectional track and on the similar-size E-Z Track, Power-Loc track and True Track turnouts. These turnouts have an 18-inch radius curve built in. While many of these larger diesels will negotiate a

steady 18-inch radius, they will derail as they lurch from a straight into a curve through a turnout, while their wheels pick at the turnout points and try to rattle out of the frogs.

PICKING THE PROPER LOCOMOTIVE

If you insist on running diesel locomotives with six-wheel trucks and steam locomotives larger than a 2-8-0, you will need more than 5 x 9-foot layout space. These locomotives will operate through Number 4-size turnouts and 24-inch radius curves but you can

Fig. 13-1. The larger HO scale locomotives will tend to derail over the turnouts used on all of the layouts in this book. You can, however, buy nearly identical locomotives that will not derail including diesels with 4-wheel trucks rather than 6-wheel trucks and steam locomotives with 8 drivers or less on relatively short wheel bases.

only squeeze a single-track oval on a 5 x 9-foot layout. A better solution is to select slightly smaller locomotives.

In nearly every instance, there is a matching four-wheel diesel for every full-size diesel with six-wheel trucks. Fortunately, the model manufacturers have made replicas of both of these types of locomotives (Figure 13-1). The black and gray Burlington diesel that is shown on the Burlington Route layout is a Proto 2000 SD7 with six-wheel trucks, the silver passenger diesel is a Proto 2000 E8A also with six-wheel trucks, and the steam locomotive is a Rivarossi 2-8-2. All three of these locomotives derail regularly over the turnouts used on all the layouts in this book. The solution is relatively simple: in place of the SD9, buy an Atlas GP7 (shown) or a Proto 2000 GP9, in place of the E8A buy an F3A from Stewart, and use an IHC 0-8-0 in place of the 2-8-2. Also shown is one of the largest full-size diesels, the Kato General Electric Dash 9-44CW in Chicago and NorthWestern paint (upper left), but Walthers has the nearly identical General Electric Dash 8-40BW (in Santa Fe markings, in front of the Dash 9-44CW) that has 4-wheel trucks. These alternate locomotives all operate well over the turnouts shown in this book.

Steam locomotives must also be relatively small to avoid frequent derailment over these turnouts, but there's a long list of locomotives that are accurate replicas of some specific prototype steam locomotives, including the Bachmann Spectrum Baldwin 2-8-0, IHC's Southern Pacific 2-6-0 and 0-8-0, Bachmann's Reading 2-8-0 and USRA 0-6-0, Life-Like's Proto 2000 USRA 0-8-0, Rivarossi's Indiana Harbor Belt 0-8-0, and Model Power's Baldwin 2-8-0, that are all ready-to-run. Nearly all of the MDC/Roundhouse and Bowser kit locomotives are also based on prototype steam locomotives. Hobby dealers sometimes carry 400 to 1000-dollar imported brass locomotives that are precise replicas of real railroad locomotives.

MAINTENANCE

If you keep your track clean, the amount of maintenance needed on your locomotives should be minimal. The major problems that affect model locomotives are oxidation of the metal wheels and track; grease and oil mixed with dirt on the wheels and track; and dirt, lint, dust, and other debris around the motor and gears of the locomotives. The only part of your locomotives that is likely to show even visible signs of wear might be the brushes on the motor, but they should last for hundreds of hours of operation. Most of the damage that occurs to model locomotives is the result of an inexperienced modeler trying to repair something that wasn't broken in the first place. The second most frequent cause of damage is, of course, accidental trips from table to floor, and accidental footwork around those floor-level layouts.

The only maintenance or repairs you should make are to see that the wheels (and the track rails) are kept spotlessly clean, that the motor and gears are cleaned frequently, and that only a small amount of grease or oil is added to replace what you wipe off in the process of cleaning the mechanism. If you have a perfectly clean engine, and if you have gone through all the troubleshooting steps in this chapter, and your locomotive still does not run, then you should take it to your hobby dealer to determine if he, one of his customers, or even the factory itself, offers repair service. At worst, you can remove the motor so the locomotive will roll, then use it as a dummy.

DISASSEMBLING

The locomotive body must be removed from the diesels and from a steam locomotive for access to the gears and other working parts. Most brands of diesel bodies can be removed by spreading the body apart with quite a lot of pressure to snap the trucks or chassis from beneath them. It's a good idea to have someone help, so one of you can spread the body while the other tries to wiggle the trucks free.

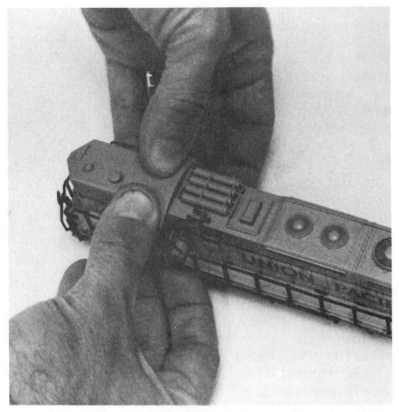

Fig. 13-2. Use both hands to spread the diesel body apart far enough so the chassis will drop free from its retaining tabs.

Screws hold the body of most steam locomotives to the superstructure. These screws must be removed to gain access to the motor and gears. You can determine the correct screws by examining the underside of the model. A screw always leads up toward the smokestack, and it must be removed, in addition to one or two more usually toward the rear of the locomotive. The rear of the cab, on some models, has a tab and a slot that attaches the rear of the superstructure to the chassis.

Be extremely careful when you remove the body so you don't break any of the wires leading to the motor or light bulbs. If you do, the wire will have to be re-soldered. You can find someone in an electronics hobby store or in a television repair shop to do the soldering for you if you do accidentally break a wire.

THE CHASSIS

Most of the model locomotives operate very nicely as shipped by the factory. Often, the models will actually run more smoothly and more quietly after they are broken in, after twenty or thirty hours of operation in one or two hour-long sessions. If the locomotive is running erratically, or if you simply like to fiddle with mechanical objects, the

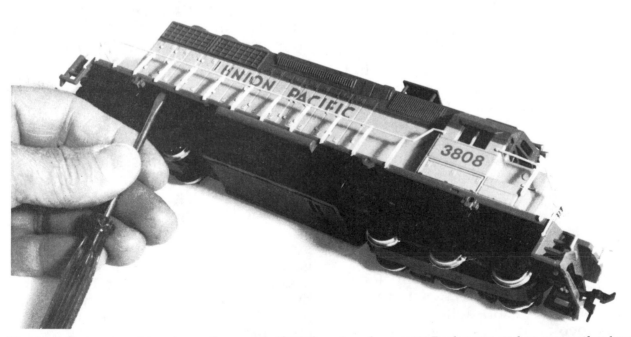

Fig. 13-3. Use a screwdriver to pry the running boards outward, on most Bachmann and on some other brands of diesels, to free the body from the chassis.

The industrial area of a small city is duplicated at Abbott on the Burlington Route Layout.

For Loads-In/Empties-Out operations on the 7 x 8-foot Burlington Route layout, the loaded hoppers are pulled from beneath the Hudson Mine tipple at Chester and loaded cars are spotted beneath the conveyor as described in Chapter 19.

The bare tabletop beginning of the 7 x 8-foot Burlington Route layout, from the plan in Chapter 20 (Figure 20-5). It has three layers of 2-inch blue insulating Styrofoam, 1/8-inch plywood shadowbox benchwork and the white Styrofoam building sites and road in place as described in Chapter 6. The flat tabletop can be left as-is for a few months while you try different track arrangements.

Two of the three layers of 2-inch thick blue insulating Styrofoam have been carved away to produce the valley in the foreground and two more layers added to create the hills in the background as described in Chapter 16. From here, the layout could be covered with a single layer of Hydrocal-soaked paper towels and plaster cloth as described in Chapter 15, or with felt as described in Chapter 17.

If you opted to cut the beige felt a bit oversize, glue it firmly in place with contact cement and let the cement dry completely. Use a utility knife to trim the felt to the edge of the ditch on each side of the track as shown.

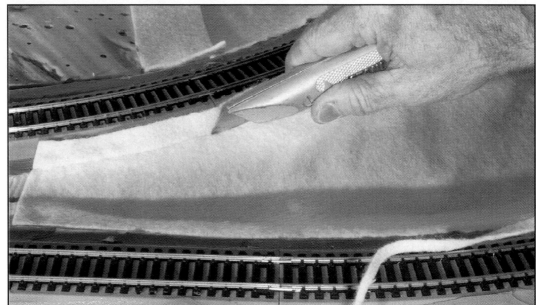

The 7 x 8-foot Burlington Route layout with the scenery shapes covered with beige felt as described in Chapter 17. The felt smoothes out the rough surface of the carved blue Styrofoam and provides a base for dirt-covered felt grass.

Use an aerosol can of earth-brown-colored paint to provide a base coat for the bare white building sites, the blue sides of any cuts, or any other areas that are not covered by green-painted beige felt. Leave the actual track and ballast gray because it will be painted and textured later.

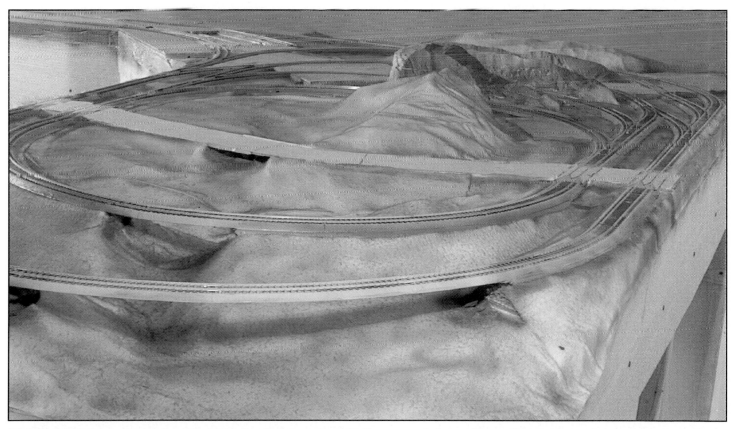

The beige felt is sprayed with a single, light coat of Kelly green ink or thinned paint to color just the top layer of fibers.

The Grass-That-Grows surface texturing shown in Chapter 17 begins with beige felt that has been sprayed lightly with Kelly green paint. Next, sift real dirt onto the felt through a tea strainer as shown, then lightly brush the felt with a wire brush to work the dirt into the felt.

The completed effect of the treated-felt Grass-That-Grows technique from Chapter 17 with an HO scale figure up to his ankles in grass.

When the Grass-That-Grows process or other scenic texturing is complete, spread the ballast, sweep it clean from the tops of the ties and away from the working parts and guard rails of the turnouts, and flood the area, as shown in Chapter 7, with a mixture of 3 parts Matte Medium to 1 part water using an ear syringe.

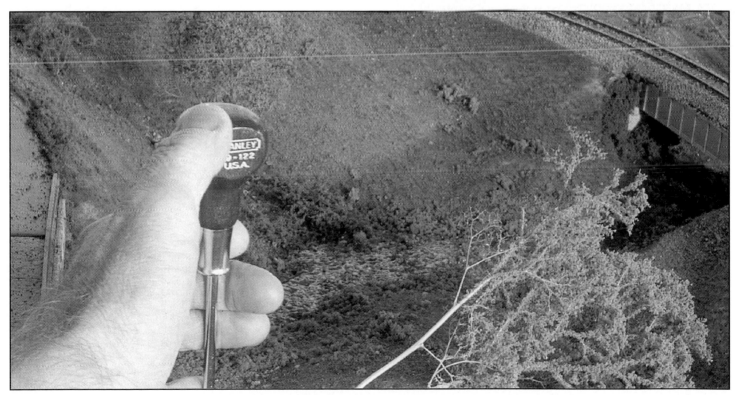

The trees are natural weeds from Noch or Scenic Express. Spray the trunks with gray primer, then spray the limbs with cheap hair spray and sprinkle on finely ground foam, spray again and add more finely ground foam. To plant the trees in the felt-and-Styrofoam scenery, simply poke holes in the earth with an awl and insert the tree.

Form the stream bed with either plaster or shaped blue Styrofoam and texture the ground with paint and ground foam or with the Grass-That-Grows felt and seal it thoroughly with artists Matte Medium applied with an ear syringe. Cover the bed of the stream with a layer of 1/8-inch-size rocks, followed by some finer sand.

Pour a 1/8-inch layer of artists Gloss Medium over the rocks and let it dry overnight (or for several days) until the milky color becomes clear. If you want to make the stream deeper, wait until the first pour becomes perfectly clear before applying another 1/8-inch layer.

For rapids, add some 1/4-inch or larger rocks and dab on some artists Gel Medium as lumps below the rocks. When the Gloss Medium dries, touch the tops with gloss pearl white paint to simulate the foam.

Add some more fresh rocks along the edge of the water before the first layer of artists Gloss Medium dries.

This stream was created with several layers of artists Gloss Medium and some lumps of artists Gel Medium for the white-water areas. The bushes along the banks of the stream are small tufts of gray macrame fiber, sprayed with hair spray, then dusted with green finely ground foam to simulate leaves.

The train set track will look more realistic if the ties are painted with a dust-on coat of gray and the sides of the rails painted Box Car Red to simulate rust. The green overspray from painting the beige felt "grass" will be disguised by the loose ballast.

Pour a minimum amount of loose ballast between the rails and spread it with a soft brush. Try to keep the ballast from the moving points of the turnouts. For the industrial area of Abbott, on the Burlington Route layout, real dirt, sifted through a fine-mesh tea strainer was used for ballast. Brush any dirt or ballast away from the moving turnout points.

The felt has been dusted with real dirt sifted through a tea strainer and the felt teased with a wire brush to create the Grass-That-Grows effects described in Chapter 17. The rocks for the stream bed are in place, with Poly Fiber and finely ground foam bushes along the creek and random patches of ground foam for low bushes and bushy weeds. The track is ballasted a shown in Chapter 7, and bridge girders and abutments beneath the two tracks and beneath the road are also in place as described in Chapter 16.

The completed Burlington Route layout with the steel viaduct completed as shown in Chapter 16. The trees are treated and planted as shown in Chapter 17, and people, cars and trains added to bring the layout to life.

The highway on the Burlington Route layout is 1/4 x 3-1/2-inch white Styrofoam painted gray with cracks and expansion joints drawn with fine-point felt-tip pen. The railroad crossing signs are from Creative Model Associates and the whistle post and yard limit signs are from Kadee. The yellow lines are painted with a Testors Gloss Paint Marker.

You can operate equipment from any era on any model railroad. Here, the Proto 2000 E8A diesel and the rolling stock define the period as about 1959 for the railroad. The vehicles also help establish a time period for the scene.

The era, here, is 1906 or later with a General Electric Dash 840B Santa Fe diesel working the hoppers at the power plant in the background, and a Life-Like Amtrak F40PH diesel pulling Walthers Amfleet coaches. The vehicles also help set the time for the scene; with a black Trident Chevrolet Step-Side pickup truck and a black Herpa Kenworth tractor on the highway. The smooth-side trailer is from Rail Power Products.

This 4 x 6-foot layout was built by Lunde Studios for the Bachmann MODEL RAILROADING WITH NICKEL SILVER E-Z TRACK, Vol. II, also by Robert Schleicher. The track plan used for this layout is a variation of the plan used for the 7 x 8-foot Burlington Route layout. This layout, however has a sky backdrop down the center of the layout, rather than across the rear, to divide it into two scenes. This is mining scene for Loads-In/Empties-Out operations. Courtesy Bachmann Industries.

The city side of the 4 x 6 layout from the Bachmann MODEL RAIL-ROADING WITH NICKEL SILVER E-Z TRACK, Vol. II book. The hopper cars for the Loads-In/Empties-Out operations lead beneath the highway overpass in the lower left. This layout was constructed using conventional open-grid bench-work with Woodland Scenics Plaster Cloth scen-ery shapes, trees and foam ground cover. Courtesy Bachmann Industries.

Larry Larson holds a power pack converted to tethered walk-around control with longer cables while he operates a Burlington freight on the outer oval of the 9 x 9-foot Burlington Northern layout (Figures 20-2 and 20-4). The freight being pulled by the Burlington Northern diesel is being operated by Bill Wright from the control panel at the town of Duncan.

Artist's pastel chalks can be used to weather freight cars, locomotives, or structures by powdering the chalk on sandpaper and dusting the powder onto the cars with a paintbrush.

For a different weathering effect, try artists' acrylic colors, thinned with about 3 parts water to 1 part paint. Apply the paint with fine-pore sponge by dipping the sponge into the color, then dabbing it lightly onto the car.

The stream on the Burlington Route layout, meandering on its twisting course beneath the geometric perfection of the railroad and highway, provides an interesting and realistic contrast between the random shapes and textures of nature and the machinery of railroading.

The towns of Abbott and Chester, on the Burlington Route layout, are supposed to be miles apart, but only a ridge and trees actually separate the two towns. The industrial buildings of the city of Abbott are visible in the background of this photo of a passenger train just arriving at Chester but, when you actually view the scene, the trees and the ridge distract your eye so you are not aware that the two towns are really that close together.

The passenger train just arriving at the Abbott station stretches back along the track to the town of Chester. The row of trees and the ridge separate the two scenes. The parked cars, figures and details at Abbott capture your attention so you are not aware that another town is that close.

Michael George is recreating a piece of real railroad, the Louisville and Nashville Railroad's Knoxville and Atlanta Division. He used a Central Valley bridge kit to duplicate the L&N's crossing of the Hiawassee River. Plans for his layout appeared in the February 1996 and September 1998 issues of *Railmodel Journal* magazine.

J.D. Smith is modeling a specific portion of the a real railroad, the Southern Railway's Rathole Division in Kentucky and Tennessee. This is his recreation of Harriman, Tennessee. His layout was featured in the February 1997 issue of *Railmodel Journal* magazine.

You can model two time periods or eras on just one layout by changing the equipment. Here, the locomotives and rolling stock are all authentic for the 1959 period at Chester on the Burlington Route layout.

By changing all the locomotives and all the rolling stock you can effectively move the era forward to about 1995. Some of the rolling stock dates to the sixties but it would have still been in operation and it has been weathered so it looks its age.

John Swanson used styrene plastic sheet, strip and milled shapes to build a replica of the grain elevator at Lawrence, Kansas. The model was part of Terry Trank's layout.

The Hudson Coal mine at Chester, on the Burlington Route layout, was kit-converted by cutting down the height of this Walthers 3051 Coal Flood Loader. The trees in this scene are Noch or Scenic Express treated with fall colors of Woodland Scenics fine ground foam.

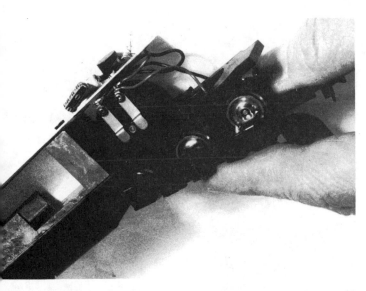

Fig. 13-5. With the bottom cover removed, the wheels and gears can be removed from the Bachmann diesels' trucks for cleaning and regreasing.

Fig. 13-4. Pry out and down on the end of the truck to free the bottom cover on the trucks from Bachmann and some other brands of diesels.

Fig. 13-6. Many diesels, like this Life-Like Proto 2000 SW9, have printed circuit boards snapped onto the top of the motor. There is usually a socket on these boards to accept the DCC decoders described in Chapter 9.

Fig. 13-7. Pry gently on the inside tab of the truck bottom cover to remove the cover from most Walthers, Model Power and from some other brands of diesel locomotives.

Fig. 13-8. With the bottom cover removed, the wheels and gears can be removed from the Walthers or Model Power trucks.

Fig. 13-9. This IHC SD40 is typical of the medium-priced diesel locomotives from IHC, Bachmann, Model Power and Walthers.

chassis can be disassembled for cleaning and inspection. Each brand of locomotive, however, has a different method of attaching the body to the chassis and of attaching the trucks and motor to the frame.

DISASSEMBLING AND LUBRICATING DIESELS

The bodies on most HO scale diesels can be removed by prying outward on the bottom edges of the body with either your fingertips or, if you can reach inside, with the tip of a screwdriver and insert a toothpick on the opposite side or end to keep the body spread apart. Spread the body, and the complete chassis should fall from the bottom of the body. It is, however, possible to clean and lubricate the gears without removing the body with some brands of HO scale diesels. Pry gently upward on the plastic tab on the inside ends of the truck and the cap covering the bottom of the truck may snap away to reveal the wheels and gears. The wheels can then be removed. When reassembling the wheels, be careful that the two copper strips contact the backs of each wheel.

DISASSEMBLING AND LUBRICATING ATHEARN DIESELS

Athearn has two distinctive methods of mounting the body to the chassis. The later production models like the SW1500, GP38-2, GP40-2, GP50 and SD40-2 have bodies that mount with four tabs extending through the chassis into the fuel tanks. To remove these bodies, insert two medium-sized screwdriver blades into the slots in the bottom of the fuel tank to engage the tabs. Pry both tabs out while you gently pull upward on the body until you can feel the body slide free on that side. Hold the body firmly while you insert the two screwdrivers in the slots on the opposite side of the fuel tank to free that side of the body. The body then can be lifted free.

The earlier Athearn diesels have bodies that are held in place with two pins that fit into tabs on the sides of the running boards on each side. Use a screwdriver or your fingertips, as described for most Atlas, Bachmann, Con-Cor, E & C Shops, IHC, Kato, Model Power, Stewart and Walthers diesels, to pry the sides of the body or running boards out to free the body.

The trucks on all Athearn diesels are held in place with a half-circle clip. Before removing the clip, gently pry outward on the long metal band on the top of the chassis to snap it away from the motor and from beneath the metal clips on the top of each truck. To remove the clip from the top of each truck, insert a screwdriver between the chassis and the truck and pry out on the bottom of the clip. If you try to remove the clip from the top of the chassis, you can break the retaining tabs. When the

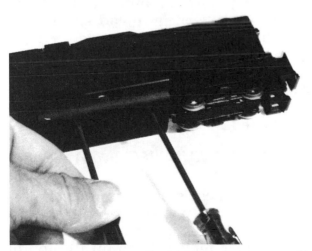

Fig. 13-10. To remove the body from the newer Athearn diesels, insert two small screwdrivers into the rectangular notches in the fuel tanks and pry gently to release the plastic body-mounting tabs.

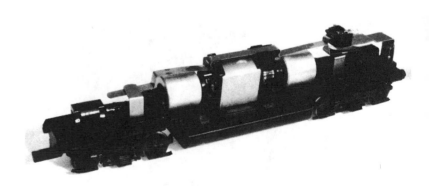

Fig. 13-11. This GP40-2 chassis is similar to most of the current-production Athearn diesels.

clips are removed, look carefully at the position of the worm gear, the washers on the ends of the gear, and the square bronze bearings so you can reassemble those parts in the proper order. The spur gears on the trucks are accessible after the worm gears are removed. To disassemble the trucks, remove the clip from the bottom of each truck using a screwdriver to pry outward on the clip's side flanges from the top of the truck.

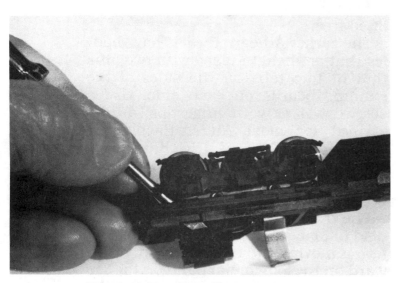

Fig. 13-12. To remove the trucks from an Athearn diesel, insert a screwdriver from below the chassis to pry and push the truck-retaining cover free from its clips.

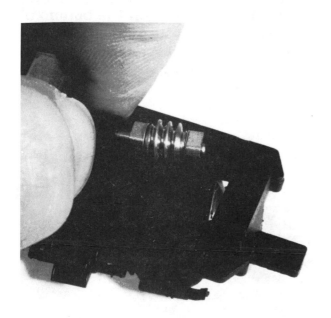

Fig. 13-13. Lift the worm gear, with its two bearings and two thrust washers, from the top of the Athearn truck.

CLEANING AND INSPECTION

Most HO scale diesel and steam locomotives have some type of metal wiper that contacts either the wheels or the trucks to carry the electrical current from the rails to the motor through the wheels or drivers. Most Atlas, Bachmann, Con-Cor, E & C Shops, IHC, Kato, Model Power, Stewart and Walthers diesels have a small copper strip that contacts the back of each wheel. Remove the wheels and notice how far the copper strip moves. That strip should move about 1/32 inch so that the wheel forces that copper strip inward 1/32 inch. Thus, the strip provides pressure on the back of the wheel when the wheel moves from side to side in the truck. If necessary, bend the clips in or out to achieve that contact. The backs of the wheels and the contacting portion of the copper strip also must be clean.

Use a hard rubber eraser like those sold by Life-Like, Model Power or Bright Boy to clean the wheels and the strips. If there is black grease inside the trucks, remove the wheels and gears and clean them in paint thinner.

Use grease and oil that will not dissolve plastic. Hobby shops carry La-Belle brand Number 106 grease and Number 108 oil that is plastic-compatible, but you may find other brands as well. Just be sure the label indicates that the grease or oil will not harm plastics. Apply one pinhead-sized dot of LaBelle Number 106 grease to each gear tooth. Also apply one drop of La-Belle Number 108 oil to the bearings on each end of the motor. All of the other bearings are plastic and should not be lubricated.

CLEANING AND INSPECTING ATHEARN DIESELS

Athearn diesels have a more complex electrical pickup system. A metal strip runs across the top of the motor to contact similar metal strips on the top of each truck. Those strips must be bent so there is pressure between them. Re-

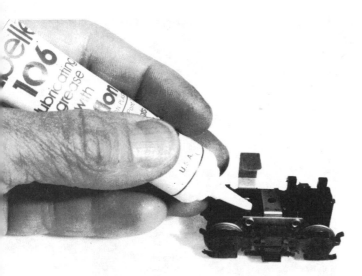

Fig. 13-14. Use one of the plastic-compatible greases, like LaBelle Number 106, to lubricate the gears and the worm in any diesel's trucks. This is the truck from an Athearn GP40-2.

Fig. 13-15. Use a plastic-compatible oil, like LaBelle number 108, to lubricate the bronze bearings on the Athearn worm shafts and on the bearings of any motor shaft.

move the strip from the motor, then push it back in place with the ends resting above the strips on the tops of the trucks. The ends of that long metal strip should be at least 1/16 inch above the strips on the ends of the truck. When the long metal strip is pushed back under the strips on the ends of the trucks it will have enough pressure to maintain contact. Be sure the contacting portion of the long metal strip and the metal strips on the tops of the trucks are clean by polishing them with one of those hard rubber erasers.

The Athearn trucks have a second electrical contact where they mount to the frame. Remove the trucks, as described earlier, and inspect the rubbing faces on the bottom of the frame and the metal strips that serve as the pivots for the trucks. Again, polish both areas with a hard rubber eraser. If they are extremely dirty or rusty, scrape the surfaces clean with a sharp screwdriver blade.

The Athearn motor also maintains an electrical contact with the chassis. To inspect that contact, remove the motor using a screwdriver to push upward through the four round holes in the bottom of the chassis to free the flexible plastic motor mounts. With the motor out, you can see a bare metal strip down the center of the chassis. That area must be perfectly clean. Clean the copper tabs on the bottom of the motor, too, and bend them, if necessary, so their ends extend at least 1/4 inch below the bottom of the motor. Those copper strips contact that bare metal strip in the bottom of the chassis.

Those areas of metal strip-to-frame contact can cause erratic operation of Athearn diesels. If you know how to solder, the performance of any Athearn diesel can be made more reliable and free from hesitation by soldering short lengths of 18-gauge insulated electrical wire from the copper strip on the top of the motor to the top tabs on the trucks. Two more wires also can be soldered from the copper strip on the bottom of the motor to the vertical edges of the metal strips that serve as the pivot points for the Athearn trucks. With this series of four wires, you are running wire connections directly from the motor to the trucks to bypass the frame itself.

Athearn diesels can surge or stumble on steep downhills with a heavy train. Sometimes this can be caused by too much end play in the worm gears. To reduce the end play, add a second Athearn Number 99201 thrust washer (available to dealers from Walthers and other wholesalers) to the stub end of the worm gear shaft (Figure 13-19). When you reassemble the worm gear, however, be sure that you can detect a perceptible end-to-end movement. If there is no end-to-end movement (end play), remove the washer so you can barely feel the worm gear move in and out.

CLEANING THE MOTOR

The only parts of the motor that should require attention are the commutator and the motor brushes that rub on the revolving commutator. I do not recommend that you attempt to replace the brushes or clean the commutator in the motors used by most HO locomotive manufacturers because the motors are enclosed (and dirt is unlikely to enter). It is difficult to disassemble these motors without breaking the holding tabs. If the motor does not run, even with the wires from the power pack touched directly to the frame contact strips on the motor, replace the motor.

The brushes on the Athearn motors are accessible by simply removing the copper clips that snap onto the top and bottom of the motor. Pry up one end while holding the center of the copper strip down so the spring doesn't eject the round sintered copper motor brush. Gently lift the strip, then the

Fig. 13-17. Use a screwdriver to press against the bottom of the plastic mounting tabs to remove the motor from an Athearn chassis.

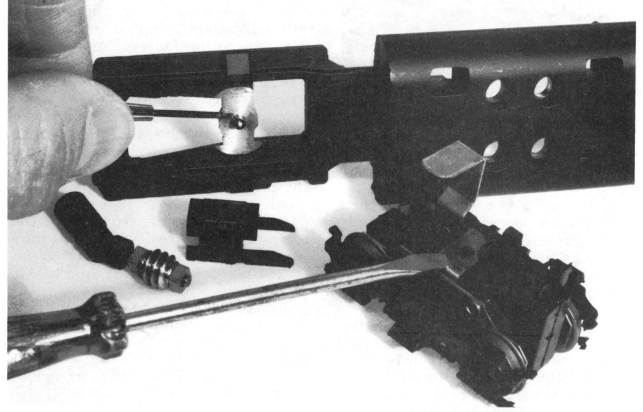

Fig. 13-16. Use a sharp-edged screwdriver blade to scrape dirt from the pivot surfaces of the Athearn chassis (top) and the trucks (bottom).

coil spring, and remove the brush from the bottom of the round hole beneath the spring. If the brush is shorter than 1/16 inch, replace it with Athearn's Number 90037 motor brush. The commutator can be cleaned without removing the brushes. Simply dip the end of a pipe cleaner in some paint thinner and gently scrub the round copper commutator (Figure 13-20).

The motor brushes in some of the older Tyco and Mantua steam locomotives are visible on motors similar to the Athearn motor. Again, the brushes should be replaced if the round copper brush soldered to the end of the brass

Fig. 13-18. Use that sharp-edged screwdriver blade to scrape dirt from the Athearn motor contact slot in the bottom well of the fuel tank on the chassis.

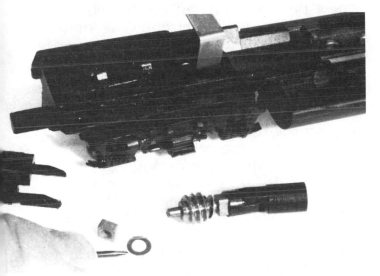

Fig. 13-19. The two thrust washers on the outer end of the Athearn worm gear shaft. If the locomotive surges when running down steep grades, it may be helped by adding another thrust washer.

Fig. 13-20. Use a pipe cleaner dipped in paint thinner to scrub the motor's commutator clean. This is a typical Athearn motor.

Fig. 13-21. The Mantua steam locomotives, like this 2-6-6-2 articulated, have a round can-style motor.

strip is thinner than 1/32 inch. The wires are soldered to the brushes on most of these motors, however, so you may want to ask your local hobby dealer if he can replace the brushes for you or if he has another customer that might be able to do the work. Most HO scale steam locomotives have a fully enclosed motor like that shown in the Mantua 2-6-6-2 articulated locomotive (Figure 13-21).

CLEANING THE PARTS

Use a tissue soaked in lighter fluid, lacquer thinner, or solvent to remove the grease and grit from the wheels and the gears. Be sure you work outdoors, away from fire or flame and away from any electricity that could cause a spark to interact with those volatile and poisonous fluids. Wear rubber gloves to protect your hands and goggles or safety glasses to protect your eyes. Wooden toothpicks can be dipped in one of the fluids to reach the tight areas. Small wooden sticks can be used, in the same way, to dislodge the worst dirt from wheels. Never scrape wheels with metal objects. You might scratch them, and the scratches will collect more dirt more quickly. Never use steel wool on any of your model railroad equipment; the tiny strands will be attracted to the motor magnets and switch rails and could cause short circuits. You only

Fig. 13-22. Use a sharp screwdriver blade to scrape-clean the treads' surfaces of diesel wheels or steam locomotive drivers or tender wheels.

need to do a thorough cleaning job once a year or so unless you're running your trains on the floor. For most tabletop layouts, a twice-a-year wheel and rail cleaning with a typewriter or ink eraser is all is needed.

ASSEMBLING THE LOCOMOTIVE

The assembly of the locomotive is the reverse of the disassembly. You must be particularly careful about the wheels, however. One wheel of each diesel wheel pair, one driver of each steam locomotive drive pair, and one wheel of each steam locomotive tender wheel pair is insulated so the wheels will not create a short circuit. The insulated wheel will have a plastic washer in its hub or, with some steam locomotive drivers, a thin band of white or red fiber or plastic near the rim. All the insulated wheels must be on the same side on the front truck and on the opposite side of the other truck on diesels. On steam locomotives, the insulated drivers must be on the opposite side (or contact the opposite rail) from the insulated wheels on both tender trucks.

If you discover that a locomotive travels in the opposite direction from all the others, that problem can be corrected by removing the wheels or drivers and turning them end-for-end before putting them back on.

TROUBLESHOOTING

The Locomotive and Electrical Troubleshooting chart in Chapter 9 (Figure 9-6) includes the probable causes of trouble that can occur in the track and the power pack as well as in the locomotive. All three components are part of the same electrical circuit. I suggest that you use a 12-volt model railroad light bulb as a troubleshooting test lamp.

DO'S AND DON'TS FOR LOCOMOTIVES

- Do clean the locomotive wheels and polish them with an ink eraser or the track cleaning erasers sold by Life-Like, Model Power and Bright Boy.
- Do clean the bearings, axles and gears of the locomotives to remove any dirt, lint or excess oil or grease.
- Do remove or mark any locomotives or cars that derail regularly for later inspection so the fault can be found before the next operating session.
- Do inspect the couplers on all locomotives to be sure they are at the proper height for coupling and that the uncoupling pin does not hang down too far.
- Do use the Trouble-Shooting Chart in Chapter 9 (Figure 9-6) and check each step, in the order presented, to pinpoint the cause of derailments or poor locomotive performance.

- Don't allow dirt to accumulate on locomotive wheels since it can cause erratic pickup and unreliable speed control.
- Don't apply oil or grease to any plastic bearings. Use oil (like LaBelle Number 108) on metal bearings and grease (like LaBelle Number 106) on plastic or metal gears.
- Don't just hope that a derailment-prone locomotive or car will eventually fix itself.
- Don't continue to operate locomotives or cars with faulty couplers since they may derail or catch on the turnouts to cause damage and derailments.
- Don't assume you know the cause of a problem without checking the alternatives on the Trouble-Shooting Chart.

PART IV: Scenery and Buildings

CHAPTER 14

Structures

THE CONSTRUCTION of buildings is almost a hobby within a hobby. The buildings on a model railroad add an immeasurable look of life to the scene, and imply industry and action. The buildings also provide the reasons for the railroad's operations because they suggest that the freight and passenger cars really are carrying commodities. All those structures, though, are really scenery in that they decorate the miniature railroad layout. Each of the structures on your model railroad serves two functions: to make the railroad seem more like a living thing and to provide a background or scene for the movements of the trains. The contrast of the angular stationary structures and the movement of the similarly shaped locomotives and cars makes both the moving and the static models more true-to-life.

You'll be a big step ahead of the game of improving the realism of your model railroad if you really think of the buildings as scenery. Structures, of course, are like any other aspect of real-life scenery; each one is a bit different from the next, just as one tree or one hill is different from another. You expect to see dozens, maybe even hundreds, of almost identical boxcars or hoppers or even locomotives on a real railroad. You can expect to see identical pieces of rolling stock or locomotives on a model railroad, too. Usually, a model railroad suffers from quite the opposite problem; far too many of its cars and locomotives are different from one another, and this often creates a circus-like atmosphere. The rule of realism suggests the use of as many of the same style, same color freight cars as you can afford, but this must be reversed when it comes to structures.

Try to do everything imaginable to make every structure different from every other structure on your railroad, and, of course, try to make each one different from every structure on everybody else's railroad! There are a few structures that are representative of generic prototype buildings including most of the kits in the City Classics, DPM, Magnuson, Rix and Walthers lines. The only modifications made to the Walthers Hardwood 933-3044 Furniture Factory or 933-3021 Northern Light and Power were made to fit the stuctures onto the layout and to allow clearances for the trains that pass next to them. Conversely, the Walthers 933-3051 Coal Floodloader mine tipple was extensively modified to lower its height. The majority of the American Model Builders laser-cut wood kits are recreations of actual prototype structures and if you find a railroad station for your favorite railroad, there's no point in altering an accurate replica.

CUSTOM-MODIFIED BUILDINGS

Very little effort is involved in making each and every building you buy or build a custom creation. It's well worth the trouble to make even a minor modification that will alter the appearance of the structure enough so at least it doesn't look like all of those in the ads and catalogs. Modifying a building can begin with your first kit-assembly job. Most plastic structure kits can be assembled in just an evening or two with the thicker liquid cement for plastics.

Fig. 14-1. The buildings at Alliance on the Burlington Northern layout are nearly all kit-conversions of two or more separate structure kits. Two of these structures along the top of the photograph are reflected in a mirror and, thus, appear as mirror-image duplicates.

PAINTING

The prelude to any assembly should be painting, even though the parts are almost always supplied in two or three or more colors. Unpainted plastic has a certain transparency that is visible and immediately identifiable to even a casual visitor. However, if you paint the plastic before assembling the pieces, an expert model builder won't be able to tell if its plastic or wood, or even real brick or stone or concrete.

Testors is just one firm that makes a subdued rainbow of flat colors in their series of Model Master II paints, and these are perfect for painting the struc-

tures on a model railroad. Floquil has a similar series of flat model railroad paints in aerosol cans. The bottled Model Master II paints are intended for military figures, but the flat-finish dark greens, beiges, browns, grays, and blues are precisely the colors you want for your model railroad structures as are the flat model railroad paints from Floquil. Most of the Floquil paints are offered only in bottles, but they're easy enough to apply with a brush because one coat is usually enough to cover the plastic. Testors also has flat black, flat white, and flat red in spray cans, and some of the primers (which don't eat plastics) come in light and dark gray and brown, so you can find most of the colors you'll need in spray cans. All of these paints are solvent-based so spray outdoors and hold the parts with disposable rubber gloves.

Floquil makes an acrylic-based line of model railroad paints, the Polly Scale series, and similar colors are available in water-based paints in Badger's Modelflex series. These paints can be applied with a brush or an airbrush.

Spray or brush-paint the windows and doors of the structures while they're still attached to the molding sprues or trees. The easiest way to paint most buildings is to assemble all the outer walls without the windows. The Model Master Liquid Cement for Plastic Models is thicker than most liquid cements but not as thick as tube-type cement. I prefer it for assembling plastic-structure kits. Let the glue dry overnight on all the seams, and pre-fit the roof, but don't glue it on. The building can then be brush- or spray-painted in a hurry because there's no tiny painting to be done. Paint the windows a contrasting color, the details like downspouts or smokestacks a third color, and the roof a fourth color. Let that paint dry overnight, too.

You cannot use plastic cement to glue a painted surface to another painted surface or to plastic, so the windows, details, and roof will have to be installed with one of the cyanoacrylate cements, such as Aron-Alpha, Hot Stuff, Zap or Super Glue, or with 5-minute epoxy. If you feel you must use plastic cement, scrape the paint away from the areas that will be joined and glue the parts in place by installing them and holding them there with a knife blade while you brush on some of the liquid cement for plastics. Use the plain white glue, or epoxy to glue the clear-plastic window glass in place. The plastic cements (either tube-type or liquid) and cyanoacrylate cements will etch or craze the clear plastic.

THE LIVE-THERE LOOK

Each of the structures on your layout should be surrounded with earth, so they look like they belong. Brush or trowel the brown-colored plaster you use for scenery (see Chapter 15) around the Homasote tabletop before the building is installed, and push the structure into the still-wet plaster. About 1/16 inch deep into the plaster is deep enough. Be sure the building is level when you sink it into the plaster. If you are using Styrofoam building sites, as shown in Chapter 16, you can coat the building site with a thick layer of artists' Matte Medium, then sprinkle real dirt through a tea strainer onto the still-wet Matte Medium and spray the area with a mixture of three parts water and one part Matte Medium, Finally, push the building into the still-wet dirt to bury its foundation. You can then use the same dirt and grass effects that you select for the rest of the scenery to blend the area around the building into the rest of the world (or to blend the rest of the world into the building area if you installed the building before the rest of the scenery).

WEATHERING

The last step is the most important; the building must be weathered by spraying it lightly and from a distance of about 2 feet with flat paint that comes close to matching the surrounding scenery. Spray a bit more of the paint near the edges of the roof to simulate rain-washed dirt that accumulates near the rain gutters, and spray a bit more near the base of the building to simulate where rain would have splattered mud around the base of the building. Practice this weathering technique on an old shoe box until you can determine just how far away you can hold the spray can to get the effect of dust. If you have an air brush, mix about three parts thinner to one part paint and apply the weathering effects with the air brush.

The entire town or industrial area should receive this roof and foundation treatment. You might want to select a different weathering shade for different towns. The town of Alliance on the Burlington Northern layout in Chapter 20 (Figures 20-3 and 20-4) has an overall touch of beige to match the nearby dirt. The areas around the Corning Mine on the Burlington Northern layout, and the Hudson Mine and the other buildings at Chester on the Burlington Route layout (Figure 20-5) have been weathered with a very light touch of black to simulate rain-washed coal dust. The town of Emmett was given a weathering tint of dark brown. This overall weathering is the single most important step in making your layout look real.

STRUCTURE CONVERSIONS

Only so many variations can be made on a structure by painting it. If you really want the majority of your buildings to look different from any others, you're going to have to learn the technique known as conversion, or kit-bashing. The fundamental principle of structure conversions is that the finished product should look unlike anything you can buy. The actual conversion could

Fig. 14-3. A bottom-side view of the Alliance Company before installation of the roofs reveals how the parts are assembled.

be as simple as adding a new roof to the Bachmann or Model Power lighted ready-built, or to a Con-Cor kit-built Freight Station. Or, it can be as complex as constructing a structure like the Alliance Company (Figures 14-2 and 14-3) from two Pola 578-616 Roth Roof Tile Factory kits. I have deliberately attempted to make most of the buildings on the Burlington Northern and Burlington Route layouts as different as possible from any existing kits so that you can see the effects of the conversion process and the simplicity of the actual work. You can refer to the photos in the various chapters for scenes of the buildings and the satellite view of the Burlington Northern layout in Chapter 20 (Figure 20-4) to locate specific structures. The key to that view (Figure 20-4) shows both the r-t-r action accessories like the log or ore car dumping devices, and the structures.

I recommend that you purchase a Walthers catalog from a hobby shop. With the catalog, you can get a better

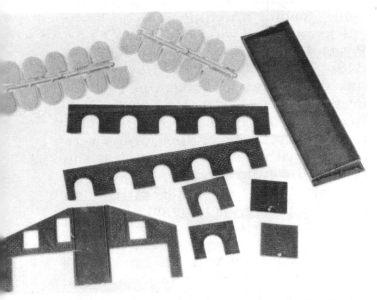

Fig. 14-2. The Alliance Company on the Burlington Northern layout is a project for the experienced kit-conversion builders. Two Pola 578-616 Roth Roof Tile Factory kits were cut and fitted to make the two-story structure, with the leftover arches cut, as shown, for the Emmett Coke Co. ovens.

idea of what the box-stock buildings look like. Refer to the current catalog to find out what is available. Most of these structures have been offered by at least four different model companies under a half-dozen different titles. I have listed the current kit's model company, part number and title in this chapter, but look for the overall shape because the titles and even the brands change every year or so.

BUYING STRUCTURES

Virtually all the structures and bridges used on the Burlington Northern HO Scale Layout (Figure 20-4) are Bachmann, IHC, Con-Cor, Model Power, or Pola kits, selected because they were the most readily available when that layout was constructed. Most of these kits are manufactured by either Heljan or Pola. Both also sell HO scale structures under their own names, as well as under the Bachmann, Con-Cor, IHC, Model Power and Walthers labels. These kits also appeared under the AHM label, but AHM is no longer in business and under the Tyco label, but Tyco is no longer producing model trains. If you compare these brands of kits, you'll often find the same kit with, perhaps, a different front, color or a change in the arrangement of multiple-building kits. In some cases, the simulated material of the walls of the kit are different. The names and brands of the kits change quite often, so it's nearly impossible to provide a number-by-number interchange. However, you can spot the shapes of the models if you look carefully. There are other brands of kits, particularly those produced by Walthers, that are just as detailed as the Pola kits but are models of completely different structures. The Atlas, Bachmann, Ertl and Life-Like plastic kits are also similar to the Pola kits in construction and ease of modification. There are also dozens of other smaller manufacturers listed in the Walthers catalog including AMI, City Classics, DPM, Faller, Kibri, Micro Engineering,

Pikestuff, Piko, Rix, Smalltown, Tichy and Vollmer. All these companies make easy-to-assemble plastic kits.

The r-t-r buildings from Bachmann and Model Power are an excellent and inexpensive source of scale-model people for all parts of your railroad. Remove the people, in the same way you would remove the roof, by applying about six coats of liquid cement for plastics to dissolve the factory-glue joints. Let the glue soak in for about an hour (but no more) and then gently pull and pry away the parts you want.

THE BUILDINGS ON THE BURLINGTON NORTHERN

Nearly all of the buildings on the Burlington Northern were converted in some major way. The IHC-brand 348-3505 Freight Station has a pagoda-style roof that is rare in real life but as common as Santa Fe diesels on model railroads. You can alter the appearance of that structure completely by replacing its roof with one cut from two IHC 348-47761 Arlee Station kits (Figure 14-4). The small roofs were joined together and cemented to plastic sign posts to make the Emmett piggyback trailer-loading and unloading dock.

The walls and windows from a Model Power 490-426 Boarding House or IHC 348-47776 Aunt Millie's House were mixed together to make the Duncan Feed & Fuel grain elevator and the Railroad Boarding House at Alliance. The end walls from one of the lean-tos were notched with a razor saw to clear the roof for the grain elevator's cupola.

Albert Hetzel created the Ford & Sons Ice Co. building by using only the long walls from two IHC 348-47798 General Store or Model Power 490-452 Western Union Office kits with chimneys and some other parts from two IHC 348-47780 Pickle Factory kits. The leftover doors from the two General Stores and one of the leftover cupolas from the Pickle Factories were used with two IHC 348-709 Sawmills and one Piggy-

Fig. 14-4. The chimney holes in the IHC Arlee Station kit were filled with leftover parts from the roof. The roof was then cut to fit the IHC Freight Station (with the Arlee Station roof supports) to create the freight station at Alliance.

back Flatcar platform to make the single-stall Engine House.

The lesson here is that each and every kit must be viewed as nothing more than a lumberyard full of walls and roofs and doors and windows that can be cut and combined in almost endless ways. You can train yourself to do this by assembling a few of these structure conversions. Then you can spot potential conversions just by looking at the catalog photos of the stock structures. All of the leftover parts can be placed in a scrap box if you can't figure out what to do with them right away. The Lumber Supply Co. was made from the two remaining buildings from the two Sawmills, Company Furniture was made from the leftover Pickle Factory main buildings. Sons Winery was assembled from the tank end of one of the Pickle Factory kits, and Alliance Coal & Fuel uses the structure from one of the Sawmills and the other General Store's brick lean-to.

The Mining Supply Co. (the flat-roofed building with the triangular staircase on the roof in Figure 14-1) is a classic. Albert Hetzel used two IHC 348-602 Interlocking Tower kits with a new flat roof cut from a sheet of Evergreen Scale Models .040-inch thick styrene plastic sheet.

Albert Hetzel used the passenger halves of the back walls (opposite the bay window) of the Arlee Station to make the simple Alliance Station. The leftover roof pieces (the chimney sides) were filled with scrap pieces of plastic shingles for the roof on the Lighted Freight Station at Alliance. The leftover baggage ends of the Arlee Station kits were used to make the Engine Tool & Supply Co. with a roof from the Pickle Factory kit.

The three dwellings owned by the Corning Mine (Figures 14-5 and 14-6) were made from two Tyco or AHM Ma's Place Kit's that are no longer produced. Nearly identical kits are, however, available. For instance, the Model Power 490-414 Billy's Garage or IHC 348-47779 Ma's Place kits. A lot of minor cutting and fitting was needed to make three buildings from two.

Figure 14-5 shows the parts ready to be assembled. The cattle pen at Emmett can be made from a modified Life-Like 433-1378 Stock Pen. The Corning Mine is the popular Pola 578-708 Old Coal Mine, with the lower level cut to create an upper level and the various supports from the kit cut to fit. The

Pola 576-704 Coaling Tower supplied the raw materials for the wood tunnel portal in Figures 15-25 and 15-26 in Chapter 15.

THE BUILDINGS ON THE BURLINGTON ROUTE

Most of the buildings on the 7 x 8-foot Burlington Route layout shown on the cover and in the plan in Chapter 20 (Figure 20-5) are also kits with major conversions. Three of the four industries along the wall at Abbott are only half-width structures to fit between the tracks and the rear wall. Obviously, cutting down the width of the side walls is a decision you must make before the kit is assembled.

LOADS-IN/EMPTIES-OUT BUILDINGS

The primary shipping and receiving industries on the Burlington Route layout are the Hudson Coal mine at Chester and the Tri-State Utility Company power plant at Elwood. These two industries are intended to be operated as coal-shipping and receiving pairs as described in Chapter 19. The power plant is on a curve and the track entering the building is supposed to end inside the building. In

Fig. 14-5. Two sets of walls and windows from two Model Power, 490-426 Boarding Houses or IHC 348-47776 Aunt Millie's Houses were used to provide the parts cut, as shown, for the three dwellings owned by Corning Mining on the Burlington Northern layout.

Fig. 14-6. The three dwellings owned by Corning Mining on the Burlington Northern layout.

Fig. 14-7. Ford & Sons Ice Co. on the Burlington Northern layout, was assembled from the parts from two IHC 348-47798 General Store or Model Power 490-452 Western Union Office kits with chimneys and some other parts from two IHC 348-47780 Pickle Factory kits.

truth, it continues around to the other side of the layout to emerge beneath the conveyor at Hudson Mine.

The Hudson Mine was modified by removing about 3 inches from it height and moving the building 90 degrees on the lattice-like supports (Figure 14-9) so the sides of the building help disguise the fact that hoppers were disappearing into the hillside behind the mine. The conveyor at the mine was modified (Figure 14-11) and the arched hole in the mine tipple enlarged to fit the conveyor. The lower end of the conveyor will disappear into a thick stand of trees and bushes on the finished layout as shown in Chapter 19 (Figure 19-12). The open track below the conveyor at the power plant disappears between two huge piles of stored coal and reappears beneath the Hudson Mine's tipple building.

The low hills and the woods (Figure 17-25 in Chapter 17) on the hills disguise the fact that the two tracks extend through the scenery so that empty

Fig. 14-8. The industries at Abbott on the Burlington Route layout, represent the types of buildings you might find on the fringe of a small city. The industries include (left to right): the Hardwood Furniture Company, a four-story barrel factory, a Teamster's warehouse, a small feed mill, a milk depot, a Workshed, a freight station and a passenger station.

hopper cars can be continually pushed into the Hudson Mine (and later picked up as empties from the power plant). The hoppers loaded with coal are picked up from beneath the tipple at Hudson Coal and delivered to the siding between the coal piles at the power plant (to be picked up again later as loaded cars at the Hudson Mine).

CHECKING BUILDINGS FOR CLEARANCES

The power plant at Elwood on the Burlington Route is located on a curve, so it is essential to check that there is clearance for the longest car or locomotive to clear the exterior and the interior of the building (Figure 14-10). In fact, the entire first floor of the right rear corner of the power plant was removed so the curved track, used by the unloaded cars, could exit the building. The cutaway wall is visible in Figure 14-9 and the upper right of Figure 14-11 but the scenery hides that part of the structure from being seen from any angle. The overhead conveyors at both the mine

Fig. 14-9. The Tri-State Utility Co. (upper left), the Hardwood Furniture Company (upper right) and the Hudson Mine (bottom) are modified Walthers kits. The power plant has the front door enlarged and the rear corner cut away. The factory has been cut down to remove its rear wall and a row of windows from each side wall. The mine has been cut down about 3 inches to reduce its height.

Fig. 14-10. The Tri-State Utility Co. at Elwood is a slightly modified Walthers 933-3021 Northern Light and Power kit, complete with a pile of stored coal made from blue insulation foam as described in Chapter 16. The conveyor from the Hudson Mine and the station at Chester are visible in the upper right.

Fig. 14-11. The conveyors from the Walthers 933-3051 Coal Flood Loader were used at both the Hudson Mine (foreground) and the Tri-State Power Co. (upper right). The conveyor at the mine was cut to reduce its length on the right and, on the left, it was cut at a 45-degree angle to fit inside the enlarged doorway on the Walthers Coal Flood Loader.

Fig. 14-12. Check all of the structures with a NMRA Clearance Gauge to be sure they clear the cars and that their loading ramps are near the right height.

Fig. 14-13. The track actually goes inside the furniture factory at Abbott and the longer cars and locomotives hit both the inner wall and the first two posts. Remove the entire corner post and the inner half of the second post. The inner wall must also be moved back 1/4 inch to clear the opposite side of the locomotive.

tipple and the power plant help distract the eye from the fact that the siding holds more than just the three or four cars it would apparently accommodate. If you intend to operate complete unit trains of coal through these structures, as described in Chapter 19, be sure that the largest locomotive, not just the cars, will clear the structures.

All of the structures should be checked with a NMRA Clearance Gauge (Figure 14-12) to be sure they clear the cars and that their loading ramps are the right height. If the structure is located on a curve, it must be moved far enough away from the track so the longest car or locomotive does not side-swipe the building. The track actually goes inside the furniture factory at Abbott and the longer cars and locomotives hit both the inner wall and the first post. It's not an elegant solution, but the best answer to this problem was to simply remove the offending post (Figure 14-13). The inner wall was moved back 1/4 inch and cemented in place.

AN INDUSTRY DIRECTORY FOR THE BURLINGTON ROUTE

The building kits used to make the structures at Abbott include (left to right): Walthers 933-3044 Hardwood Furniture Company, a four-story barrel factory made from walls cut from several Con-Cor 222-9028 Two-Stall Enginehouse kits, a Teamster's warehouse from a modified Life-Like 433-1351 General Store, a small feed mill made from an IHC 348-812 Barn, a milk depot from a Life-Like 433-1347 Train Station kit and an AMI 129-106 Worksheed kit.

The freight station is cut from a two-story IHC 348-47798 General Store or Model Power 490-452 Western Union Office kit with a Pikestuff 541-17 Loading Dock, 541-1100 Roll-Up Freight Doors, 541-1010 Concrete Staircase, and 541-3101 Downspouts parts.

John Welther built the passenger station (Figure 14-14) at Abbott from an American Model Builders'152-138 Springfield Depot kit. These kits (Figure 14-15) are laser-cut from thin sheets of wood so only assembly is required. They are a delight to assemble but they do require some time because there are a lot of parts. American Model Builders has a large range of kits, most based on actual prototype structures.

The power plant at Elwood is 933-3021 Northern Light and Power (modified to clear the curved track as shown in Figure 14-9 and 14-11) and the

Fig. 14-15. American Model Builders is one of several manufacturers of kits whose parts are laser-cut from thin sheets of wood so only assembly is required. There are a large number of parts, but the major components have tabs and slots for easy assembly and alignment, and some of the smaller parts are self-adhesive.

small office is an AMI-brand 129-103 WIlliamsburg Yard Office,

The Hudson Coal mine at Chester is a Walthers 933-3051 Coal Flood Loader (modified to reduce its height as shown in Figures 14-9 and 14-11). The canning plant next to the mine is a Pikestuff 541-4 Warehouse, the Chester passenger station is a Con-Cor 222-901 Two Brothers Restaurant cut to a single-story with a roof from the Bachmann 160-35106 Texaco Station kit. The small freight station is a much-modified shed from the Pola (ex-AHM, Ex-Tyco) 578-702 Sand House-Loader kit.

STRUCTURES THAT SPEAK

The weathering steps suggested earlier will help bring those painted plastic buildings into the realm of reality. You will want to carry it a step further, however, to make those buildings come to life. Populating the buildings with people can make that happen. And the final touch will be added when the various signs of the

Fig. 14-14. The passenger station at Abbott is built from an out-of-the-box American Model Builders 152-138 Springfield Depot kit.

FIG. 14-16. STATION AND INDUSTRY NAMES FOR SIGNS.

ALLIANCE	BUILDERS	ALLIANCE	BUILDERS
ARLEE	CHEMICAL	ARLEE	CHEMICAL
BEDFORD	COAL	BEDFORD	COAL
CORNING	COKE	CORNING	COKE
DUNCAN	CONCRETE	DUNCAN	CONCRETE
EMMETT	DAIRY	EMMETT	DAIRY
FALLS	FARMING	FALLS	FARMING
GURNSEY	FEED	GURNSEY	FEED
HASTINGS	FUEL	HASTINGS	FUEL
ISLAND	FURNITURE	ISLAND	FURNITURE
JUNCTION	GROCERY	JUNCTION	GROCERY
KIMBALTON	HARDWARE	KIMBALTON	HARDWARE
LAKE	ICE	LAKE	ICE
MASON	IRON	MASON	IRON
NEW	LUMBER	NEW	LUMBER
ONEIDA	MINE	ONEIDA	MINE
PADUCAH	MINING	PADUCAH	MINING
SPRING	OIL	SPRING	OIL
TIMBER	PACKING	TIMBER	PACKING
TREES	STEEL	TREES	STEEL
UDELL	STORAGE	UDELL	STORAGE
VALLEY	STOVES	VALLEY	STOVES
WOODWARD	SUPPLY	WOODWARD	SUPPLY
YOUNGSTOWN	WHOLESALE	YOUNGSTOWN	WHOLESALE
	WINERY		WINERY
BAKING		BAKING	
BOX	SUPPLY	BOX	SUPPLY
BREWERY	SONS	BREWERY	SONS
BREWING		BREWING	

AND AND AND AND & & & & & &						AND AND AND AND & & & & & &				
CO. CO. CO. CO. CO. CO.						CO. CO. CO. CO. CO. CO.				
COMPANY COMPANY COMPANY						COMPANY COMPANY COMPANY				
INC. INC. INC. INC. LTD. LTD.						INC. INC. INC. INC. LTD. LTD.				

buildings and industries are in place. These include the railroad station signs, a few advertising posters, and perhaps a billboard or two. Make a photocopy of the signs in Figure 14-16. Then you can cut out the various signs to supplement those supplied with the majority of the buildings.

You can piece together the names of all the industries on the Burlington Northern and hundreds of others from the words on that page. Cut the words out and paste them to pieces of a file card or postcard with rubber ce-ment. If you want a color, add it with a felt tip pen. Spray the signs with a light coat of Testors DullCote, and, when dry, attach them to your buildings with 5-minute epoxy. When the waybill tells your pedlar freight's switching crew to spot a car at Ford & Sons Ice Co., all the crew needs to do is find the right car and look for the industry's sign. Your empire is now a part of the real world.

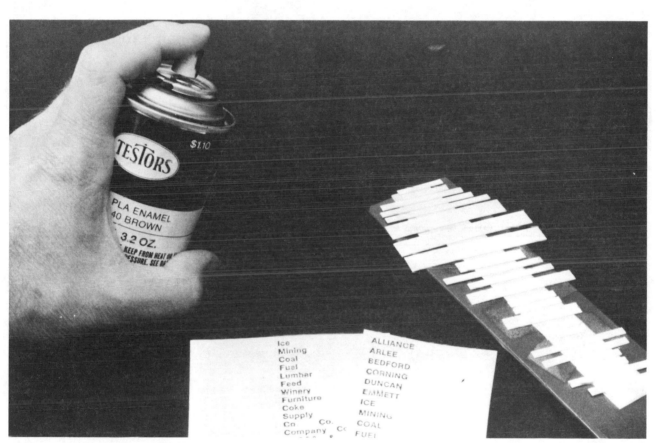

Fig. 14-17. Cut backings for the signs from file cards and hold them to a scrap of wood with masking tape, sticky-side-up, while you spray-paint them brown or gray.

DO'S AND DON'TS FOR MODEL BUILDINGS

- Do use cement for plastics to assemble even the snap-together building kits.
- Do paint every building on your layout so each looks like solid material rather than translucent plastic.
- Do apply enough dirt around the base of any building so the building appears to be resting in the earth.

- Do arrange buildings in small groups to match the style of industrial, downtown or residential areas with open areas of scenery between clusters of buildings.
- Do modify all the buildings, before you assemble them, so they are at least a bit different from the stock kit and, thus, unique to your model railroad.

- Don't rely on just a few plastic tabs or pegs to hold a plastic building together.
- Don't use buildings just as they come from the box. Paint the building and or the trim a different color.
- Don't drop buildings on top of the layout so they look like oversize children's building blocks sitting on carpet.
- Don't spread houses, stores and industries at random around the layout.

- Don't use buildings exactly as found in the kits; they will look like the buildings on every other model railroad. With freight cars, that's realistic because freight cars travel from town to town. Buildings, however, are unique to specific areas.

CHAPTER 15

The Earth in HO Scale

IT'S NO WONDER that model railroaders have to devise so many construction, design, and operating tricks to make their miniatures look like the real thing. The whole construction process is backward when you compare the building of a real railroad to the building of a model. We arrange the world to suit our tracks, while the real railroads must arrange their tracks to fit the world. Nobody is a natural scenery expert. The only way to learn about scenery is to look at it—really look at it. Don't try to place your railroad in the Rocky Mountains if you can't get there to see what they look like, or, at the very least, if you're not willing to study books on geology and geography at a college library. Nature is one of the more difficult things to duplicate unless you have a model or sample readily available.

THE FIELD TRIP

Try to select geography that is either near your home or that you can visit at least once a year. Take some photographs and make some plan-type sketches to show the scene in the photographs. Let those photographs encompass the terrain for a quarter-mile or so on either side of the tracks, and take some close-ups of just the cuts and fills and bridges next to the tracks. It's a good idea to even take some samples of the soil both for color and to actually use on your layout.

Pay particular attention to the way cuts (through mountains or hills) and fills (over valleys or streams or hollows) begin and how they blend in with the edge of the track and with the surrounding terrain. These are the most difficult-to-capture aspects of real scenery. It's relatively simple to use latex rubber molds to cast rocks or to spread plaster around a hillside. However, the abrupt change from almost vertical sections of scenery to the gentler slopes and the edges of the railroad right-of-way are not so easy to capture on a model railroad. If you have a color photograph, some samples of the rocks and soil in the area, a bird's-eye-view sketch of the area, and a few notes to tie it all together, then you're prepared to make a model of the area.

I recommend that you try to include at least three or four of these real-world vignettes in your scenery. Finish them before you complete the rest of the scenery so you'll gain the experience of creating scenery yourself. The rest of the layout's scenery can then be freelanced, drawing on your experience with those proven-to-be-genuine scenes from the real world. Please do not try to duplicate any of the scenery you see on other model railroads. You'll be translating only what someone else has interpreted to be real, and you'll lose much of the realism in the process.

Go directly from your research in the real world to the methods and techniques that other modelers have developed. You don't have to invent new ways to make scenery. What you do have to do is to try to capture the shape and color and texture of the part of the real world that you have selected as your prototype. You will need to make several trips back to that source for information you forgot to get the first time and, perhaps, to collect more dirt and rocks for the layout. While you're on those field trips, you can also collect rocks to be used as molds (this will be discussed later in this chapter) and a variety of weeds and twigs to be used for tree trunks and bushes on your layout.

THREE SCENERY SYSTEMS

The techniques in this chapter are the established methods of making scenery in the least amount of time. Briefly, the scenery is shaped with wadded-up newspapers and covered with either plaster-soaked paper towels or gauze with plaster, like Woodland Scenics Plaster Cloth, impregnated into it. Two newer methods are shown in Chapter 16: the first utilizes blue insulation extruded-Styrofoam like that made by Dow-Corning. You carve away anything that doesn't look like a valley or mountain. The second utilizes white expanded-Styrofoam from Woodland Scenics and is called their Subterrain system. The scenery techniques for the Subterrain system are nearly identical to those in this chapter but Woodland Scenics recommends, of course, that you use their Plaster Cloth rather than paper towels soaked in plaster for the scenery contours.

MIX-AND-MATCH METHODS

There are also two possible choices for finishing the surface of the scenery. The first method requires a plaster surface for the scenery shapes. The plaster is then painted with latex wall paint and textured with real dirt, and ground foam or flocking to model grass and weeds. Those are the methods used for the 9 x 9-foot Burlington Northern layout (Figure 20-3). The second method is the Grass-That-Grows method shown in Chapter 17. This method can be used with either plaster-covered contours or with the bare blue extruded-Styrofoam shapes from Chapter 16. The carved blue Styrofoam and Grass-That-Grows texturing are the methods used for the 7 x 8-foot Burlington Route layout (Figure 20-5).

So, there are three methods of making the basic scenery shapes in this book and two methods of finishing the surface for earth and grass effects. You can mix and match all of them or build part of the layout with one system and part with another. Each has its advantages. The paper towel method in this chapter is the least expensive and allows you to pre-color the plaster so chips and areas you miss with paint will not be so visible, but it is the messiest and the heaviest. If you substitute Plaster Cloth, you avoid most of the mess and it's just as quick, but is still fairly heavy. You also cannot pre-color it as effectively and it is more expensive. However, the Plaster Cloth method can be about as light as blue extruded-Styrofoam if you also use the Woodland Scenics Subterrain system for supporting the roadbed and use the techniques shown in Chapter 16 for building a tabletop from blue extruded-Styrofoam. The carved blue extruded-Styrofoam method is the lightest (especially if the surfaces are textured with the felt Grass-That-Grows techniques), and it is the least messy, but it takes some practice to learn to carve out the contours. It is also slightly more expensive. Confused? Just pick the methods that seem the most fun to you.

THE PLASTER AND PAPER TOWEL SYSTEM

Model railroaders have developed a very simple scenery system that, like the Homasote roadbed, requires an industrial compound you may have to search for. There is a special building plaster called Hydrocal that becomes virtually as hard as rock after it sets; in fact, it becomes a type of alabaster. Some building-supply firms will order it in 100-pound bags if you ask them. Hydrocal is almost self-supporting; no chicken wire or screening is necessary as with other systems. Woodland Scenics sells smaller packages of Hydrocal through model railroad dealers. If you cannot find Hydrocal, settle for

Fig. 15-1. Use a tall box car and a long locomotive or passenger car to check clearances on the mock-up scenery.

the best grade of regular gypsum plaster you can find. You'll need gypsum plaster for some of the details described later in this chapter; the finished Hydrocal is too hard to carve into rocks and erosion gullies.

THE FULL-SIZE MOCK-UP

The scenery system that was developed for use with Hydrocal only requires piles of wadded-up newspapers to create the shapes of the hills and mountains and valleys. You will need some sort of 1-inch or thicker Masonite or plywood profile boards to match the shape of mountains and valleys where they meet the edge of the table. Alternately, you can use 1-inch-thick white extruded-Styrofoam from a lumber yard for the Profile boards, or use the ribbed white expanded-Styrofoam Profile boards from Woodland Scenics Subterrain system, shown in Chapter 16. You will also need a few vertical braces to support the tops of the hills or mountains in the center of the layout. The system allows you to actually mold the shapes of the hills and valleys with old newspapers before you apply any plaster. The profile boards can be cut to match the profiles you've made with the paper towels. When you think you're satisfied with the shapes, drape the layout with a single layer of wet brown industrial paper towels. The brown towels will give you a much better idea of the shapes than the camouflage effect produced by the pictures, ads, and headlines in the newspaper.

The basic humps and lumps are wadded-up newspapers. The almost-final surfaces of the hills and valleys are then shaped by draping wet newspapers over the wads of newspapers. If you see that a hill is too high or a cut is too close to the tracks, all you have to do is shove the newspapers aside. Strips of masking tape will help to hold the wads of newspapers down, and strips of tape can be used to make a netlike support to carry the newspaper wads over any large gaps or access holes in the benchwork.

Be sure to operate the highest boxcar and the longest locomotive or passenger car you have over the railroad while the scenery is still in the mock-up stage. This will allow you to determine whether there is enough clearance through all the cuts and tunnels. Often an overhanging pilot on a diesel locomotive or the skirt on a passenger car will hit scenery placed too close to the track.

TUNNELS

Every model railroad can benefit from the use of tunnels because they help disguise the fact that the trains really don't travel as far as they should and that they really don't connect with the outside world. Here, again, you'll find yourself working in the opposite direction of the real railroads, which try to avoid the expense of a tunnel whenever possible. Very few model railroads are large enough to have a mountain that's gigantic enough to warrant a tunnel; the real railroads would have used cuts in almost every example you see on a model railroad. If you expect those mole hills to look like mountains large enough for a tunnel or two, you'll have to be careful to apply the practices the real railroads use, although in somewhat smaller-than-true, HO scale proportions.

You'll see that there are several smaller buildings in the Alliance area of the Burlington Northern layout because the clutter of a dozen buildings is far more realistic than the three or four structures that would fill that size area if everything was in exact scale. The windows and doors are precise HO scale, and the proportions are correct for 1/87-scale people, but most of those buildings are closer to the size of a two-car garage than to that of the gigantic factories they represent. That same principle must be used for the hills and valleys on your model railroad. Use several smaller hills rather than one large mountain, for example.

Copy the dirt or rock cuts through the earth that lead to every real railroad tunnel (including the rather deep cut leading to the top of each tunnel portal), but don't make the mountain above the tunnel as large. You can disguise the size of the mountain, to some extent, by planting smaller trees on its upper slopes to give the illusion of distance.

TUNNEL PORTALS

Each tunnel must have some type of tunnel portal. A few tunnels are blasted through solid rock, so the rock itself forms the shape of the portal. Most tunnels, however, have wood, concrete, brick, or stone portals and linings through the length of the tunnel. When you build the portal, don't forget to extend the material far enough into the tunnel to give the illusion that the tunnel is lined through its entire length. Real mountains aren't hollow like those on a model railroad, and that mass is what you are trying to duplicate.

Model railroad shops sell a large selection of simulated wood, cut stone and rock tunnels portals, or you can make your own. The 1/4-inch-thick white expanded-Styrofoam sold by Woodland Scenics makes a fine material to use for tunnel portals. Carve the foam with a common kitchen steak knife to create the graceful arch over the top of the tunnel portal, and make the arch at least 3 inches high and the vertical walls at least 2 inches wide (2-3/4 inches if the tunnel is on a curve). The portal can be covered with the same plaster you use for your scenery. Smooth on the plaster to simulate a concrete tunnel portal and lining, or rough it up to simulate a tunnel carved through solid stone.

A wooden tunnel portal can be made by cutting the parts from a 578-704 Pola Coaling Tower (with a razor saw as shown in Figure 15-25). Use some 3-inch-wide strips of cardboard to simulate the vertical walls or linings of each tunnel for at least 6 inches into each tunnel. You can decide whether to include the tunnel portals in the mock-up stage and plaster around them, or to make the mountain look as though it really was there before the track and install the tunnel portal after the plaster is in place.

PLASTER MOUNTAINS

When you're satisfied with your newspaper mock-up scenery, cover every inch of the tracks with 2-inch-wide masking tape. You can tape plastic trash bags over large flat areas, such as the Alliance yard and around any bridges. You will want to apply some plaster near the tracks on most flat areas to simulate hills and cuts, however, so use just the masking tape over the track in most places. You will also want to cut through the Homasote to make any small lakes or streams at this stage, and, of course, all the bridges should be in place with plenty of space below them for the bottom of the river or stream.

The Hydrocal plaster will remain self-supporting if it is soaked into industrial-grade paper towels (usually brown or beige and much tougher than the household kind). Industrial paper towels are available from restaurant and hospital-supply distributors. Perhaps you could persuade your local service station to sell you a few bundles. If you cannot find Hydrocal

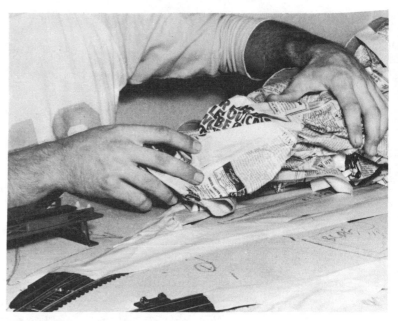

Fig. 15-3. Crumple and wad newspapers to form the shapes of the hills. If the newspapers are too bouncy, wet them with a mist of water.

plaster, use common gypsum plaster, but build some 8-inch plywood supports for the interior of the mountains before you finish the newspaper mock-ups. The mock-ups will help you to decide if more supports are needed. Use the mock-ups, regardless of what type of plaster you use, to help you decide on the shape for the upper edges of the 8-inch plywood or Masonite profile

Fig. 15-2. Cover every inch of the track with wide masking tape to protect it from the plaster.

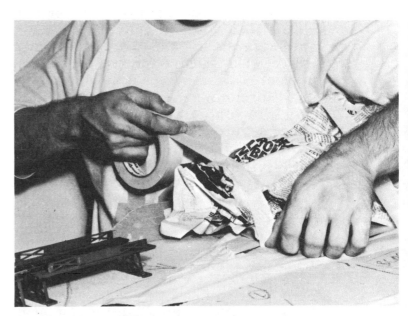

Fig. 15-4. Tape the wadded-up newspapers to the 1/2-inch Homosote boards of the roadbed and also tape them to the edges of the layout.

Fig. 15-5. Roads through the hills can be cut from corrugated cardboard and taped in place before applying plaster.

panels. They should be nailed and glued to the sides of the benchwork (like those near the river and bridges on the Burlington Northern layout in Chapter 20). Two or three layers of Hydrocal-soaked paper towels will be self-supporting but it may take four or more layers of paper towels soaked in conventional gypsum plaster to come close to the self-supporting strength of the Hydrocal method.

You can use these same techniques with Woodland Scenics Plaster Cloth or Activa's Rigid Wrap gauze impregnated with Hydrocal. The gauze adds enough strength so you can get by with just a single layer in most areas to save weight. The plaster-impregnated cloth is also less messy because you simply dip the cloth in a tray of water and avoid mixing any powdered plaster. There is no way to color the Plaster Cloth or Rigid Wrap except to add powdered colors to the plaster a light tint and then apply paint as described later in this chapter or simply cover the finished plaster surface with felt using the Grass-That-Grows system from Chapter 17.

Mix the plaster for soaking the industrial paper towels in flexible plastic pans that you can throw away or purchase a large Pyrex glass mixing bowl. The Pyrex can be washed clean much more easily than regular glass, and it is

somewhat stronger. Purchase some dark-brown powdered pigment for plaster from the same building-supply dealer who sells you the Hydrocal or gypsum plaster. Buy enough to give a light-brown color to all the plaster you purchase. The powdered pigment should have instructions to tell you how much is needed for that particular brand, or you can ask the dealer.

Pour about four cups of water into your mixing bowl and slowly sprinkle in about an equal amount of plaster while you stir. Always add the dry plaster to the water; not the water to the plaster. The exact ratio of plaster to water can vary considerably, so keep stirring while you add the plaster. You want a mix about the consistency of thick cream. When the consistency is right, stir in the proper amount of the dry pigment. With practice, you'll learn how much plaster is about right, and then you can stir in both the plaster and the pigment at the same time.

Submerge each paper towel in the plaster mix to thoroughly wet it and drape the plaster-soaked paper towel over your mock-up scenery. Overlap each additional paper towel about halfway across the area of the first one and place the third paper towel almost directly over the first. This interweaving technique will give you the three layers you need for strength. If you're using

Fig. 15-6. Dry coloring pigment is available where you buy the Hydrocal plaster. Use enough of the coloring to make the plaster darker than you'd like because it will become much lighter when the plaster dries.

Fig 15-7. Add the plaster and the dry-coloring pigment to the water as you stir.

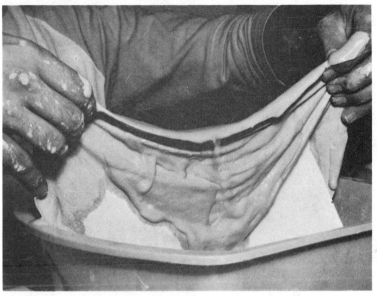

Fig. 15-8. Submerge each paper towel in the tub of wet plaster so the plaster completely covers every inch of the towel.

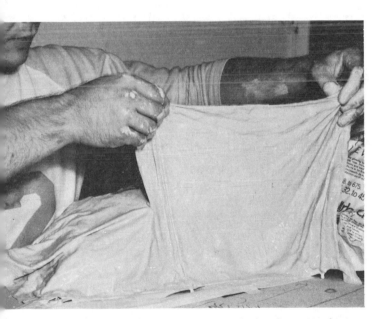

Fig. 15-9. Dip the paper towels in the wet plaster, then drape them over the mock-up scenery.

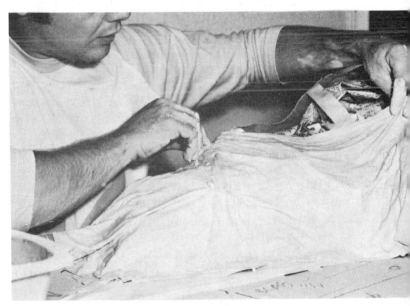

Fig. 15-10. Each additional plaster-soaked paper towel must overlap the adjacent towel by about half the width of the towel for strength. At least two layers of Hydrocal-soaked paper towels will be needed for self-supporting scenery.

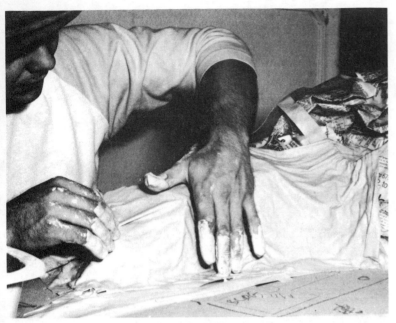

Fig, 15-11. Smooth each paper towel's plaster where it meets the masking tape that is protecting the tracks.

conventional gypsum plaster rather than Hydrocal, add two more paper towels to the area in the same overlapping pattern. Continue to add paper towels around the layout until the scenery shapes are complete.

You will undoubtedly have to mix many batches of plaster to complete the scenery work on any layout. The new plaster will stick nicely to the old if you continue the work on the same day. If the job takes more than a day, be sure to spray some water on the places where you will add new plaster to the old so that the two will bond together nicely. I suggest that you rub the surface of the last layer of paper towels with your hand during the last few minutes of the hardening or setting stage to roughen the surface. When you do this, the particles of just-hardened plaster will act like very rough sandpaper to roughen the rest of the surface. It's a bit hard on your hands, so apply some hand cream or salve to replace the natural body oils the plaster leaches out. The roughened surface can be used as-is for just about everything, but for those nearly vertical walls and cliffs, you'll want to carve or cast rock or erosion marks into the plaster.

REAL ROCKS

It's possible to carve simple rock structures like the layers of sandstone and the erosion marks that water makes on smooth earth cuts and fills. More complex rock structures are best duplicated with latex rubber molds taken from real rocks. Chunks of coal can often provide rock-like strata that is even more realistic than genuine rocks when applied to a model railroad. Spray the portion of the rock or the piece of coal you want to duplicate with silicone spray or with one of the non-stick cooking sprays, such as Pam.

Liquid latex can be purchased in cans from many craft-supply stores. If you cannot find the liquid latex, you can substitute artist Matte Medium, but the resulting mold won't last for more than one or two castings. Brush a thick layer of the latex or white glue over the rock, apply a layer of gauze or cheesecloth to act as reinforcement, and brush on another layer of latex or white glue over the gauze or cheesecloth. Repeat the process until you have a total of three layers of liquid latex or Matte Medium and two layers of gauze or cheesecloth. Allow the mixture 24 hours to dry before gently peeling it away from the rock. You now have a mold of the rock, which can be duplicated in plaster.

Use gypsum plaster for the rock castings so that you can carve the edges to help them blend into the surrounding scenery. You might want to use a shade of gray or beige dry-color pigment for the rocks rather than brown. Use only about half as much of the pigment as you did to simulate dirt on the rest of the scenery so the rocks will be almost white. Mix the plaster until it is just a bit thicker than before (but it should still be pourable). Pre-wet the area where the rock casting will be placed with a spray bottle or plant atomizer. Pour the wet plaster into the mold and immediately slap the mold and the plaster against the place where you want the rock. Hold it there until you can feel the plaster harden (it will take only a minute or two) and immediately peel the mold away before the plaster is completely hard. You can add as many appli-

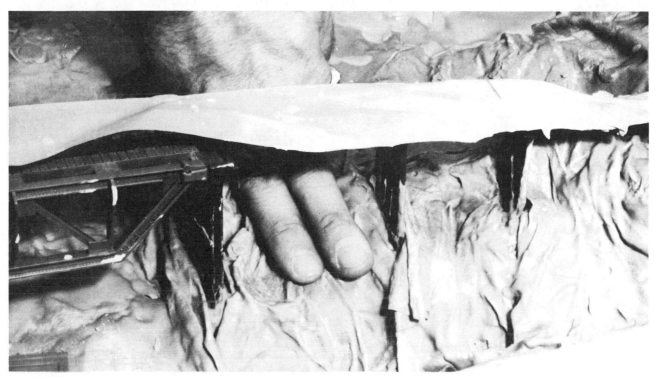

Fig. 15-12. Tuck the still-wet, plaster-soaked paper towels in around the trestle and viaduct bents to make the earth beneath the bridges. It would be wise to protect the bridges from the plaster with small pieces of clear plastic wrap.

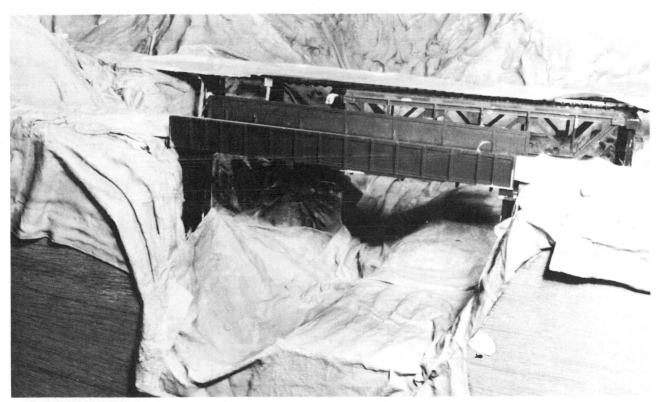

Fig. 15-13. The gaps between the paper towels and the bridge abutment and trestle bents can be filled with a a thick putty-like mixture of plaster.

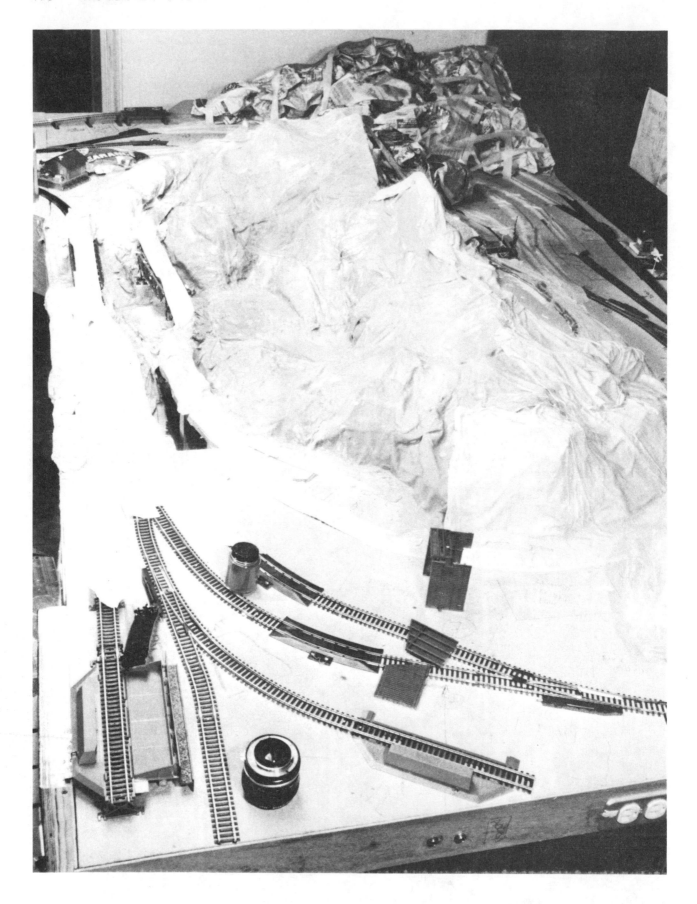

Fig. 15-14. Complete one area of the scenery at a time. If you're not satisfied with the shapes, simply add more wadded-up newspapers and apply the plaster-soaked paper towels on top of the finished scenery.

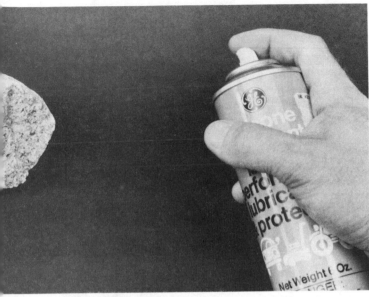

Fig. 15-15. Find a rock or a piece of coal with suitable rock texture and spray it with several coats of silicone dry lubricant.

Fig. 15-16. Pour a thick layer of liquid latex (or Matte Medium, or even white glue) on the silicone-treated rock surface.

Fig 15-17. Cover the rock with alternating layers of liquid latex and gauze to make a mold for casting rock surfaces.

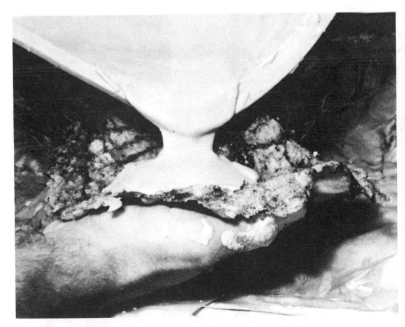

Fig 15-18. Fill the rock mold with gypsum plaster.

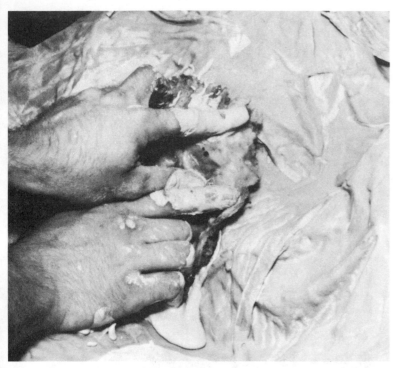

Fig. 15-19. Push the plaster-filled rock mold onto the face of the scenery and hold it there until you can feel the plaster just begin to harden, then gently peel back the rock mold.

Fig. 15-21. Crumple aluminum foil and use it as a mold to create some types of rock texture

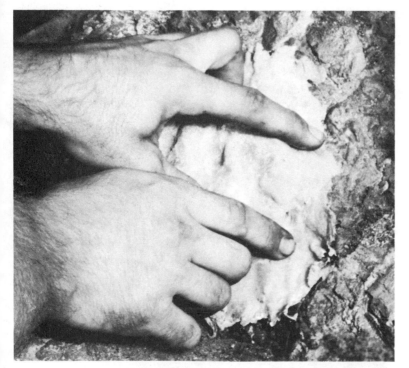

Fig. 15-20. Overlap the next rock casting over the first to help disguise the seams between the two. Keep adjacent castings aligned so the major cracks or flaws in the rock are parallel to one another.

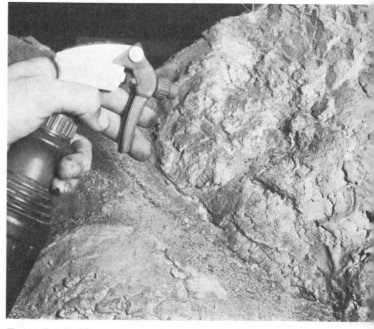

Fig. 15-22. The rock can be colored with an initial wash of black or dark brown Rit dye or acrylic color thinned with about 9 parts water to accent the depressions and crevices in the rock molding.

cations of rocks made from the same mold as are needed to give the cliff the face you want. Overlap each casting slightly, and, perhaps, tilt each one a few degrees to give a slightly different appearance to each segment. You can, of course, use many different rock-casting molds on various parts of the layout or even on a single cliff face. Remember that the rocks must match the texture of the rocks in the cuts and cliffs you see in the geographic area you have selected as the prototype for your layout. Crumpled aluminum foil can be used in place of the latex or Matte Medium-and-gauze molds to duplicate one specific type of rock texture with this same casting procedure.

Fig. 15-23. Slightly lighter tones can be dabbed onto the rock face to create the speckled appearance of some types of real rock.

GROUND COLOR AND COVER

If you were able to pre-color the plaster, you won't need to paint the surface. If, however, you cannot locate pow-

Fig. 15-24. A typical wood tunnel portal on the Southern Pacific Railroad in 1978.

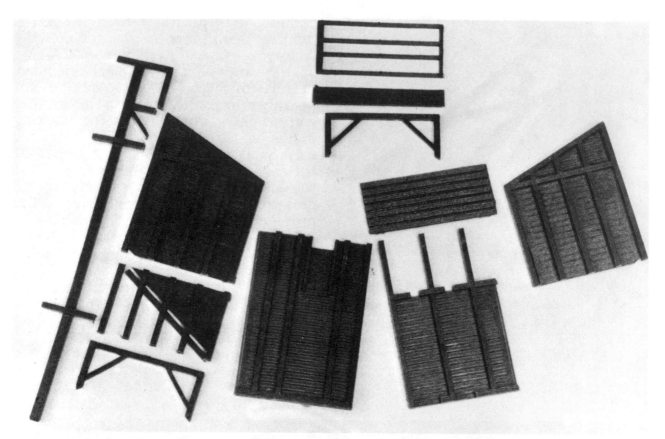

Fig. 15-25. The parts from a Pola Coaling Tower were cut like this to make a wood tunnel portal.

Fig. 15-26. The two wings on either side of the tunnel portal would normally be positioned as shown. The angle of the hill on the Burlington Northern suggests a reverse angle for the right wing.

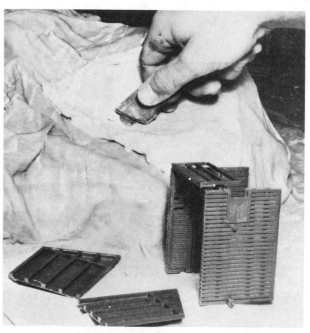

Fig. 15-27. The plaster mountain covers the tracks just like a real mountain might, so a cut must be made (with a utility knife) for the tunnel.

Fig. 15-28. The tunnel portal area on the Burlington Northern layout after the scenery is completed.

Fig. 15-30. Spray the areas that will become the bottom of any stream or lake with several heavy coats of Testors DullCote to seal the surface so loose plaster or texturing materials won't form air bubbles in the bottom of the resin water.

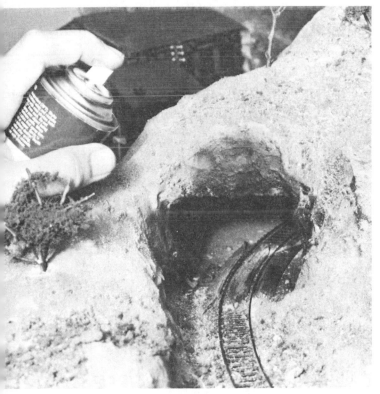

Fig 15-29. Spray a light mist of dilute acrylic black paint over the tops of each tunnel portal to simulate the stain from diesel exhausts or steam locomotive smoke.

Fig. 15-31. Decoupage fluids, such as Envirotex, can be used to make lakes or streams. Mix according to the instructions on the bottles or cans.

Fig. 15-32. The tiny hair-like interior of cattail plants can be used to make realistic weeds on the banks of ponds and streams.

dered colors or if you use Plaster Cloth or Rigid Wrap, you must paint the stark-white scenery surface. Paint every square inch of the plaster surfaces with latex wall paint to match the color of earth you will be using. Use a floodlight to help accent any of the white that shows through.

Rocks can be colored by simply spraying on a wash of ninety-five parts water and five parts dark-brown or dark-gray acrylic paint. The wash will collect in the crevices and hollows of the rock castings and the almost-white plaster will show through as highlights for some incredibly realistic rock effects. Brush equal parts of water and white glue over the horizontal surfaces of the rocks, and use a strainer or flour sifter to sprinkle real dirt on those areas.

Cover the areas of the scenery that are not occupied with buildings, track, or cliffs with real dirt in this same manner. When all the dirt is in place, you can remove the masking tape from the track and add whatever matching or contrasting shades of dirt you have selected for track ballast, as described in

Chapter 7. Part of the earth and even some of the track sidings should be covered with grass and weeds, as described in Chapter 17.

WET WATER

The material that produces the most realistic water with the least effort is artists Gloss Medium. This is essentially a clear latex paint that dries to a high shine. It looks and acts like plain white glue but it does not dry as hard so there's little chance it would crack. Unfortunately, it can remain milky if you try to pour it over about 3/8 inch deep. You can minimize the cloudy effect by pouring only 1/8-inch layers and let each dry for a week. This technique is illustrated in the color section of this book.

For deeper water and for more realistic rapids and faster water, use the epoxy sold by craft shops for use in decoupage. This material differs from the resin sold to repair fiberglass boats in that the epoxy requires only a few drops of the catalyst per cup of resin, while the fiberglass material demands a nearly equal mix of resin and catalyst. The two look the same when cured, but the decoupage epoxies do not produce the horrible odors of fiberglass resins while they cure. Both run like water until they cure or harden, so the bottom of any lake, river, or stream bed must be sealed and perfectly watertight where you intend to pour the resin. If the river runs right to the edge of the table, you can build a dam by sealing the end with plastic garbage bags covered in silver-colored air-conditioner duct tape. If the stream is deep, back up the duct-tape dam with a temporary sheet of plywood or Masonite. Add any sunken boats, old tires, weeds, or logs that you want to see submerged. Spray the entire submerged portion of the river or stream with several coats of Testors DullCote to seal any loose dirt or debris so that trapped air cannot form bubbles in the bottom of the epoxy-resin water. Let the DullCote dry for at least two days before pouring the epoxy resin. Mix the resin and the catalyst exactly as shown on the side of the can. Mix several small batches so you can build up deeper water in layers that are no more than 1/16-inch thick. If you try to pour too much of the resin, it will crack as it cures. You can

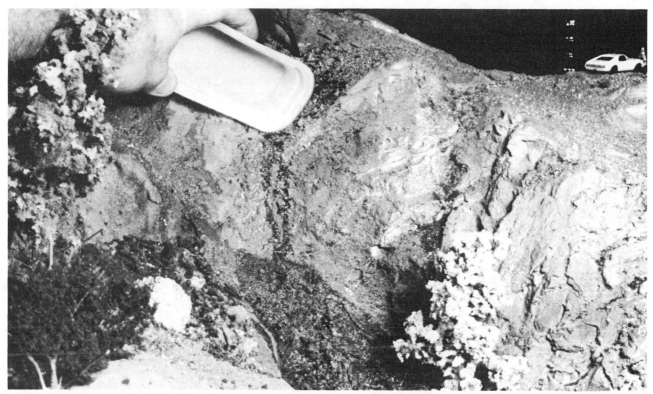

Fig 15-33. Steep steams can be poured (or brushed) with as many as a dozen applications of epoxy resin.

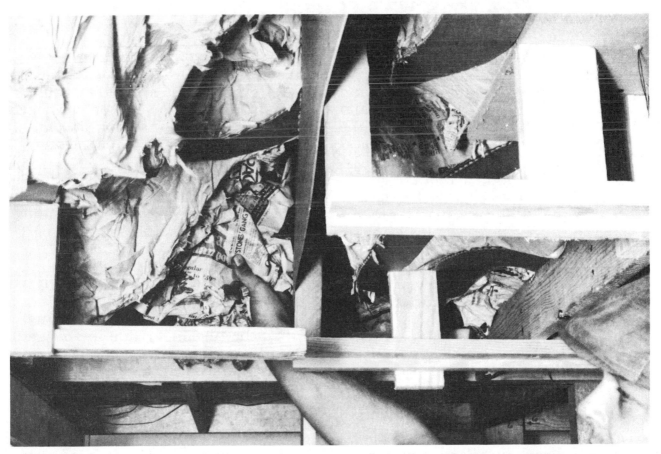

Fig. 15-34. When the scenery is complete, the wadded-up newspapers can be pulled from beneath the mountains and hills.

Fig. 15-35. This fast-flowing mountain stream was created using Artist's Gloss Medium as shown in the color section.

add another pour to help disguise the crack, but it will never look quite right. You should be ready to insert a few weeds cut from hemp rope and a bit of ground foam rubber dyed green into the edges of the last layers of the resin while the resin is still wet. Wiggle a wooden stick around on the last layers, just as they are becoming hard, to simulate ripples on the water's surface. If you pick at the resin right through the hardening stage, you can even simulate rapids and white caps. Touch a few of the hardened tips with a wash of white oil paint and turpentine to give a white-water effect. Very steep streams can be cast by tilting the entire layout so that the stream itself is level. If you cannot do that, then build up the stream by applying a dozen or more thin layers of the epoxy resin with throw-away paint brushes, which hardware stores sell for use with acids. Artist's Gloss Gel also can be used for steep streams.

DO'S AND DON'TS FOR CREATING SCENERY

- Do use real dirt sifted through a fine wire screen to simulate dirt.
- Do check the clearances beside and above the tracks, at tunnels, and cuts through the hills by running the longest locomotives and the longest cars over the layout.
- Do spray any of the too-bright greens with a fine mist of light beige wash (a mix of about nine parts water to one part beige acrylic paint plus a drop of dish washing detergent) to blend the colors of the layout and avoid too much contrast between earth and leaves or grass under the relatively dim indoor lighting.
- Do have color photographs, postcards or magazine illustrations of the general area you wish to model beside the layout so you can match colors, shapes and plant/earth textures with model materials.

- Don't attempt to create scenery by using only the packaged model scenery materials arrayed by whim.
- Don't build rock walls or cliffs so close to the tracks that long locomotives or cars will sideswipe the scenery and derail.
- Don't use dyed sawdust or ground foam to simulate dirt.
- Don't settle for bright greens and deep browns as the only scenery colors.
- Do apply ballast to any mainline tracks (and dirt to industrial sidings) but keep the ballast well away from the moving parts (the switch points) of all the turnouts. Glue the ballast in place with a mixture of nine parts water to one part artist's Matte Medium with a drop of dish washing detergent.

CHAPTER 16

Lightweight Scenery

THERE ARE TWO BASIC TECH-NIQUES FOR BUILDING scenery shapes. With the first, you start with an open-grid benchwork or tabletop and build the mountains, hills and valleys as shown in Chapter 15. The second method begins with a more-or-less solid block of dense, blue-colored, extruded-Styrofoam and you carve away anything that doesn't look like a mountain, hill, or valley. That second method is the one you'll learn by studying the techniques in this chapter. It is particularly effective when used with the Grass-That-Grows surface texturing shown in Chapter 17, and it is extremely lightweight because there's no need to use an ounce of plaster.

THE FLAT EARTH ALTERNATIVE

Honestly, it is not necessary to carve valleys or build hills. Most of the real world is relatively flat. If you elevate the track on roadbed (an automatic process if you use track with built-in roadbed like E-Z Track, Power-Loc track or True Track), add building sites and elevate the roads as shown in Chapter 6, you can simply texture the surface and use trees to provide a view block between

Fig. 16-1. There is no real need to carve the blue extruded-Styrofoam tabletop if you don't want to. On the 7 x 8-foot Burlington Route layout, you can create a simple view block between the coal mine at Chester and the power plant at Elwood with r-t-r trees. If you wish, cover the rest of the layout with felt, as described for the Grass-That-Grows system in Chapter 17, but do not glue the felt to the tabletop in case you want to lift it later to add a valley or build a hill.

scenes (Figure 16-1). All of the trees in the photo are ready-made products available from Life-Like, Woodland Scenics, AMSI, Noch, Faller, Scenic Express, Faller, Heki, Busch, Accurate Dimensionals and others.

None of these scenery-construction methods are permanent so you can rip up the surface textures and cut a valley or remove the trees and add hills years later. That's one of the many joys of model railroading; there's no construction schedule so you can build and finish any part or all of the layout on your own timetable.

CARVING THE MOUNTAINSIDE

The conventional scenery-construction methods shown in Chapter 15 allow you to mock up the hills and valleys with wadded-up newspapers covered with brown paper towels. You really cannot do that with the blue Styrofoam system. I would then suggest you make a scale model of the scene shapes you hope to achieve. Use a block of child's modeling clay (Figure 16-2) and carve the valleys with the end of paper clip. I used this technique to see if it was possible to produce both the valley at one end and the mountains in the middle of

a 4 x 8-foot layout and still retain relatively gentle slopes.

THE STYROFOAM SCULPTOR'S TOOLS

It is possible to use these techniques to create mountains and valleys from the white expanded-Styrofoam of beadboard, but I would not recommend that for a model railroad because it is just too weak. The white Styrofoam material can be carved for dioramas or small scenes and it works well for roads and for the basics of Woodland Scenics' Subterrain system shown in Chapter 6. The blue Styrofoam is the material used to build the lightweight benchwork in Chapter 6. If you have planned on having rivers and valleys, you have included 4 to 8 inches of the blue Styrofoam beneath the track as shown in that chapter. Use the same material to make the mountains.

The blue Styrofoam can be carved with a hacksaw blade or a serrated kitchen knife. These tools will produce some nearly weightless dust that can be readily removed with a vacuum cleaner. An alternative method is to use a special hot wire cutter that produces only a few drips of melted plastic foam and wisps of white smoke. The hot wire softens the microscopic air bubbles

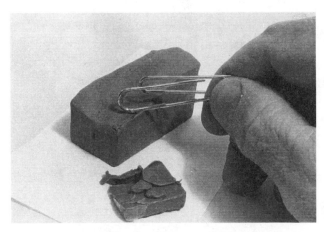

Fig. 16-2. It is difficult to envision what the scenery carved from blue foam will look like on the finished layout. Make a simple mock-up from a chunk of child's modeling clay, sculpted with a paper clip. That's how I determined that the valley would, indeed, slope up into the hill on the Burlington Route layout.

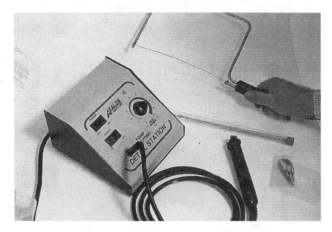

Fig. 16-3. The Avalon Concepts Detail Station is a transformer with adjustable controls so you can vary the amount of heat produced by the heated wires in the Detail Wand (shown at the end of the coiled cable) or the Shaper Tool (top). The Detail Station provides power to heat the wires in the two cutting tools so they can melt their way through the Styrofoam with little mess. Do, however, work outdoors because the fumes may affect allergies or cause other health problems.

that are trapped in the Styrofoam to produce a cut. The hot wire produces fumes that can be toxic, especially to anyone with allergies, so always work outdoors.

I used Avalon Concepts Foam Sculpting Detail Station set to cut the Styrofoam for the Burlington Route 7 x 8-foot layout. It is relatively expensive but it is the only hot wire tool that can be used to cut into the center of a 2 x 2-foot or larger panel. The Avalon Concepts set includes a transformer to reduce the 110-volt current to a usable level, the Detail Wand and a single, short blade. You will want to purchase at least two of the Avalon Concepts Wand Wire packs that include three 12-inch pieces of wire that can be bent into any shape. The hacksaw-shaped Shaper Tool is optional and, frankly, really not needed for this type of modeling work (Figure 16-3).

The wire can become as hot as an electric stove and the melted plastic that can drip off the wire is hotter than melted candle wax, so burns are possible. Wear cloth gloves and long sleeves so no skin is exposed. Caution: do not try to use a hot wire cutter with the urethane foams because the fumes produced can be toxic.

I bent three different cutting wires for the Detail Wand Bend (Figure 16-4). The 4-1/2-inch long U-shaped piece that is clamped in the Detail Wand was used for carving the valleys and mountains and for drilling holes for wires as shown in Chapter 8 (Figure 8-1). Be sure the parallel wires are at least 1/2 inch apart so there's less chance they can accidentally touch if you push the heated wire through the blue Styrofoam with too much force. Bend a similar hot wire cutter but with only a 2-1/2-inch deep U-shape and bend the ends at a 90-degree angle to make a cutter that will make right-angle cuts in 2-inch thick sheets of blue Styrofoam as shown in Chapter 6 (Figure 6-7). Finally, bend a multiple-Z-shaped piece with the full 12-inch wire to make cuts for the drainage ditches on each side of the railroad roadbed (Figure 16-4).

DIGGING RAILROAD ROADBED DITCHES

The real railroads always provide drainage ditches about 8 to 10 feet (that's about 1-1/8 to 1-3/8 inches) out from the bottom of the ballast. In fact, the railroads maintain a piece of equipment called a ditcher that has conveyor-belt mounted digging scoops to clean out those ditches. Few model railroads have these drainage ditches but they lend an incredible degree of realism. Also, the drainage ditches will help ensure that you do not place any cuts, tunnels or buildings so close to

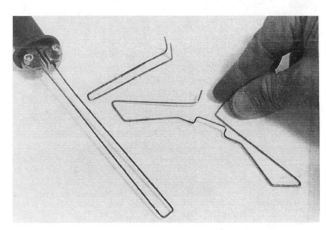

Fig. 16-4. Use needlenose pliers to bend three pieces of the Avalon Concepts Detail Wire for making 90-degree cuts in the Styrofoam (top) as shown in Chapter 6 (Figure 6-7). Also use this method for making deep cuts, for carving scenery (left) and for making drainage ditches on either side of the E-Z Track roadbed (right).

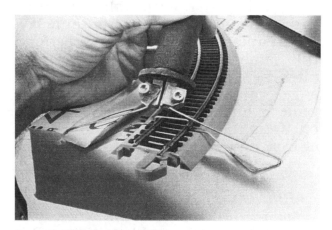

Fig. 16-5. Clamp the ditch-cutting wire in the Detail Wand and adjust the temperature at the Detail Station so the heated wire will make steady cuts through the Styrofoam. The U-shaped loop rides on the rails to position the cutting wire.

the tracks that they interfere with the passing trains. Bend the wire so it has a square-cornered U-shape that will just clear the outside of the rails. It's almost impossible to make a really tight bend here, so make one about 1/4 x 3/4 inch as shown, and bend it 45 degrees sideways after the wire is mounted in the Detail Wand to make the U-shape shallow enough so it just clears the molded-in spike heads of the track. Make the other angle bends to match the wire in Figure 16-4.

To use the hot wire ditcher, simply pull it along the track so that both sides cut equally wide ditches in the blue Styrofoam. It is, of course, essential that the track be located precisely where you want it so it will be centered over these two ditches. I would advise waiting until you are confident enough to glue the track down before cutting the drainage ditches. I allowed a full 1-1/2 inches on either side of the track because I knew the loose ballast would spread further than the plastic ballast on the E-Z Track. Adjust the controls on the Avalon Concepts Detail Station so the wire is just hot enough to cut as described in Chapter 6. If you used the hot wire to cut the blue Styrofoam panels for the layout, you should already be familiar with the technique. Practice cutting the ditches, however, on the bottom side of some of the removable blue Styrofoam panels to get the feel of using this cutter. I was able to trace all the tracks on the Burlington Route layout in about an hour. You can perform this same cutting task with a serrated kitchen knife by simply marking the edges of the roadbed and using the knife to cut the ditches in two passes, one from the roadbed side and the other from the opposite side to remove the V-shaped ditches.

CARVING OUT THE VALLEYS

Again, you can carve the blue Styrofoam with a hacksaw blade (Figure 16-13) or a serrated kitchen knife. I used the U-shaped, 4-1/2-inch-long wire (Figure 16-4) to shape all the valleys and

hills on the Burlington Route layout. One of the detriments to realism that is common to many model railroads is the sight of nearly vertical slopes on the mountains and cuts. In the real world, only rock cuts are that steep. I wanted the Burlington Route layout to represent the gentle slopes that are common to most of North America so I used a 1/2-inch block of plywood to support the end of the Detail Wand (Figure 16-6) while I made the initial cuts. With some practice, I would make these shallow

Fig. 16-6. Use a block of wood to keep the Detail Wand at a shallow angle for more gentle slopes. The cutting wire is only about 4 inches long, so you will need to make two or more passes in some areas to cut all the way through a 2-inch layer of Styrofoam. All of the cuts can be made using a hacksaw blade, which is far less expensive than a hot wire-cutter, but produces a bit more mess.

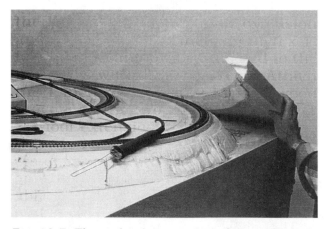

Fig. 16-7. The embankments that elevate real railroad track are usually sloped at about 30 degrees. The first cut will extend only through the first 2-inch layer of foam. When the cut is complete, remove the foam. If you use a hacksaw blade for these cuts, lift the foam about an inch so you can see the bottom of the blade while you saw around the curve. Make all the embankments first, even if some parts of them will be replaced by bridges.

cuts without using the block of wood, but it helped give me a feel for the work. Most real railroad-cuts in the earth and earthen fills or embankments are no steeper than 30 degrees, so I used a 30-60-90 triangle to guide the cutter when making those cuts. The hot wire is only long enough to make a cut at 30 degrees through a single 2-inch layer of blue Styrofoam. If you are making shallower cuts, use the cutter vertically to remove the material and make a second pass. When the cut is complete, lift the layer of blue Styrofoam (Figure 16-7) away and resume cutting through the second layer.

One of the secrets of working with blue Styrofoam for scenery is that you can replace or add material as well as remove it. If, for example, you discover that you have made any portion of the valley too deep, find the chunk of blue Styrofoam you removed and slice off the bottom of it to fill in the bottom of the valley.

PREPARING FOR BRIDGES

This scenery construction system allows you to make decisions about bridges and tunnels after you see that there would be a need for such features. The long, curved embankment on the Burlington Route layout crosses a shallow valley that would, logically, have been the course of a small stream. That was the place where the real railroad would have installed a bridge. A

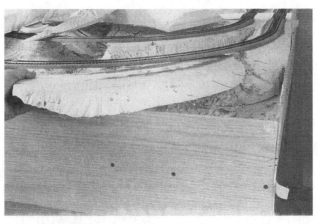

Fig. 16-9. Use the Avalon Concepts Detail Wand with the 4-1/2-inch, U-shaped wire or a hacksaw blade to cut through the embankment. Wiggle the cut portion of the embankment from beneath the roadbed. You can cut deeper into the next layer of foam to carve out the final floor of the valley and the course of the stream.

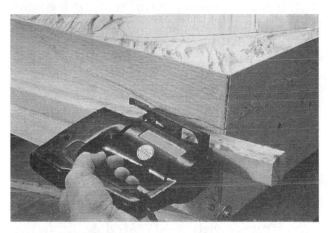

Fig. 16-10. When you are satisfied with the valley contours, hold a piece of 2 x 2 wood against the plywood while you cut through the 1/8-inch plywood with a saber saw along the contours or profiles of the scenery.

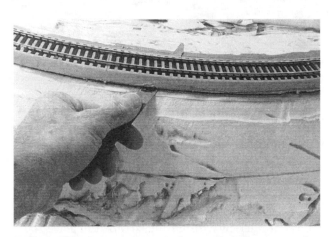

Fig 16-8. You can remove the track at any time by simply wiggling a serrated kitchen knife between the roadbed and the Styrofoam. Loosen the track that will be on bridges, but leave the track in place.

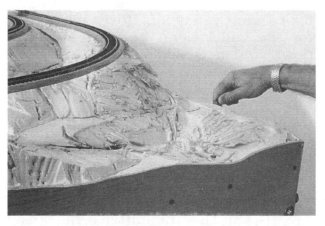

Fig. 16-11. Final shaping of the Styrofoam, particularly along the edges of the layout, can be done with the serrated kitchen knife.

real railroad probably would have installed a small culvert down near the level of the stream. I postulated, however, that the stream flooded frequently, so a steel viaduct was needed to span most of the valley

Determine the length of the bridge and wiggle a serrated knife between the roadbed and the blue Styrofoam (Figure 16-8). Remember that the embankments beneath the bridge should be no steeper than 30 degrees, and make the cuts through the embankment with the hacksaw blade or hot wire. The embankment can then be removed (Figure 16-9) from beneath the track and roadbed. The shapes of he valley sides and floor can be sculpted by trimming off a potato chip-sized piece of the blue Styrofoam with either a hot wire or a hacksaw blade or, for smaller cuts, a serrated knife.

When you are satisfied with the shape of the valley, the edges of the 1/8-inch plywood shadowbox can be trimmed to match the shape of the blue Styrofoam. Use a piece of 2 x 2 lumber to keep the saber saw blade from digging more than 1/4 inch or so into the Styrofoam while you make the cut (Figure 16-10). Small corrections can be made in the areas where the Styrofoam meets the plywood by carving with a serrated knife or by adding on some of the chips to build the area up.

CARVING THE MOUNTAINS AND HILLS

The hills are carved with a process that is almost the reverse of that used for carving valleys. Leftover pieces cut for the valleys can be turned upside down and used for small hills (Figure 16-12). To make larger hills, begin by laying a fresh sheet of 2-inch-thick blue extruded-Styrofoam over the layout. Use a marker to indicate where the building sites are located. Use spare pieces of track to duplicate the pattern of tracks beneath the Styrofoam, and mark the locations of the edges of he drainage ditches beside the track (Figure 16-13). Use the cutter or hacksaw blade at a gentle angle (Figure 16-6) to cut around the Styrofoam to the edges

of the buildings or the drainage ditches. I made some of the cuts to the track at a 60-degree angle because I knew these steeper cuts would be hidden by trees and buildings. When the hill is completely cut, look to see if there is still a flat top. If so, you can pin another piece of blue Styrofoam to the cut piece with 4-inch-long concrete nails. Turn the two pieces upside down (Figure 16-14) and use the slopes from the original piece as a guide for the hacksaw blade or hot wire to cut into the new piece. When the cuts are completed, turn the two pieces over and position them beside the tracks (Figure 16-15). Secure them on the tabletop with 4-inch-long concrete nails.

Fig 16-12. Leftover pieces of Styrofoam from the valley can be inverted and used as small hills.

Fig. 16-13. For taller hills, place a layer of the 2-inch-thick blue Styrofoam over the tracks and use a spare set of track sections to mark the position of the track hidden below the Styrofoam. Mark a second line about an inch away from the roadbed to leave room for drainage ditches. Use the hot wire Detail Wand or the hacksaw blade to cut slopes through the blue foam that taper away from these lines to carve the sides of cuts through the hills.

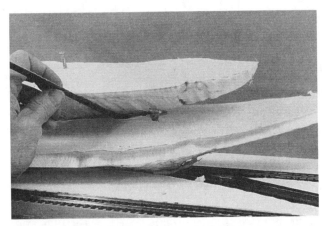

Fig. 16-14. The very small hills on the Burlington Northern layout were barely 2 inches high by the time the realistic gentle slopes were cut. A few areas, however, still have flat tops and they can be extended higher with a second layer of blue foam. You can use leftover scraps of the blue foam for this. Pin the scrap to the bottom of the hill with concrete nails and use the slope of the hills (bottom) to guide the hot wire cutter or the hacksaw blade while you cut through the hilltop.

Fig. 16-15. Invert the two-piece hill (Figure 16-14) and pin it to the layout with 4-inch long concrete nails. The slopes next to the track in this area are steep because they will be hidden from view by buildings and trees.

BORING TUNNELS

If you find that two layers of carved Styrofoam still allow a flat top, you may have a place where a tunnel can be used. Repeat the process used for carving the hills to carve the top of the tunnel (Figure 16-16).

If there are areas where you simply must have steep scenery beside the tracks, you can use the Mountains-In-Minutes pre-painted urethane foam rock. Do not ever attempt to cut these products with a hot wire because the resulting fumes are toxic. The urethane

Fig. 16-16. If you want to make tunnels, use a third layer of blue Styrofoam to span the tracks. There was not enough room on the Burlington Route layout, with its gentle slopes, for mountains high enough to accept tunnels.

Fig. 16-17. If you want visible rock outcroppings, you can use the pre-painted and weathered urethane foam castings for Mountains-in-Minutes. Cut the foam rocks with a hacksaw. Never use a hot wire cutter with urethane foam because the fumes can be toxic. Cap the rocks with pieces of the blue foam cut to fit.

foam is, however, easily cut with hacksaw blade. The tops of the rock cuts can be finished off with small pieces of blue Styrofoam (Figure 16-17).

When the scenery is complete, check all the tracks for adequate side clearances by pushing the longest passenger or freight car you will operate around the tracks (Figure 16-18). These two hills will become piles of coal at the power plant. Mark the locations of all the buildings and other non-earth items like the two piles of coal. The coal piles were finished by painting the Styrofoam with black latex paint, then covering the surfaces with a thick layer of Artist's Matte Gel. Real coal was then poured over the piles and pressed into the still-wet Matte Gel. Remove the coal piles and buildings and the scenery, which now looks very much like ice blue surfaces of the Arctic (see the color section). It is now ready for final texturing (Figure 16-20). If you cover the surface with plaster, paper towels dipped in plaster or Plaster Cloth, you will be

Fig 16-19. These two coal piles were made with the same foam-cutting techniques used for the hills and valley. Paint the piles black and cover them with Artists Matte Gel. Then press real coal into the still-wet gel. Position the coal piles and mark their edges so you are sure they do not interfere with the hills or with adjacent structures.

adding unnecessary weight to the layout. I would recommend that you use the Grass-That-Grows system of treated felt for as much of the surface as possible because it adds only ounces of weight.

BUILDING BRIDGES

Bridges are best installed, or at least their abutments put in place, before

Fig 16-18. Push the longest cars and locomotives you will operate around the track to be sure none of the new hills interfere with the equipment. It's a simple matter now, to trim away any offending areas. Leave at least an extra 1/8 inch of clearance to allow for surface textures.

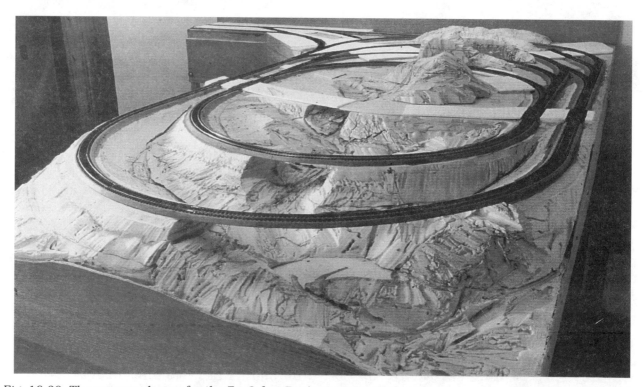

Fig. 16-20. The scenery shapes for the 7 x 8-foot Burlington Route layout are complete. Right now, it looks like something from the blue side of the moon or from the arctic. Leave the layout in this condition for a week or so to allow time for some additional carving in the valley or to modify the scenery before you apply the final textures.

Fig. 16-21. Test-fit the bridges. The steel viaduct on the Burlington Route layout is a Micro Engineering kit that has been cut down to about one-third of its original height.

the scenery surface is textured. I wanted a steel viaduct over this valley. I used the Micro Engineering 255-75514 Tall Viaduct. Hold one of the bents for the bridge against the track (Figure 16-21) to see how much of the bent can be used. I needed only the center section, which allowed the wider top piece to match the wide bridge needed for a curve. Frankly, this bridge is a kit for experienced modelers because there are a lot of very similar parts to differentiate, then cut from their sprues and assemble. You could build a simpler version using one of the wood trestle kits or steel trestle bents cut from the conveyors of Walthers 933-3051 Coal Floodloader's conveyor towers.

Deck girder bridges are good choices for use as bridges on tight-radius, 18-inch radius curves because nothing protrudes above the rails to foul overhanging cars or locomotives. These bridges can be cemented directly to the bottom of the E-Z Track roadbed with

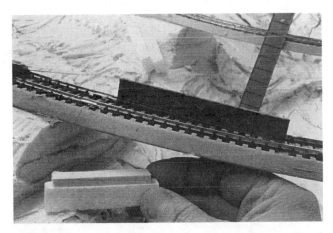

Fig. 16-22. Make bridge abutments from Woodland Scenics' 1/4-inch white Styrofoam cut into 1/2 x 2-1/2-inch pieces with a piece of 1/8 x 3/16-inch balsa glued on top. Paint them a concrete gray.

clear silicone bathtub caulking compound. Make bridge abutments that will appear to support the ends of the girder bridges from 1/4-inch, white Styrofoam and pieces of 3/16 x 3/8-inch balsa (Figure 16-22). The girder bridges included in the Micro Engineer viaduct kit were used beneath the viaduct and

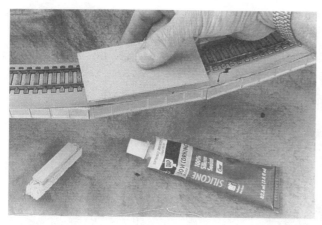

Fig. 16-23. I made a rectangular cardboard template for the two Micro Engineering viaduct towers so I could be certain the bride girders would be cemented in their proper places. Paint and weather the girders before installation. Cement the deck girders to the bottom of the roadbed with clear silicone bathtub caulking. Ballast the track after the girders are in place.

beneath the road on the Burlington Route layout.

I made a rectangular cardboard template the length of the deck girders in the Micro Engineering 255-75514 Tall Viaduct kit to be sure that the two deck girders for each tower would be square. I then cut the remaining deck girders with a razor saw to lengths that would fill in the spaces between the towers. Next, I attached all the girders to the bottom of the roadbed (Figure 16-23) with clear silicone bathtub caulking compound.

Paint the bridge abutments a concrete gray and cement them to the bottoms of the bridge girders and the blue Styrofoam. Now, finish all the scenery beneath the bridge as described in Chapter 17.

To finish the steel viaduct, follow the instructions in the Micro Engineering 255-75514 Tall Viaduct to assemble the bents and the cross bracing and cut the bents so they fill in the spaces between the scenery and the trestle (Figure 16-24). Build the bridge right on the layout to fit that distance between the bottom of the bridge girders and the surface of the scenery (Figure 16-25). I deliberately cut the embankment on the inner oval so the valley would be spanned by the length of one of the girders in the Micro Engineering 255-75503 50-foot Deck Girder Bridge. Just install the two girders by gluing them to each edge of the bottom of the roadbed, then glue the abutments to the bottoms of the girders.

Fig. 16-24. Finish the scenery before assembling the bents for the viaduct so you can cut the bent to precisely the right height. Paint the bents and braces before this final assembly. Cement the bents to the girders and the cross-braces to the bents with clear silicone caulking compound.

I used two leftover girders from the viaduct for the bridge beneath the highway but Micro Engineering offers that bridge as a separate kit 255-75504 30-foot Deck Girder Bridge if you do not use their steel viaduct kit.

Fig. 16-25. Weather the completed bridge with a bit of black and, perhaps, a few rust stains.

CHAPTER 17

Trees, Shrubs, and Other Greenery

MUCH OF MOTHER EARTH is covered with some type of living foliage. It's what prevents this planet's surface from becoming just a cloud of dust. The dirt and rocks, of course, underlie all that greenery, and that's why greenery is one of the last scenic effects to be added to a model railroad. If you're following the suggestions in this book, your entire model railroad is now covered (in your mind, at least) with either track, structures, ballast, rocks, dirt, or simulated water.

In practice, I suggest that you complete just a few square feet of the layout to this stage so you can apply your lessons to the rest of the railroad after you have learned through practice. There's no real reason why you cannot create scenery in just one small corner of the layout, from the plaster stage right through water and foliage. When you feel like making more scenery, begin another section and gradually work your way around. You can also use this period to experiment with other techniques like the Grass-That-Grows method of

Fig. 17-1. The majority of the exposed areas of the Burlington Route layout were treated with the Grass-That-Grows earth and grass and all of the trees are Noch or Scenic Express weeds treated with finely ground foam.

providing both earth and grass effects shown later in this chapter. If you decide to use plaster, I suggest you place pre-colored plaster just about everywhere in order to get the messy part over and done with. If you find later that you need to change a mountain or add a river, it's easy enough to break through the plaster to mock-up a change in the scenery and cover it with plaster. Apply the final touches of foliage to only those areas where you're pleased with the rest of the scenery. Those finished areas will include the tracks and their immediate surroundings.

GROUND COVER

Scenery begins at the ground. Far too many modelers skip right ahead to bushes and trees and wonder why their layouts look like deserts with trees on them. I suggest that you use at least two different kinds of ground

Fig. 17-2. Use a plastic squeeze bottle or Woodland Scenics' Scenic Sifter to apply the strands of polypropylene grass to surfaces treated with artist Matte Medium while the Matte Medium is still wet.

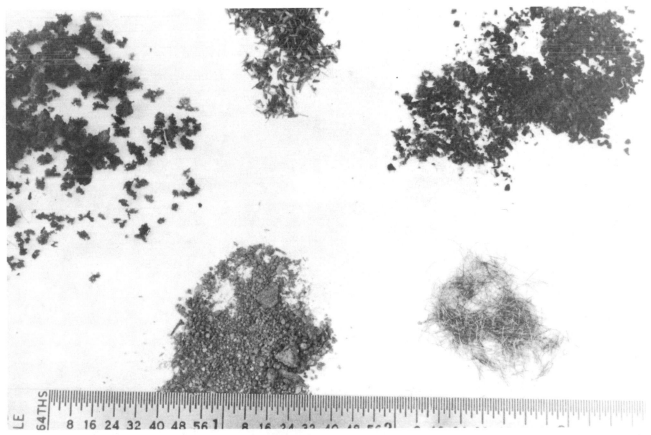

Fig. 17-3. Five scale-model ground covers (clockwise, from upper left): ground foam, sifted sawdust, sifted coffee grounds, 1/8-inch cut strands of polypropylene twine, and real dirt.

cover in addition to real dirt: ground (chopped) foam rubber dyed green and 1/8-inch strands of polypropylene macrame twine. The real dirt and the ground foam can be held in place on the layout by spraying the area with a mixture of three parts water to one part Artist's Matte Medium and a drop of dish washing detergent to break the surface tension of the fluids. Or you can use Woodland Scenic's Scenic Cement or Champ Decal Company's Resibond Spray.

You can find real dirt anywhere. I would suggest, however, that you bring along a magnet to be sure the dirt is not some iron oxide that is magnetic enough to be pulled into the motors of your locomotives. Sift the dirt through a fine-mesh tea strainer and save only the dirt that passes through the strainer. It is possible that some microorganisms are living in the dirt, so it's a good idea to bake the dirt in an oven at 400 degrees for an hour to kill anything that might be in there.

Fig. 17-4. Use a tea strainer to apply most types of ground cover, tapping the side of the strainer to sift the material onto the surface of the scenery.

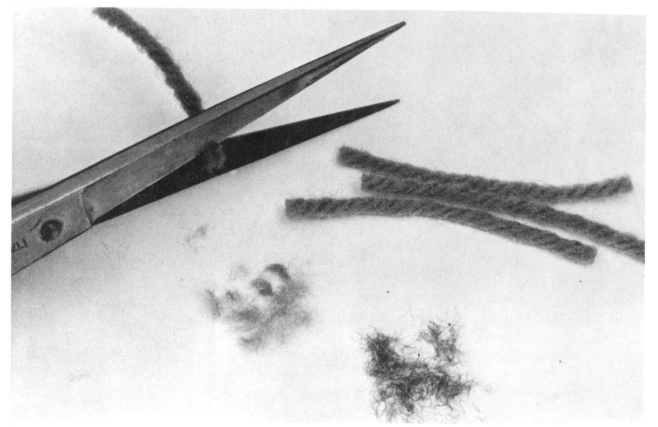

Fig. 17-5. The polypropylene twine will fall in individual strands when cut (bottom), while most synthetics tend to collect in scale-model tumbleweeds (center).

The ground foam rubber is available in a variety of grinds (sizes of the foam pieces) and colors to match summer foliage, as well as spring and fall colors, and the bright hues of flowers. The foam is even available in earth or dirt colors and it makes a surprisingly realistic substitute for sifted real dirt. Hobby shops carry the foam under the AMSI, Bachmann, Life-Like, Plastruct, Scenic Express, and Woodland Scenics labels. The foam can simply be sprinkled on trees, shrubs or ground for now.

WEEDS AND GRASS

Polypropylene twine is available from macrame shops and craft departments. The twine must be cut into 1/8-inch lengths. Polypropylene is the only material that will retain the individual strands after it is cut this short. You can do this with other synthetic macrame or knitting twines, but they'll bunch together to form clumps very similar to tumbleweeds. Polypropylene, on the

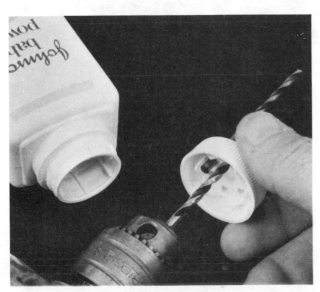

Fig. 17-6. Enlarge the holes in the top of a baby powder dispenser to 1/8-inch diameter so the plastic bottle can be used as a squeeze-type applicator for the fiber grass.

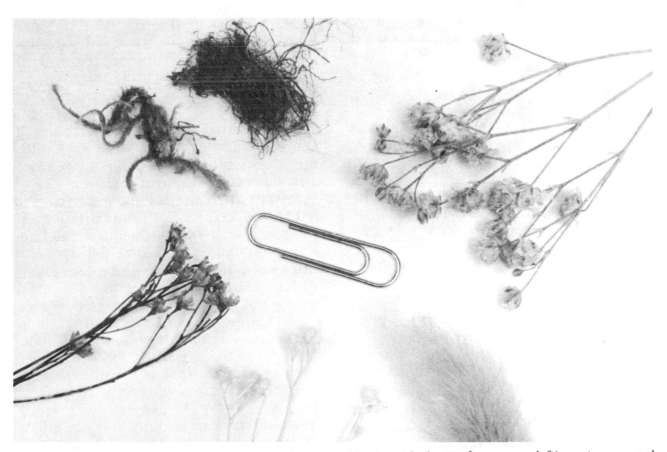

Fig. 17-7. Some natural growths for scale-model trees and bushes (clockwise, from upper left): peat moss, real grass roots, flowered baby's breath, bottle brush, dried Caspia, dried and dyed Caspia.

other hand, will simulate grass, hay, wheat, and similarly textured weeds. Buy dark green, light green, and avocado colors if you can. Faller, Kibri, Noch, Preiser, Vintage, and Woodland Scenics (available to dealers from Walthers), and Scenic Express (1001 Lowry Dr., Geanette, PA 15644) sell similar materials, already cut.

A squeeze-bottle applicator is the best tool to use to apply the 1/8-inch strands because the squeezing action creates some static electricity on the strands, which makes them stand up like a crew cut when they come in contact with the glue. Use Woodland Scenic's Scenic Sifter (Figure 17-15) or you may be able to find a flexible plastic container with a half-dozen 8-inch holes in the lid. A container from bathroom cleanser or table salt will do, or you can make your own from a plastic baby-powder bottle. Drill 1/8-inch holes in the lid, using a second drill bit to keep the two layers of the lid from rotating (Figure 17-6). When the lid is snapped back onto the bottle, each of the little sawtooth tabs must be positioned so they fit inside the neck of the bottle. Lightly squeeze the bottle to spray the simulated grass onto the glue-dampened earth.

THE GRASS-THAT-GROWS SYSTEM

If you are modeling an area where the predominant surface texture is grass or grass-like weeds, consider using this Grass-That-Grows system. The system begins as soon as you have finalized the shapes of the scenery using the Hydrocal-dipped paper towels, the Woodland Scenics Plaster Cloth in Chapter 15 or the shaped-Styrofoam in Chapter 16. The next step is to cover all the areas you wish to be grass (or mostly grass) with beige-colored felt from a fabric store (Figure 17-8).

COVERING YOUR WORLD WITH GRASS

To apply the felt, simply drape a 4 x 4-foot sheet over the layout and mark

Fig. 17-8. Drape beige felt over the scenery shapes and make rough cuts where the bridges and track will fit to begin the Grass-That-Grows system of providing both earth and weed textures.

where the track, bridges and buildings are located so you can cut the felt with heavy scissors to avoid these areas. You want to have plenty of felt for this method and it works well with hills and valleys. Test-fit the felt to be sure it covers all the areas you want, then lift the felt and spread on a thick layer of latex contact cement (Figure 17-9). Work quickly now, because you want to apply the felt before the contact cement dries. Press the felt firmly into the contact cement over every square inch of the layout and let it dry overnight. Next, use a utility knife to slice along the edges of the roadbed, along building sites and along roads, to remove any excess felt (Figure 17-10).

An alternate method of applying the felt works well for flat areas and for areas where there will be a lot of small areas of grass (felt). Lay the felt over the tracks, building sites and roads, and use a green felt pen to mark precisely where you wish to cut the felt (Figure 17-11). Use scissors to cut the felt to this shape, apply the contact cement, then press the pre-fitted felt firmly into the still-wet contact cement. Cover all the areas of the layout with felt where you want grass or weeds, especially those narrow areas between the edges of the roadbed and the edges of the table. Even if you want mostly dirt with just a few weeds, the felt will serve as a

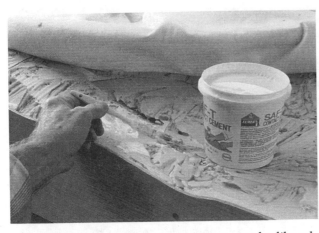

Fig. 17-9. Lift the felt so you can apply liberal amounts of latex-based contact cement to the scenery shapes. Press the felt onto the contact cement while the cement is still wet.

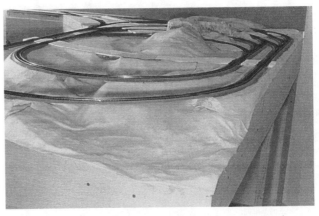

Fig. 17-12. The beige felt was used to cover virtually all of the visible surfaces of the 7 x 8-foot Burlington Route layout except the highway, the building sites and the steeper faces of the railroad's cuts through the hill. Next, spray the top layer of fibers with Kelly green paint.

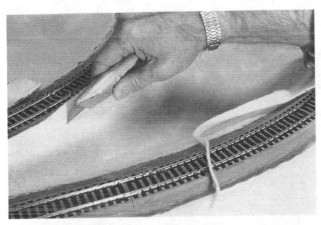

Fig. 17-10. Allow the contact cement to dry for three or four days, then use a utility knife to slice away any excess felt right up to the flat portion of the drainage ditches beside the track.

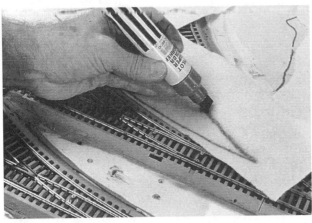

Fig. 17-11. For smaller areas, simply lay the loose felt over the tracks and mark the exact edges of the felt with a marking pen, then use scissors to cut the felt to shape. Check the fit, trim it if needed, and cement the felt in place with latex-type contact cement.

base. You can even cover it with narrow dirt roads, but leave the larger areas of dirt around industries and roads bare. When you are satisfied with the coverage, spray the beige felt with green acrylic paint or artist's inks. I found that inks like Badger's Air-Opaque worked especially well and left little odor. Do work outside, however, because there is a lot of spray and it can get caught up in the house's heater system and spread everywhere (as I discovered for myself!). I mixed one part Chrome Oxide Green with about nine parts Green to make a Kelly Green. I used two of the one-ounce bottles of Air-Opaque for this layout. The idea is to color only the very top layer of the individual fibers of the felt so the beige is still very visible.

MAKING THE GRASS GROW

To make the grass appear to grow, spread a layer of dust-like dirt over the felt. Use a tea strainer with the small screen so mostly dust falls on the layout. Vary the amount of the dirt that you sift onto the layout, with the steeper slopes receiving more dirt and the flat areas receiving very little. Next, use a stiff steel-wire brush, like those used to clean files, to work the dirt into the felt so that layer of green-painted fibers

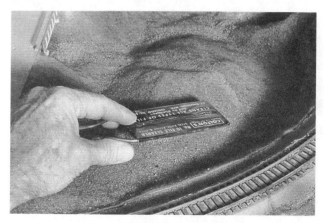

Fig. 17-13. When the contact cement is thoroughly dry, use a tea stainer to sift real dirt onto the felt. The powdery dirt can then be worked into the felt by brushing the felt with a stiff wire brush like this file cleaner. The dirt will cover the majority of the felt, with only the few fibers growing up through the dirt.

shows through the dirt. Look closely and you'll see that it looks like those fibers really are growing up through the dirt (Figure 17-15). If you want a bit more dirt, sift on some more and brush it in. For dirt roads, trim the felt's fibers and apply enough dirt to completely bury the felt. Except for lawns and pastures, there are various types of weeds scattered through the grass fields. Use the various weed textures shown later in this chapter to add those effects to the felt (Figure 17-16).

When you're completely satisfied with the grass effects, spray the entire area with a mixture of five parts water to one

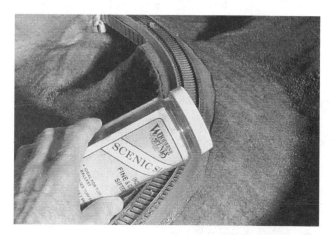

Fig. 17-14. You can disguise any visible felt edges with some fine green foam. Most of these edges will, however, be hidden by the final step in the texturing process—ballast for the track and roadbed.

Fig. 17-15. Sprinkle ground foam in the hollows to represent bushy-type weeds and add any other fiber weeds or texture details like those described earlier in this chapter (Figures 17-5 and 17-7). When you are satisfied, spray all of the treated felt with a mixture of 4 parts water, 1 part Artists Matte Medium and a drop of detergent (or use Woodland Scenics Scenic Spray or Champion Decals Resibond Spray).

Fig. 17-16. The Burlington Route layout is now covered with treated felt to complete the Grass-That-Grows system, and the girder bridges and ballast are installed. The final steps will be to install the lower portion of the bridges and add the trees.

part Artist's Matte Medium and a drop of dish washing detergent to act as a wetting agent. Or use Woodland Scenics Scenic Cement, or Champ's Decal Company's Resibond Spray to bond the dirt and textures to the felt. Use enough spray so the entire area turns a milky color. Use a pump sprayer from a hair salon supply store or Woodland Scenics' Scenic Sprayer to deliver just a mist so you don't disturb the loose dirt and texture materials. Let it dry for at least a week and the layout is ready for bridges, trees and bushes (Figure 17-16).

TREES AND BUSHES

Natural materials such as weeds and lichen mosses and even some root systems work well for simulating trees and bushes. In some cases, the tiny flowers or ends of the natural material are fine enough to be almost-to-scale leaves. However, most of these materials must be used only as the branch systems for the trees or bushes on a model railroad, with the actual leaves formed from finely ground foam rubber, dyed sawdust, or a combination of the two materials.

BRANCHES AND TWIGS

The most critical part of most miniatures of trees and bushes are the tiny intermediate twigs that branch off from the main trunk to hold the leaves. There are some natural growths that have very delicate structures, including the Noch 5228-23800 Large and 528-23820 Medium Natural Tree Forms. Similar tree forms are available in larger quantities from Scenic Express. These are a Scandinavian weed that makes incredibly realistic trees, espe-cially when the weeds are covered with two or three layers of finely ground foam. These trees are more realistic if the trunks are painted a dark gray using automobile primer from a spray can. For variety, use both the rust-colored Oxide Primer and conventional gray primer on the same trunks. Work outdoors for this process and let the trees dry overnight. To apply the foam, spray the tree with the cheapest hair spray you can find and sprinkle the foam onto the tree. Spray it again and sprinkle on more foam. Repeat the process a third time if you want a more dense tree. An alternate method is to dip the trees in that mixture of four parts water to one part Artist's Matte Medium and then sprinkle on the foam. The Matte Medium helps to soften the relatively brittle weeds and preserve them. These are the trees that were used on the Burlington Route layout on the cover of this book.

Realistic trees can also be made using natural weeds like sagebrush and some hedge trimmings for the main

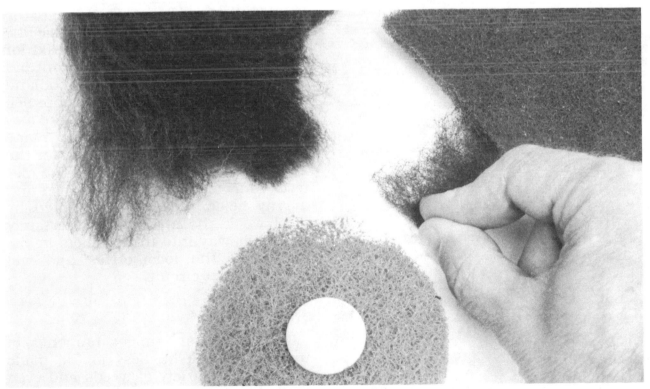

Fig. 17-17. Bulk macrame rope (before weaving, upper left) and plastic scouring pads are some materials to use for the small twig structures for trees.

Fig. 17-18. Dip the largest pieces of plastic wool, macrame fiber, or Woodland Scenics' Poly Fiber in Artists Matte Medium before placing them in the ravines of the scenery.

Fig. 17-19. Carefully select weeds and small twigs, which can be used to simulate tree trunks, and use ground foam for the foliage.

trunk and major limbs. To simulate the twigs on these heftier weeds, use the hair-like plastic cloth that is used for some types of packing insulation and for plastic scouring pads or Woodland Scenics' Poly Fiber. Macrame shops sell bulk skeins of a coarse, cotton-like material some macrame rope is made from, which can be substituted for the Woodland Scenics' Poly Fiber. The material is available in both a brown and a gray/beige. Do not be tempted by steel wool; the strands will certainly find their way into the magnets in the motors of the locomotives and will cause a short circuit.

TREE TRUNKS

The trunks and major branches of trees and large bushes can be made from a wide variety of weeds and even the twigs of small bushes or trees. If you cannot find sizes and shapes that suit the types of trees in the geographic area of your model railroad, then make your own. Stranded steel clothesline can be cut into 4 to 8-inch lengths with diagonal cutters. Unwrap the individual strands for about half the length of the piece of wire and bend them into the shape of branches. Bend out all but two of the strands at the bottom of each piece to form roots. The two remaining strands will be inserted into the plaster or Styrofoam to support the tree. Use the putty-style, 2-part epoxy and catalyst to make the trunk texture for each tree, and paint the trunks with brown, gray, and beige acrylics to simulate bark.

The unwoven macrame fiber or Woodland Scenics' Poly Fiber can be applied two different ways to simulate two different types of branch structures. The material can be cut and wrapped into a very loose ball or cloud and then glued to the tree-trunk structure, or the macrame material can be cut into short lengths and fanned out before being glued to the trunk structure.

Fig. 17-21. Woodland Scenics' Poly Fiber is one of the better materials to use in creating twig structures for trees or bushes.

LEAVES

The final step in making the tree is to spray the twig portion with a mixture of 4 parts water to 1 part Artists Matte Medium with a drop of dishwashing detergent, (to break the surface tension of the fluids) or you can use Woodland Scenic's Scenic Cement or Champ Decal Company's Resibond Spray.

Let the glue dry until it is just becoming tacky, then dip the tree into a box of

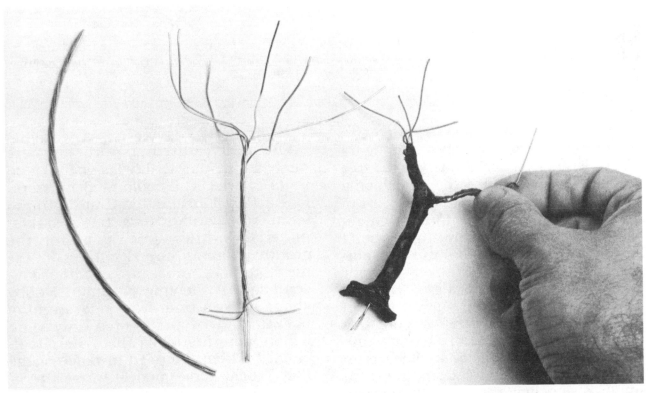

Fig. 17-20. Shape the basic tree trunk from pieces of wire clothesline and cover them with putty-type epoxy and catalyst (right) to simulate the thicker area of the tree trunk and its bark

Fig. 17-22. The unbraided macrame rope can be pulled into rounded shapes (top) or cut and spread into fan-like shapes (bottom) to simulate different types of tree structures.

Fig. 17-23. Spray the trees with cheap hair spray and dip them into a box of ground foam to simulate leaves.

dyed ground foam rubber. This creates the individual leaves, as shown in Figure 17-23. Drill or punch a hole for the tree in the plaster or Homosote and dab on a bit of precolored plaster to be worked in around the root system. Finally, glue a bit of ground cover around the base of the tree. Pay attention to nature's examples when you plant the trees on your model railroad. Most trees grow in small valleys or hollows, and they are often clustered in groups of three or more. Use some of the gray-colored twig and trunk trees without the application of leaves to simulate an occasional dead tree in a small grove of living trees. Now your layout has really come alive!

COMMERCIAL TREES

The trees featured up until now were made with either real twigs or the dried roots of weeds. Woodland Scenics offers a Poly Fiber material and ground foam. Woodland Scenics has a similar material in their tree kits, but the ground foam is already glued to the mesh to save you a step in the construction of the tree or bush. Hobby shops also carry at least one brand of packaged, dyed and treated Norwegian lichen moss (usually called, simply, lichen) that can be used in place of the Poly Fiber. Some modelers use the lichen as-is for trees and bushes and it is part of some of the ready-made trees

Fig. 17-24. Woodland Scenics' Foliage Material is essentially their Poly Fiber with the ground foam already glued in place. Stretch the material as much as possible for maximum realism.

in the plaster scenery to accept the trunks. Use about a dozen trunks for every square foot of forest to simulate a few visible tree trunks. Spread the Poly Fiber over the nails and pull out some tufts to suggest the tops of individual trees. Do not use balls of the stuff because that's the best you can hope for, a hillside covered with furry balls. Spray the Poly Fiber with hair spray and sprinkle on some fine ground foam. Finally, plant completed individual trees all around the Poly Fiber to disguise the base. If you are using the Noch or Scenic Express weeds for trees, use some of the broken-off tips to simulate individual branches sprouting out of the dense Poly Fiber forest. Simply tuck a dozen or so broken-off ends into the Poly Fiber.

from firms like Bachmann, Life-Like, and Model Power. The lichen looks far more realistic, however, if it is also covered with a bit of ground foam to disguise the lichen tip texture.

Most of the ready-made trees have a wire core with bristle limbs similar to a baby bottle brush. These trees can be made more realistic by trimming their shapes with scissors to create a rougher, more natural form and by covering them with ground foam for a more random texture.

BUILDING FORESTS FULL OF TREES

You can simulate an entire forest with just a dozen trees and some Woodland Scenics Poly Fiber. Stretch the Poly Fiber so it has the see-through quality of the edges of real trees. This is the technique used for the forest on the Burlington Route layout, a forest so dense it actually hides the two Loads-In/Empties-Out tracks that connect the mine at Chester with the power plant at Elwood (Figure 17-25).

Paint some nails or 1/16-inch wooden dowels with gray primer and push them into the Styrofoam scenery or drill holes

Fig. 17-25. Spread Woodland Scenics' Poly Fiber and support it with a few 4-inch concrete nails to cover the tops of hills like this one on the Burlington Route layout. Spray the Poly Fiber with cheap hair spray and sprinkle on ground foam. Finally, surround the Poly Fiber with a few dozen HO scale trees. Stick any broken-off limbs into the Poly Fiber to suggest that the trees surrounding the Poly Fiber are also deep inside it and sprouting through the forest canopy.

PART V: Miniature Empires in Action

CHAPTER 18

Automatic Coupling and Switching

THE REAL EXCITEMENT that model railroading offers is not only running the trains but the actual coupling, uncoupling, and switching, just as real railroads do each day. Some model railroaders place a string of cars and a locomotive and caboose on the track and never uncouple a car until they take that train off the layout to replace it with another. Of course it is exciting to watch any train move around a model railroad layout, particularly one that has some buildings and scenery for that train to pass. This makes it seem like it's really going somewhere. But there is much more to a realistic model railroad than that.

If you are one of the many model railroaders who consider switching to be nothing more than simply running a train forward, backward, and forward again, I think you are missing one of the more fascinating aspects of the hobby. The real excitement of switching comes from the duplication of all the movements of the real trains—and for precisely the same reasons. If you want your model railroad to be authentic, you will want to switch that train back and forth.

THE HANDS-NEAR APPROACH

One of the many differences between a toy-train operator and one who is running a real railroad in miniature is a hands-off approach. That's why those endless laps around the layout with the same old trains become boring. There's a thrill in sitting or standing at a control panel while you flip levers to switch

trains in and out of sidings or stop one train while you start another. The towerman's job is always going to be a part of both real and model railroading. Please don't let that be the only part of the hobby for you, though. Step down from that tower (here is where the walk-around control from Chapter 9 is a big help) and try the engineer's or brakeman's jobs for awhile. You still won't have to destroy the illusion that yours is a real railroad by actually touching the miniature trains. The true model railroader is the person who practices a "hands-near" approach, which means that he or she remains close enough to the moving train to be a participant rather than a mere spectator at a control panel.

COUPLERS

Most HO scale locomotives and cars are now equipped with a working knuckle coupler that can be coupled anywhere, uncoupled with a small screwdriver or by remote-control over a hidden magnetic ramp. The uncoupling can be delayed after pausing at the hidden ramp and the car can be uncoupled on down the track. These couplers are similar to the coupler pioneered by Kadee several decades ago. Kadee makes the widest variety of these couplers, but there are now many brands including Accurail, Bachmann, InterMountain, Life-Like Proto 2000 and McHenry. Some of the older train sets, locomotives and cars, and some of the least-expensive train sets, locomotives and cars still have a horn-hook style coupler (Figure 18-1, left). If you never intend to couple or uncouple, these couplers are fine. If,

Fig. 18-2. The Kadee magnetic uncoupling ramp can be glued directly between the ties. Be sure to position the ramp a tie or two in from the end of any track section so the ramp will not be caught by the plastic webs that join the end ties.

Fig. 18-1. The new operating knuckle couplers are all similar to this Kadee Magne-Matic coupler (right). All are designed to be uncoupled with a special magnet mounted between the rails. These couplers also have a delay action so you can cock them over the magnetic ramp, then push the car ahead to where you want to spot it. The coupler on the left is the horn-hook that is only found on the least-expensive toy locomotives and cars.

The couplers will uncouple without derailing the train by using a magnetic ramp that is buried beneath the track or placed between the rails so it looks like a highway crossing (Figure 18-2). Just stop the car and locomotive with the couplers over the 2-inch-long ramp and the two couplers open to disengage. That leaves a lot of room for error, and the train doesn't have to be spotted very carefully to catch part of the ramp.

These knuckle-style couplers have a small bent steel wire that hangs below the coupler. This uncoupling pin is repelled by the magnetic ramp and that action is what pivots the coupler knuckle open to uncouple. The wires

however, you really want to enjoy your model railroad, replace the horn-hook couplers as soon as possible. Bachmann makes a truck-mounted Kadee-style knuckle coupler that can be used to replace the truck-mounted couplers if you would rather not mount the Kadee-style knuckle couplers on the body as described later in this chapter.

These couplers look like real railroad couplers, although they are about 25 percent larger than they should be for truly accurate HO scale couplers. The coupler knuckle actually opens like a real coupler, too. The real magic of these couplers, however, is that they really will couple with a gentle force.

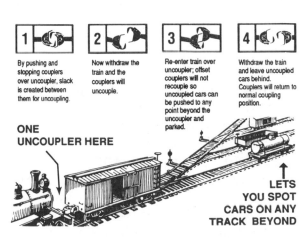

Fig. 18-3. This shows how the Kadee couplers (and most other brands of HO scale operating knuckle couplers) operate over the ramp (1 and 2) and how the delayed-action principle functions (3, 4 and the lower drawing). Courtesy Kadee Quality Products

vaguely resemble the air hoses that hang beside the couplers on real trains. But honestly, the uncoupling pin does not look realistic when a single car is seen from the end. Still, the appearance is vastly more realistic than that of the horn-hook couplers.

The knuckle-style couplers on your HO scale cars and locomotives will couple together just about anywhere, except on a curve or a downgrade. Coupling, then, can always be a hands-off operation as long as the couplers are working properly. Uncoupling is a bit tricky to do from a distant control panel because you have to be able to judge exactly where the couplers and the cars are on the track. The couplers on your HO scale models will only uncouple by remote control when they are directly over the magnetic uncoupling ramps. When you pull the train away, the uncoupled car or that portion of the train will stay at the uncoupling ramp. You must perform a quick succession of moves for reliable uncoupling. Stop at the ramp, back up just a fraction of an inch, then pull forward immediately. You can put the magnetic ramps on any 6-inch or longer piece of straight track. Most of these couplers have a delayed action that allows you to cock the coupler open over the ramp and shove (but not pull) the car to any location on the railroad (Figure 18-3). When you stop the train and reverse it, the coupler will uncouple.

MANUAL COUPLING

There's a better way of uncoupling that will let you get even more involved with the operation of your trains. Simply use a small screwdriver, an ice pick, or an awl to operate the couplers (Figure 18-4). Accurail and Kadee also make special uncoupling picks that work very well for manual uncoupling. You're still not actually touching the models but you are performing the function of the brakeman, in addition to your other duties as towerman (or dispatcher) and engineer. This may

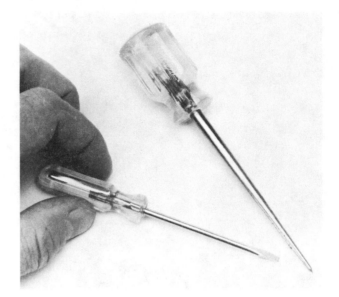

Fig. 18-4. A small screwdriver or an awl (right) can be used to uncouple most of the brands of automatic knuckle-style couplers. Kadee and Accurail offer inexpensive tools that will be more reliable for this purpose, however.

sound simple, but don't laugh until you've tried it for several operating sessions.

You don't have to put your miniature railroad equipment through those toy train gyrations of lurching backward and forward to get the couplers to open, and you don't have to try to figure out how to place an uncoupling ramp every place you want or need one. You really should use the uncoupling tool in conjunction with the walk-around throttle (in Chapter 9) so you can use the throttle to set the locomotive in motion when you have the couplers open. It will take some practice to determine the best ways to use the screwdriver or ice pick. The trick is to push the point straight down to get it just into the gap between the couplers, then twist or lean the tool slightly to pry the couplers apart. The movement should be very delicate.

COUPLER MAINTENANCE

The couplers are the most vulnerable parts of your models, and it's easy for them to be knocked out of alignment. You should check every coupler on every piece of equipment you own, and make it a habit of checking the couplers whenever you put a new piece of equipment into operation. Be sure the coupler is free to pivot from side to side without any binds or jerks. Try coupling it to a coupler on another car by pushing the two cars together on the track, by hand, so you can feel if it takes too much pressure to get the two to couple. Sometimes small wisps of plastic or small ridges of flash must be sliced off cleanly with a sharp hobby knife in order to get the coupler to work properly.

The couplers, like the trucks beneath freight and passenger cars, are self-lubricating, so if someone has applied any oil or grease, it should be cleaned away before it has a chance to attract dust and lint.

MAGNETIC UNCOUPLING RAMPS

Kadee offers three styles of uncoupling ramps. One that is placed between the rails after the ties have been cut away with a razor saw, another that is buried in a 3 x 3-inch cavity cut about 8 inches deep in the roadbed (before the track is laid), and an electromagnetic ramp that is mounted in a 2 x 3-inch slot cut through the roadbed and tabletop. The first two ramps are permanent magnets. The third is activated electrically with a small push-button. The ramps include instructions on their installation and suggestions on where to place them.

INSTALLING AUTOMATIC KNUCKLE COUPLERS

Kadee manufactures approximately two dozen different coupler mounting designs, including Numbers 26, 27 and 28, which are designed to be mounted on the trucks of inexpensive ready-to-run rolling stock (and locomotives) from Bachmann, Life-Like and Model Power. The couplers require some slight trimming on the stock trucks for some applications and they are furnished with complete instructions. I suggest you buy all three so you'll have a proper coupler for any truck-mounted coupler pocket design.

Most modelers, however, prefer the more realistic coupler mounting on the bottom of the car. All of the plastic car kits have coupler pockets designed to

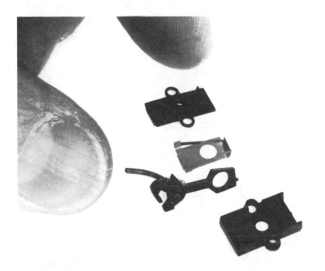

Fig. 18-5. The Kadee Number 5 coupler pocket (top and bottom), flat bronze spring and coupler.

Fig. 18-6. Use a hobby knife to remove the small peg from inside most Athearn freight and passenger car coupler pockets before installing the Kadee Number 5 coupler and spring.

accept a Kadee Number 5 coupler. This mounting design or coupler pocket has become a standard for nearly all HO scale cars and locomotives. If you are fitting the knuckle couplers to a car that has its couplers mounted on the trucks, you will have to cut the original coupler and pocket from each truck with a razor saw or diagonal cutters. The coupler pocket supplied with most brands of knuckle couplers, including the original Kadee Number 5, can then be mounted by drilling a small hole and threading that hole as shown later in this chapter.

Some Athearn cars have a coupler pocket that will accept the Kadee Number 5 coupler and most of the other designs of knuckle couplers, but there is a small tab inside the pocket that must be cut off with a hobby knife (as shown in Figure 18-6) before using the new coupler and copper spring. Athearn's metal coupler cover is used.

These couplers also will fit the coupler pockets on most HO scale locomotives and cars. If the model does not have a coupler pocket, or if the knuckle coupler will not fit the pocket, use the pocket supplied with the new coupler

Fig. 18-8. Use a Number 50 drill bit in an electric drill to make the hole for a Kadee coupler in the coupler-mounting pad of most Athearn diesels.

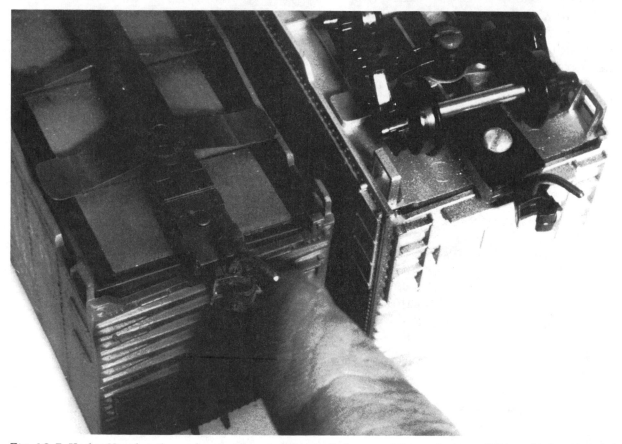

Fig. 18-7. Kadee Number 5 couplers (and springs) installed on an Athearn box car (left) and MDC/Roundhouse box car (right).

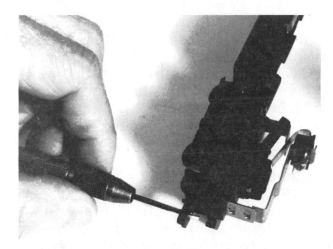

Fig. 18-9. Hold a Number 2-56 tap in a pin vise to cut the threads in that Number 50-sized hole in the Athearn diesel's coupler-mounting pad.

Fig. 18-10. Use a razor saw to remove the back 1/8 inch of the Kadee Number 5 coupler pocket to mount the Number 5 coupler and spring on the Athearn coupler-mounting pad.

Fig. 18-11. Use a 1/4 x 2-56 flat head screw to mount the Kadee Number 5 coupler on the Athearn coupler-mounting pad.

Fig 18-12. Use the Kadee Number 205 Coupler Height Gauge to check the height of the coupler and the uncoupling pins on every knuckle-style coupler.

Fig. 18-13. If the coupler is too high, remove it and use a file to remove enough material to lower the coupler.

or the Kadee Number 5 coupler's pocket. Use an electric drill with a Number 50 (size) drill bit to drill a hole where the new coupler should mount and pivot. Thread the hole with a Number 2-56 tap held in a pin vise. Install the new coupler, spring and pocket with a 1/4-inch-long, 2-56 screw. The Number 50 drill bit, the 2-56 tap and the 1/4 x 2-56 screw are available from hobby shops and larger hardware stores.

Kadee sells a Number 205 coupler height gauge (Figure 18-12) that is an essential tool for reliable coupler operation. The gauge is a cast metal device that holds a coupler and rests on the track. Some modelers glue a 12-inch-long piece of track to a board and mount the Kadee Number 205 gauge permanently to the track as a test track. Place the car or locomotive with the new Kadee couplers installed on the track and roll the coupler up to the gauge. The height of the coupler and the height of the uncoupling pin must match the gauge. If the pin or coupler is too high, the couplers won't operate properly. If the pin is too low it can catch on the turnouts and cause derailments. To lower the coupler, install some thin plastic or cardboard shims between the coupler pocket and the bottom of the car. On some locomotives, the coupler can be lowered by filing the top of the coupler-mounting pad (Figure 18-14). To lower the coupler, add washers between the trucks and the underframe on rolling stock. On some locomotives the frame can be filed to raise the coupler. If the coupler is too low on a freight or passenger car, you may be able to install washers between the trucks and the bolsters to raise or lower the car (and the coupler). Kadee also makes offset couplers that can be used to raise the coupler about 1/16 inch. Kadee includes lubrication and installation instructions with each package of couplers.

TRAILING SWITCH MANEUVERS

Once you understand how to perform switching maneuvers, you'll discover why those freight trains make so many back and forth movements. And once you know the reasons for them, you'll realize that it can be an important part of your model railroad operations. When you've learned how to perform switching movements, you may find you like that kind of action far more than just running trains. When you learn how to operate the Waybill switching system (discussed in Chapter 19), you may want to spend most of the time at any operating session just switching cars in and out of trains. Even without the Waybill system, though, you'll need to learn the basic switching moves. Then you can make up trains and break them down, using a locomotive, rather than your hands, as a switch engine.

There are really only three basic switching moves, the trailing-point move, the facing-point or run-around move, and the reverse move, which reverses a train through a wye. Since most track plans group these three, there are endless combinations. These are the only ways to move railroad cars on railroad track by pushing or pulling them with locomotives. When you get really good at switching, you may want to duplicate at least the Timesaver portion of the 10 x 10-foot track plan in Chapter 20 (Figure 20-6). The three-track Timesaver is a 10 x 68-inch track arrangement that has been developed over the years for use in switching contests, so it's deliberately challenging.

TRAILING-POINT MOVES

The trailing point simply describes the direction of the turnout's points of the siding relative to the direction of the train on the main line. If the siding (and the turnout's points) trails off behind the train as the train passes it, it is considered a trailing-point siding. The direction of the train determines the type of maneuver; if the train were traveling in the opposite direction (counterclockwise in the illustrations), the siding and the turnout points would be facing the train. This would become a facing-point turnout. However, the movements nec-

Fig. 18-14. The locomotive and stock car are uncoupled from the train at this point on the Burlington Northern layout.

essary to get a car in or out of a siding that is a facing point are much more complicated than those moves needed to switch a car in or out of a trailing-point siding. Figures 18-14 through 18-17, on the 9 x 9-foot Burlington Northern layout, illustrate where the locomotive is uncoupled and switched. The locomotive stops its train so it can uncouple, however, much of the train is behind the car that is to go onto the trailing-point siding (Figure 18-15). The car happens to be next to the locomotive in the illustrations, but there could just as well be one or two or more cars be-

tween the locomotive and the car that is to be switched or spotted on the siding. The locomotive then moves forward with the car to be spotted on the siding until the wheels of the car clear the points of the turnout (Figure 18-15). The locomotive stops while the brakeman throws the turnout from the main line to the siding. The locomotive then reverses to shove the car into the siding and stops while the car is uncoupled (Figure 18-16). The locomotive pulls forward again until it (or the last car) clears the turnout points, where it will stop. The brakeman then moves the turnout from the siding position to the main-line alignment. The locomotive reverses until it

Fig. 18-15. The stock car is pulled forward just enough to clear the turnout points.

Fig. 18-16. The stock car is pushed back into the siding and uncoupled.

Fig. 18-17. The locomotive pulls forward to clear the turnout, then backs up to couple onto the remainder of the train.

gently couples back to the remainder of the train (Figure 18-17). It then stops while the brakeman sets the couplers and connects the air hoses. The train then moves forward to its next destination. Every time the train starts or stops, it is counted as a move; the fewer moves in a complex switching situation, the quicker the time.

Most of the sequence for switching the car into the siding would, of course, be reversed if a car was already on the siding waiting to be added to the train. When you become proficient at switching maneuvers, you may want to set up situations where two or three cars need

to be moved in or out of any given siding. For instance, imagine how many moves it would take if that empty log-dumping car at the Lumber Supply Company's log pond was supposed to be picked up by the same train that spotted that stock car at the cattle pens. The loaded car of lumber wasn't quite ready for pickup, of course, so it would have to be put back where it is before the train could proceed. It can be done in eleven moves or less, including the single move of stopping and starting the train for the beginning and end of the maneuver. Here's a hint: pick up the flat car and the log car at the same time (two moves). Remember, you want to leave with the log car in the train, the flat car loaded with lumber at the saw-mill, and the stock car at the cattle pens.

RUN-AROUND OR FACING-POINT MOVES

The switching moves are more complex when the siding is facing the direction in which the train is traveling. In the old days, the train crews would make such a move with a flying switch. This means running the locomotive forward past the switch, throwing the switch just as the locomotive clears it (but while the train is still moving), and uncoupling the car so it will roll on into the siding. That's no longer legal on real railroads, and it's impossible to do on a model railroad because there's no way to uncouple while the train is still in motion. The only way to get that car

Fig. 18-19. The locomotive uncouples from the train, pulls forward to clear the turnout, then backs up and moves on across the distant bridge (top).

Fig. 18-18. The lone hopper car full of coke is waiting for a pick up.

into or out of a facing-point siding is to run around the car at the nearest passing siding so you can push the car into its siding. A passing siding is generally considered to be a siding that has a switch at both ends, although a train can back into a stub-ended siding (and they often do) and wait while another train passes by. The siding with a switch at both ends is needed so the locomotive can literally run around its train to couple onto the back of it.

The sequence of the run-around moves shown in Figures 18-18 through 18-23, and again on the 9 x 9-foot Burlington Northern layout, show the essential moves that are used to pick up the loaded hopper and to place it in the train. The illustrations skip one or two of the obvious start-stop moves. You can understand, from studying these moves and from trying them on a section of your own railroad, how complicated even this basic switching situation can be.

You will notice that there is at least one passing siding on nearly every layout plan in this book, as well as one or two stub-ended sidings. Both types of track configurations are needed if you want to operate your layout like the real thing. That's why I suggested in Chapter 1 that you consider the purchase of a pair of turnouts as they are more important to the enjoyment of the hobby than having an additional locomotive. Even the simplest of layouts should have at least four turnouts to provide a passing siding and two stub-end sidings. Position those turnouts for

the stub-end sidings so that one will be a facing point when the other is a trailing point. This will provide the maximum amount of operating action.

The facing-point or run-around sequence can be completed in a total of eleven moves if done in the manner shown in the illustrations. It would also be possible to use one of several alternate methods, such as leaving the remainder of the train back on the main line behind the bridge. The moves shown are typical of those used by the real railroads' switch crews, who must leave the main line clear for as long as possible.

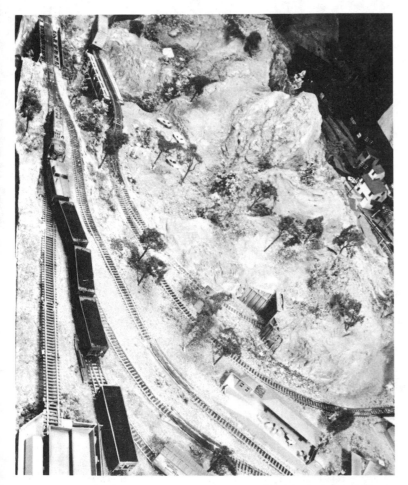

Fig. 18-20. The locomotive pulls forward, couples to the train, backs up until the first car clears the turnout just in front of the bridge, then pushes the train forward.

Fig. 18-21. The locomotive uses the entire train to pick up the single loaded hopper car, then it uncouples the train to leave the train on the passing siding.

Fig. 18-22. The locomotive backs up to the bridge, then heads forward and on past the train to the right of the passing siding's turnout.

Fig. 18-23. The locomotive couples back onto the train to complete the move.

WYE-SWITCHING OPERATIONS

The wye that is shared by switch crews in Alliance and for reversing trains for holdover at Points East on the 9 x 9-foot Burlington Northern layout (and the wye shared by switch crews in Abbott and Chester on the 7 x 8-foot Burlington Route layout) are examples of the type of double duty that trackwork must do on a typical model railroad. The situation is often seen in the tight trackage in older industrial areas and yards on the real railroads, so the problems are as real as any you'll duplicate on your model railroad. The reversing sequence for turning trains (or just for turning locomotives or cabooses, when the stub end of the wye is short) is simple enough. The train moves forward along the main-line leg of the wye (Figure 18-24), backs up the stub end through the far switch until the stub-end switch is cleared (Figure 18-25), then moves forward down the near leg of the wye and back out to the main line (Figure 18-26), traveling in the opposite direction from the way it entered the wye.

This wye at Alliance, although it does have a stub end, actually functions like the main/branch-style wye in Figure 9-11 in Chapter 9. The straight portion of the wye is the main line out of Alliance, and the leg of the wye that curves from Emmett toward Corning is the branch line (actually the main line again). You'll see that the wye is wired so that the short, curved portion with the Freight Unloading Depot (F. C. Rode & Co. concrete pipe, Figure 20-4) is the electrically isolated reversing section. When trains arrive at the wye from Emmett, they take the left leg past F. C. Rode & Co. so they can be turned back into the holding track called Points East (the track with the f block on the plans and control panels), and will be ready for a later return trip over the layout. There's a deliberate switching problem here because the main line beyond the switch points on that leg of the wye is only about 24 inches long, which is just long enough for a typical four-car train but not enough for its locomotive. There would be room for another car or for the locomotive if the Alliance Freight Station were not where it is, but that's the easy solution to the problem. You'll enjoy this layout more because it does have a few problems incorporated into the design. If you get tired of switching every train at the wye, just add another length of track to the stub end of the wye at Alliance and put the freight station somewhere else.

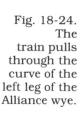

Fig. 18-24. The train pulls through the curve of the left leg of the Alliance wye.

Fig. 18-25. The locomotive backs its train down the straight leg of the wye to clear the far turnout.

Fig. 18-26. The locomotive now pulls the train forward through the second curved leg of the wye to complete the move.

CHAPTER 19

Trains in Action

THE MOVEMENTS of the train are what make any model railroad a truly living replica of real railroading. You have nothing more than a three-dimensional sculpture until you add the action of the trains. Your railroad will revert back to that toy-like state if the action doesn't at least represent the way real trains move. That's what this chapter is all about.

There's also an almost-magic method of installing four switches and some track so you can switch loaded cars into an industry and pull unloaded ones out (or vice versa). This is called Loads-In/Empties-Out.

All of these operations can, of course, be performed with a temporary layout on the floor or a movable one on a tabletop. You really do not even need the actual industry buildings, just small cards with the name of the industry beside the siding will do for now. You may even want to try operating for awhile before you decide what industries you actually want to build for your layout and exactly where you want to locate industrial sidings. With the built-in roadbed track system described in Chapter 4, you have the option of changing your mind with hardly any rebuilding time required.

ACHIEVING AUTHENTICITY

One of the problems that a model railroader faces is a lack of credibility. We have to keep reminding ourselves that our miniatures often aren't real enough, and we don't need some glaring, toy-like sight to make it more difficult for our imaginations to work. The switching suggestions you'll find here in the Waybill system will allow you to move freight cars into and out of industrial sidings almost exactly as though the cars were indeed carrying freight. That scene will be silly, though, if you try to imagine that an empty flatcar really does have a load after it leaves the factory that was supposed to have loaded it. The Loads-In/Empties-Out system is one way around the problem because it really puts loads in those cars.

There are easier ways of doing almost as good a job of tricking even your own imagination. First, try to include as many industries as you can that would ship and receive something in the same kind of car. A furniture factory might receive fine hardwood in a boxcar and ship furniture out in the same car. A sawmill might receive rough-cut lumber and ship finished lumber on the same flatcar. A coke oven might receive hopper carloads of coal and ship almost identical-appearing carloads of coke. A Trailer Train terminal is just as likely to receive flat carloads of full trailers as it is to ship similar loads. Second, try to load flat cars and gondolas with only a partial load, so they can be considered either empty or full. Load a few of those intermodal, Piggyback-style flat cars with just one trailer. Both methods will add to the power of suggestion.

THE WAYBILL SYSTEM

Each shipment made by rail is the result of dozens of papers that order the shipment and the car that will hold it and route that car to the customer. Paperwork is seldom enjoyable enough to become a hobby, and we certainly don't

Fig. 19-1. The waybill tells the engineer where that car should go.

need it to operate a model railroad. But you should have some system of directing the flow of each and every car over your railroad so that your line will have the appearance of really moving goods, not just freight cars.

The waybill system will assign each car a definite purpose as it moves, empty, or loaded with a specific commodity bound for a specific destination. The system requires only a 2-1/4 x 3 - 1/2-inch clear plastic envelope (billfold photo-carriers will do) for each and every freight car you operate. A self-adhesive white sticker is applied to the upper-left corner of each of the clear plastic envelopes and shows the car's railroad initials and the car number. The envelope then follows that car wherever it goes on your layout. A small box can be glued to the side of the table near every town to hold the envelopes for any cars that may be sitting in that town. The envelopes for cars in trains are simply carried by the engineer (that's you) along with the walk-around throttle.

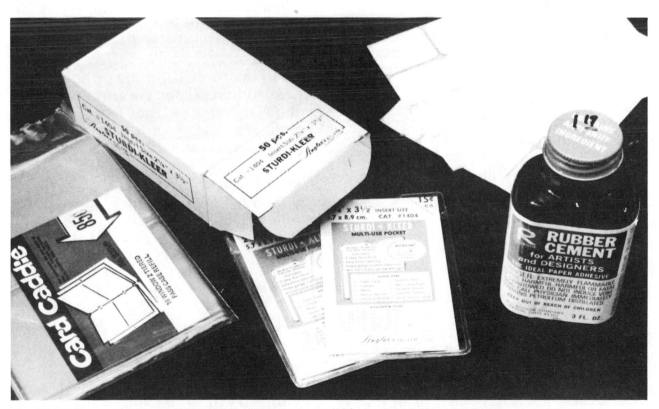

Fig. 19-2. The materials for the waybill system are available at any stationery store.

Place a larger file box near whatever area you consider to be your main yard to hold the cars stored there. Put some dividers in the box for stock, refrigerator (reefer), tank, flat, box, gondola, hopper, and covered hopper cars to make it easier to find them when you need a specific car and its corresponding card. That main yard may well be the shelf or box where you store the cars that you don't have room for on the layout!

WAYBILLS

The second part of the system is the waybills themselves. These are patterned after the waybills the real railroads use with most shipments, but they are somewhat simpler and are much more powerful and versatile in directing the railroad crew's actions. Four blank waybills are included in Figure 19-3. Have photocopies made of that page so you will have about four times as many waybills as you do freight cars. Because waybills are supposed to be folded in half, you need only one-sided copies. You can then cut the waybills apart, apply some rubber cement to the backside, and fold them to produce a two-ply piece of paper that is about as stiff as cardboard. You might want to spray them with clear paint (the same kind you use on your models after decal applications) so they will last forever — without any fingerprint-grease smudges. Save the clear coat, though, until you've used the waybills for a week or so and you know the information on them is the information you need. Each of the waybills must be filled out to indicate how its particular commodity should be transported.

SHIPPING AND RECEIVING

You will use the waybills to decide what cars to move and where to move them. The first consideration when creating the waybills, however, will be the industries and other sources of freight on your own railroad. On a pad of paper, list each of the industries you plan to locate on the sidings of your layout. The industries don't have to be there

yet, but the sidings must be, so you'll have a place to spot that freight car. The copy-and-cutout station and industrial signs in Chapter 14 will give you an idea of the different types of industry you might choose, and there are others indicated on the key (Figure 20-4) to the 9 x 9-foot Burlington Northern layout in Chapter 20.

Write down the goods or commodities that each industry might receive under an IN column and the goods or commodities it might ship under an OUT column. There is no reason why any industry would ship or receive everything by rail, however. A power plant, for instance, would receive coal, but it would ship electrical power over wires rather than over rails. And some firms, like warehouses, would ship small boxes of manufactured products by truck or, a concrete plant might receive raw materials like coal or ore by barge or conveyor. You'll need to do this paperwork only once; when it and the waybills are completed, operations will only involve placing cards in the clear plastic envelopes. You can also add more goods or commodities to the list to make more waybills after you have used the system for a few months and are more familiar with the kind of freight traffic your railroad needs.

Add two more columns beside each of those industries for TO and FROM. List all of the places that each industry might ship those commodities to in the OUT column and the places where it might get it from in the IN column. Those places can be other industries on your own railroad. A fuel dealer for instance, might receive its coal from the coal mine on your layout. About half of the places should be off your layout because that's a bit more like real life; few railroads are lucky enough to have both the shipper and the receiver.

INTERCHANGES

It is most common for a shipment to be loaded on one railroad and transferred (railroads use the word interchanged) with three, four or more other

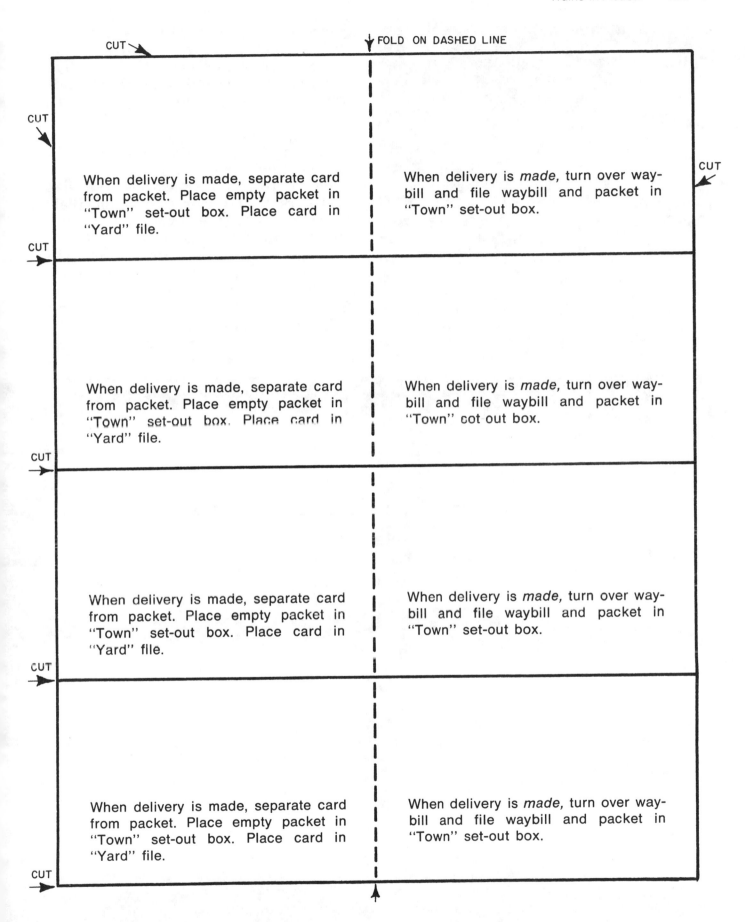

Fig. 19-3. Four waybills that can be photocopied and cut apart.

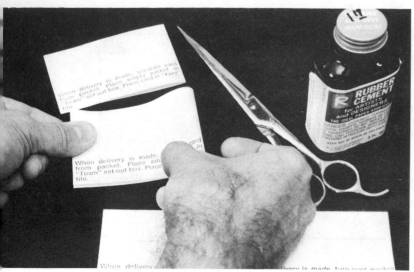

Fig. 19-4. Cut apart the photocopies of the waybills, then fold them as shown and glue the backs together with rubber cement.

railroads before it reaches its final destination. For our purposes, the off-line places can be marked simply "interchange," and one end of a stub-end siding can be designated as the industry interchange.

I suggest that you put a rerailer track section at the end of that siding so your interchange area can be the box or shelf where you store extra cars. That way, cars destined for interchange really do travel off the layout. The interchange track may also be a simple tunnel, such as track j (the interchange with the Union Pacific Railroad) on the Burlington Northern layout in Chapter 20 (Figure 20-3). You can use a passing siding (such as the track J, the AT&SF RR interchange) on the Burlington

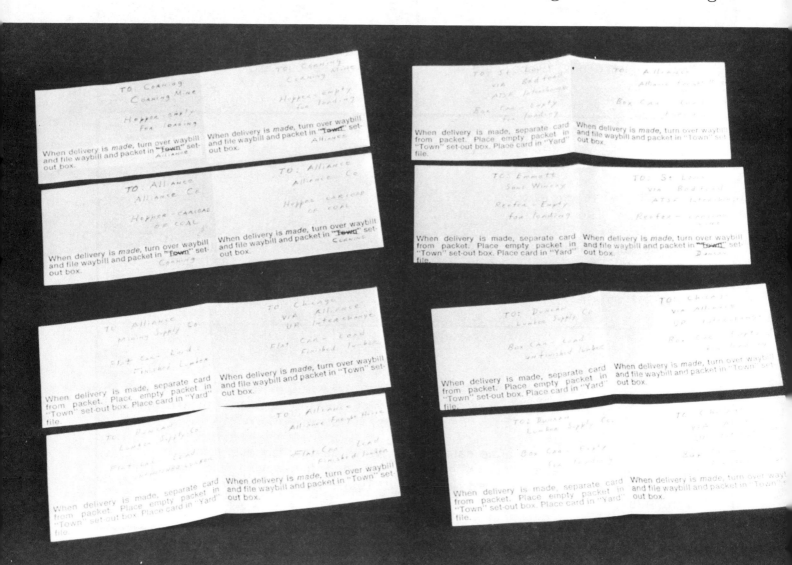

Fig. 19-5. Samples of eight waybill variations (unfolded only so you can read both sides).

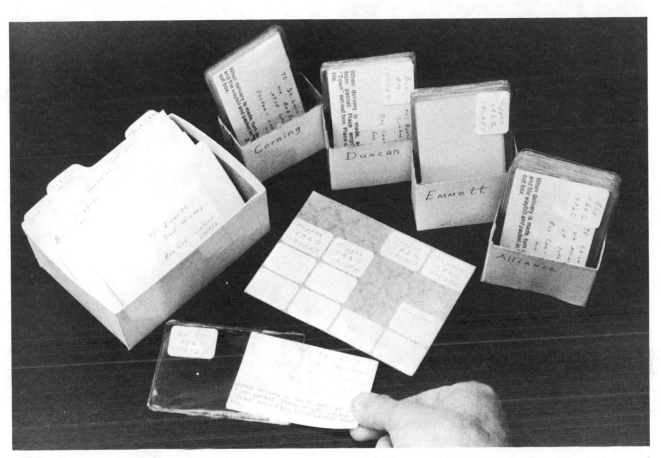

Fig. 19-6. A waybill file box is needed for each town, plus a master or yard file for the waybills themselves and for empty-car envelopes.

Northern layout. Designate one end as IN (it's at Bedford on the Burlington Northern layout), so you can just keep adding cars until they appear for pick-up at the other end of the siding (at Duncan on the Burlington Northern layout). On the 7 x 8-foot Burlington Route layout (Figure 20-5), the siding nearest the edge of the table at Abbott can be designated as an interchange track with the ATSF, the Union Pacific or any other railroad that might connect with your empire. If you want a second interchange track on the Burlington Route layout, you could designate the stub-ended siding at Chester as another interchange.

FILLING OUT THE WAYBILL

You can now use your list of industries and their shipments to fill in both sides of the waybills. Begin on the side of each waybill that ends with the sentence, "Place card in Yard file." Then follow these steps:

1. Write "TO:" and list the name of the town where the industry is located, followed by the name of the industry.

2. List the type of car that would be used for the commodity that specific industry receives. (This is the "IN" commodity from your list.) Then write, "Empty For Loading."

3. Turn the card over, and write "TO:" and the destination for that industry's products. The destination can be a bit tricky, but it's logical if you think it out: List the name of any city (say, Chicago) as the destination, write VIA (meaning through), the name of the town on your layout, and the interchange track in that town (write Interchange).

4. Note the type of car, just as you did on the opposite side of the waybill, but here add the words "Carload" (or Loaded) and the commodity the car will actually carry.

Fig. 19-7. A computer keyboard drawer is used to support the Digital Command Control power pack and to hold the yard file on the 7 x 8-foot Burlington Route layout.

Fig. 19-9. Use a larger clear plastic envelope to hold the waybills for an entire train.

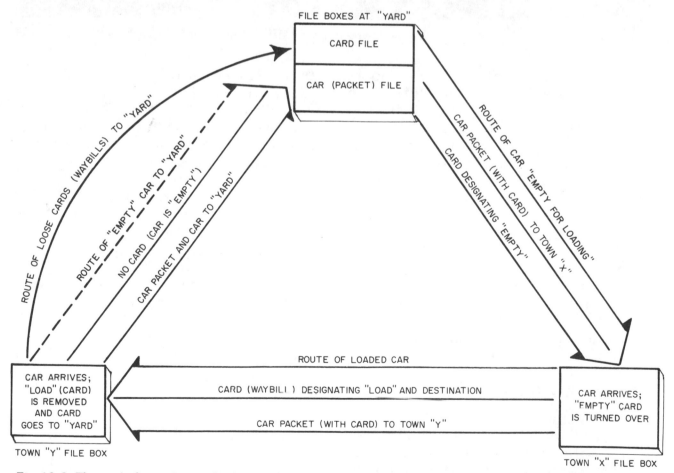

FILE BOXES AT "YARD"

CARD FILE

CAR (PACKET) FILE

ROUTE OF LOOSE CARDS (WAYBILLS) TO "YARD"

ROUTE OF "EMPTY" CAR TO "YARD"

NO CARD (CAR IS "EMPTY")

CAR PACKET AND CAR TO "YARD"

ROUTE OF CAR "EMPTY" FOR LOADING

CAR PACKET (WITH CARD) TO TOWN "X"

CARD DESIGNATING "EMPTY"

ROUTE OF LOADED CAR

CARD (WAYBILL) DESIGNATING "LOAD" AND DESTINATION

CAR PACKET (WITH CARD) TO TOWN "Y"

CAR ARRIVES; "LOAD" (CARD) IS REMOVED AND CARD GOES TO "YARD"

TOWN "Y" FILE BOX

CAR ARRIVES; "EMPTY" CARD IS TURNED OVER

TOWN "X" FILE BOX

Fig. 19-8. The cycle for each standard type of waybill and plastic envelope for each cars follows this pattern.

That completes the standard waybill. A variation would be to simply list the town and industry name for a receiver industry that is actually on your layout. Make about four cards, each with a different destination, for each industry on your layout.

You will also want to make some variations on those standard cards to suit particular industries and track situations. If the car is a flat car or a gondola, try to list a load on both sides of the waybill so there will be no Empty--- For Loading's—just two different loads. You can do the same thing for any type of car that might appear on both the IN and OUT lists for a specific industry.

EMPTY-IN FOR LOADING

If you do add a pair of passing sidings for the Loads-In/Empties-Out operations, you'll need a special card for the cars that are always empty. It should read: "Empty--- For Loading" on both sides. It should list the town the empty is picked up from in place of the pre-printed word "Yard" on both sides of the card. Cross out the sentence "Place card in Yard file" because the car (and the card) will never get back to the yard. Make another type of card for the cars that are always loaded, which reads: "Carload of Coal" (or whatever the commodity) on both sides of the card. Cross out the word "Yard" on both sides of this card and list the name of the town that ships that load. Cross out the sentence, "Place card in Yard file" on these cards, too. The cars that have these special cards will be cycled back and forth through their industry until you decide to pull the cards and insert them in some other cars' clear plastic envelopes. The cards in Figure 19-5 that read "TO: Corning" on both sides and "TO: Alliance" on both sides are examples of the Loads-In/Empties-Out cards.

THE YARD FILE

The Waybill system of operation begins when you pick some of the waybills at random that match the types of cars in your yard area. On the Burlington Northern (Figure 20-3), the yard would be the trackage at Alliance and on the Burlington Route layout (Figure 20-5), the yard would be the trackage at Abbott. Follow the directions on those cards to switch the now-loaded cars onto the appropriate sidings. From that point on the system is self-perpetuating, so long as you follow the instructions on the waybills. Keep the extra waybills in that yard file and return the used waybills to the rear of the pack of waybills. Draw fresh ones each time you're ready to operate a train. Figure 19-7 shows how the car (and its clear plastic envelope) originates in the yard where the waybill is inserted. The waybill is then turned over (according to its own printed instructions), and that car is ready to be picked up by the next train through town. In some cases, the car may go directly back to the yard, or, in the case of Loads-In/Empties-Out, operations, the car may never go back to the yard. If you want the car to sit on the siding for awhile, add another hold card with a note stating it is to be picked up after one or more passes (days or weeks) by the freight trains through town.

LOADS-IN/EMPTIES-OUT

Most of the commodities that are loaded into hoppers or gondolas are raw materials that are used by another industry, so the flow of traffic is mainly a repetitive pattern of loaded cars traveling to the industry and empty cars traveling back to the commodity source for reloading. Some examples of popular heavy traffic flow prototypes for model railroaders are hoppers of coal destined to be dumped into ships or taken to power plants, gravel traveling from a quarry to a cement plant, iron ore being taken to a steel mill or to be dumped into ships and logs traveling from the mountains to the sawmill.

All of these involve the use of cars that are obviously loaded in one direction and unloaded in the opposite direc-

Fig. 19-10. The Alliance Company (far left) power plant and the Corning Mine on the 9 x 9-foot Burlington Northern layout are served by the same pair of sidings, which are connected inside the mountain.

Fig. 19-11. The Tri-State Utility Co. on the 7 x 8-foot Burlington Route layout has two sidings that are connected to the Duncan Mine but their connections are hidden by a thick grove of trees. Here, an unloaded hopper is being pulled from the Tri-State Utility Co.

Fig. 19-12. The Duncan Mine on the 7 x 8-foot Burlington Route layout has the same unloaded hopper shown in Figure 19-11 now ready for pick up. The loaded hoppers are picked up from the Duncan Mine beneath the coal tipple itself while those same loaded cars are delivered to the Tri-State Utility Co. on the track between the two large piles of coal.

tion—a difficult challenge for the modeler, because even the operating type of cars would be too time consuming to load or unload three or four or more at a time. The answer to this is the concept known as Loads-In/Empties-Out.

The Loads-In/Empties-Out concept requires a model of both the shipping industry (a coal mine, for example) and the primary receiving industry (say, a power plant). Either industry may also use cars to or from other sources, but the majority of the traffic is between the two. The unit trains that carry a hundred carloads of coal, and that never uncouple as they cycle from Colorado mines to Illinois power plants, are a modern example of such traffic.

Each industry must have two tracks of its own, and the two must be located near each other on your layout. They could be separated visually by a mountain, like the Burlington Northern layout (Figure 19-10), a tall and thick forest, like the Burlington Route layout (Figures 19-11 and 19-12), by a painted sky backdrop (like the Bachmann E-Z Track

layout in the color section), or some other feature that breaks any visual connection between the two industries. The two sidings appear to be stub-ended at each industry but, in fact, they connect inside a tunnel between the two industries. The two tracks that lead into the Corning Mine on the Burlington Northern layout in Chapter 20 are actually the same two tracks that lead into the Alliance Company.

You can see the two tracks on the Burlington Northern Layout in the satellite view in Figure 20-4, but the mountain effectively blocks any connection between the two from normal viewing angles. It helps the illusion if the tracks enter each industry from slightly different directions. The right-hand track into the mine receives only empty hoppers; and loaded hoppers are picked up only on the left-hand track at the mine. Those loaded cars are actually shoved through the mountain by other loaded cars being delivered to the power plant. The empty hoppers that are pushed into the mine will eventually be pushed out from the

Fig. 19-13. The coke ovens at Cardiff, Colorado, about 1900. Coal is dumped into the top and super-heated to make coke, which is then loaded into box cars or hoppers. Photo courtesy of Library, State Historical Society of Colorado

Fig. 19-14. The r-t-r "action" coal-dumping car ramp (now available from Life-Like with a section of Power-Loc track) was elevated to simulate a coke oven, where coal is baked into coke for steel-making, for making cement, for producing sugar from sugar beets and for pickling.

power plant as empties. It takes about nine cars to fill each track in this example, so the ninth car into the mine will always push the first car out the power plant's end. The system provides an endless supply of loaded hoppers at the mine and an endless supply of empty hoppers at the power plant.

The Loads-In/Empties-Out system does exactly what its name implies. It allows you to have extremely realistic operations, which includes empty cars traveling toward a mine and carloads of coal traveling toward the power plant. Notice that no locomotive actually travels through the tunnel that connects the mine and the power plant. The cars alone are pushed by other cars through the tunnel.

If you want to simulate the operation of modern unit trains, you could just as well operate a single complete train of loaded hoppers with a permanently coupled locomotive and caboose. You would need matching trains with identical car

Fig. 19-15. The track on the far right (near the right edge of the 1 x 3-foot extension) on the Burlington Route layout can be designated as an interchange track. Here it's being used as a team track, the place where real railroads unloaded freight cars directly into waiting trucks.

numbers and identical weathering, however. One set of cars would be filled with coal and the other set would be empty. When the train of empty hoppers entered the mine on the right track, you would hold it there and wait a moment before flipping the block switch, which would allow the second train of loaded cars to exit on the left track, thus simulating the loading cycle. The process would be repeated when the loaded train reached the power plant, except that the train of empties would appear after the train of loaded cars disappeared. I prefer the individual-car method over the unit-train operation, but you can take your choice with the same trackwork and industries. You would alter only the shape of the industries to duplicate the Loads-In/Empties-Out coal-hauling with gravel, ore, or logs.

TIMETABLE OPERATIONS

You can establish a timetable just like the real railroads when you establish a point-to-point run, such as that for the layouts in Chapters 3 and 20. Time the amount of seconds it takes for a train to travel from one town (siding) to the next and call the seconds minutes. Duplicate the general format of any real railroad timetable. There is, I feel, a better way to run a railroad in miniature than to spend your leisure hours watching the clock. Timetable operations really are necessary on some of the gigantic club layouts, where there may be as many as twenty trains on the tracks at the same time. The timetable that helps to keep the real trains from running into each other works on these club layouts as well. Most home layouts, however, are operated by just one person for most of their sessions, and, at most, there may be three operators.

The Out-and-Back track plan in Chapter 3 (Figure 3-5) and the 9 x 9-foot and 10 x 10-foot plans in Chapter 20 (Figures 20-3 and 20-6) are large enough to keep three operators busy. One person is in the yards making up trains, while the other two are operating

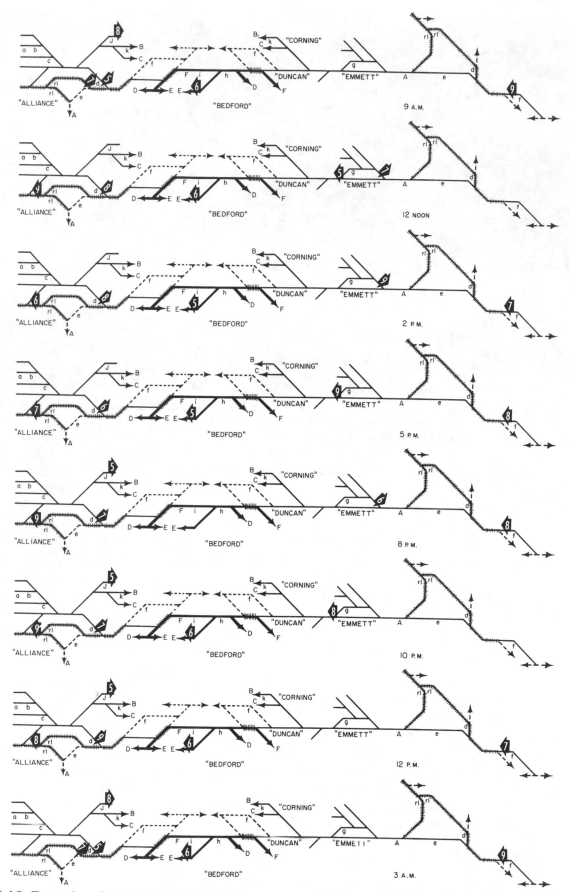

Fig. 19-16. Examples of where Trains 5, 6, 7, 8, and 9 might be on the Burlington Northern layout at some specific times during a 24-hour operating session with the use of a sequence timetable. This is similar to playing musical chairs, but with trains.

trains out on the main line. Another blocking switch must be added to allow the yard areas to be operated by a third power pack unless you are using the Digital Command Control System described in Chapter 3. There's little need then, for more than two trains to be out on the main line at any one time.

THE SEQUENCE TIMETABLE

If you have as many as six trains waiting on the holding tracks or passing sidings, no more than two ever need to be running at one time. With that in mind, you can stage what I call "sequence timetable operations." The sequence timetable merely means that you establish an operating pattern for your trains, such as that on the 9 x 9-foot Burlington Northern layout. Those trains originate in Alliance and travel over the route described in Chapter 1, to be turned and held on the Points East track (f), and shown in the schematic diagram (Figure 19-16).

Two additional patterns can be applied to this particular layout. Every fourth or fifth train can be routed into the tunnel at the terminal track j, which leads to an imaginary interchange with the Union Pacific. The operator in the Alliance yard then makes up a new train in the tunnel by hand-carrying cars to and from storage shelves. (The single track qualifies as a Fiddle Yard for just that reason—cars are fiddled on and off the layout.) The second interchange path routes trains into the passing siding at the terminal track i for an imaginary interchange with the Santa Fe Railroad. The two alternate routes allow you to use locomotives from different railroads to break up the pattern of running Burlington Northern trains alone from Alliance to Points East and back. The Union Pacific train can be a once-a-day Amtrak passenger train for even greater variety.

A TYPICAL DAY

Figure 19-17 shows the locations of five trains on the Burlington Northern plan in Chapter 20 (Figure 20-3) at purely imaginary times of a 24-hour day. By stipulating that it takes 1 hour for a train to travel from Alliance to Points East, you can create your own 24-hour day by completing twenty-four train movements over the railroad. The arrows indicate the direction of travel of Trains 5, 6, 7, 8, and 9 at eight random hours during a typical day. When any arrow changes direction, that train has been reversed at the Alliance wye.

Train 5 would be the best one to pick as that Amtrak streamliner. Train 5 makes an imaginary trip off on your layout and onto the Santa Fe at 2 p.m., to reappear about 7 p.m., before heading back to the Union Pacific. Train 8 has a similar route and timetable. Train 6 is a "through-freight" going cross-country over our railroad. Cars would be added or taken off this train only at Alliance. Train 7 is a "pedlar" freight, or "way" freight, which means that it makes switching moves at almost every town (where there's a car ready to be picked up or scheduled to be dropped off—all through the waybill process). Train 9 can be another pedlar freight.

FROM IMAGINARY TO REAL

The waybill system, as well as every operating and construction idea on these pages, is based on the actual operations of the prototype. None of this was created for toy trains. You are running a real railroad in miniature when, first, you operate with the quick through-freight system of endless oval operations to simulate cross-country trains, secondly, you make up trains using a switch engine in the yards, and finally, you move every freight car with the waybill system or you operate with a sequence timetable. Combine all these types of operation with, perhaps, one of those Santa Fe interchange freight trains or an Amtrak passenger train added to the sequence timetable, and you can keep yourself busy for years before you even think about building another railroad.

CHAPTER 20

Miniature Empires

THIS IS THE PLACE where you might just bring some of those dreams of real railroading to life. Any of the three layouts you see in this chapter are attainable goals for anyone who has successfully completed and operated that first 4 x 8-foot tabletop model railroad.

You can in fact, build a 4 x 8-foot table using the techniques in Chapter 6. If you choose, stop at the flat, tabletop stage while you experiment with various track plans in that space. I settled for the plan in Figure 20-5. Five alternate plans for a 4 x 8-foot spaces are shown in Chapter 3.

The three model railroad empires in this chapter (Figures 20-2, 20-4 and 20-5) are designed to be free-standing with just one of the shorter ends against a wall. Understand then, that you need at least a 2-foot access aisle for the three sides of these layouts. A simple 4 x 8-foot layout really requires an 8 x 10-foot area of floor space. The Burlington Route plan (Figure 20-5) was designed to take advantage of the need for an aisle by including a 3-foot extension on one of the ends that would be against a wall. This layout then, would require a minimum of 9 x 10 feet of floor space. The 9 x 9-foot Burlington Northern layout (Figures 20-2 and 20-4) would require an additional 2 feet of aisle space on two sides; so it would require an 11 x 11-foot area. The plan in Figure 20-6 is an around-the-wall layout, designed to have at least its two longest edges against walls in an 8 x 10-foot space.

The around-the-wall layout illustrates an alternative use of this space. It leaves the access in the center and places the layout around the edges of the space. It is designed to have three of the four sides against a wall. This layout can be extended into a 10 x 10-foot C shape by adding the Alliance and Corning portion of the layout (Figure 20-3). The around-the-wall layout can be extended in any direction, at the points shown on the plan, to fill, for example, the walls in a 12 x 15-foot room. The plan can also be reversed or mirrored so you can relocate the entryway to suit an existing doorway.

MODULAR BENCHWORK

The 9 x 9-foot layout (Figures 20-2 and 20-4) and the around-the-wall layout (Figure 20-6) should be assembled in modules of open-grid benchwork (such as that discussed in Chapter 4) no larger than 30 x 60 inches. Figure 16-1 shows how to cut the 1/2-inch Homasote roadbed and 1/2-inch plywood tabletops for a 5 x 9-foot layout from 4 x 8-foot sheets of both materials. You'll need both Homasote and plywood in the shapes and sizes A through G to duplicate the 9 x 9-foot layout. The around-the-wall layout can be cut from a single sheet each of Homasote and plywood by cutting them into 2 x 4-foot panels and arranging them in the L-shape of the plan. The open-grid benchwork for any of these layouts should be assembled in modules to match the sizes of the Homasote and plywood pieces. The 30 x 60-inch maximum is just small enough to fit through any door, even with mountains of scenery. You will probably want to move the layout some day, and

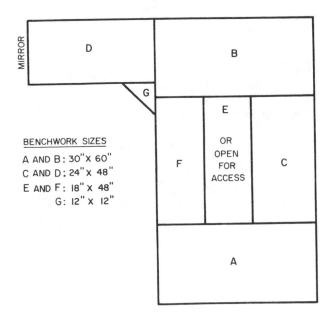

BENCHWORK SIZES

A AND B: 30"x 60"
C AND D: 24"x 48"
E AND F: 18"x 48"
      G: 12"x 12"

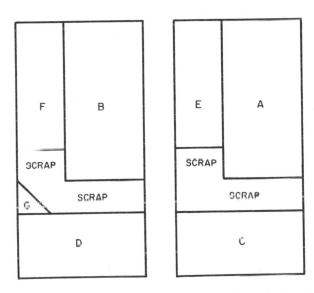

Fig. 20-1. Method for cutting two 4 x 8 foot sheets of plywood panels for a 9 x 9-foot layout

the planning stage is the time to prepare for it.

The Burlington Route layout (Figure 20-5) is designed to be built in only two modular sections, a single 4 x 8-foot section and a removable 1 x 3-foot extension. The 4 x 8-foot portion will, however, probably be too heavy to move easily unless it is built with the lightweight construction techniques shown in Chapter 6. For instance, build scenery (like part of the layout itself) with blue extruded-Styrofoam, as shown in

Chapter 16 and texture the scenery surfaces with felt, as shown in Chapter 17.

BUILDING TABLETOP LAYOUTS IN STAGES

The Burlington Northern and the Burlington Route empires both have almost anything you could want in a model railroad, from walkaround control to scenery to most industries served by the real railroads. Their greatest assets, though, are the track plans. The 9 x 9-foot Burlington Northern has a far more complex track plan with four passing sidings at Alliance, Bedford, Duncan and Emmett. The sidings at Bedford and Duncan overlap near Duncan. What appears to be a pair of passing sidings at Corning is really a pair of Loads-In/Empties-Out industrial sidings described in Chapter 19.

The 7 x 8 foot Burlington Route is a simplified version of the larger Burlington Northern layout. The Burlington Route layout has only a single passing siding that serves both Chester and Elwood. What looks like a second passing siding inside the inner oval is a pair of Loads-In/Empties-Out industrial tracks between Chester and Elwood. The wye can be used (on either layout) as a runaround track to get the locomotive from one end of the train to another, but the locomotive will be reversed each time it travels through the wye.

The final plan, for either the Burlington Route or the Burlington Northern, will provide just about every type of real railroad operation you could ask for, including:

1. Trains can operate in the orbiting style popular in Europe and in toy departments, with two trains circulating endlessly on the inner and outer ovals.

2. A single train can operate over a rather lengthy route using both the inner and outer oval for a two-lap trip around the layout. That same route can add extra miles to any type of train operation you choose.

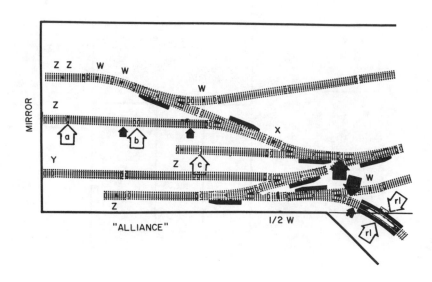

Fig. 20-2. The track plan and wiring connections and electrical installation gaps for the 9 x 9-foot Burlington Northern layout.(See Figure 9-9 for the key to track symbols.)

Track Sections Required

9-inch straight	32
9-inch Rerailer straight	4
3-inch straight Z	29
2-inch straight X	10
1 1/2-inch straight Y	10
*3/4-inch straight	
Full 30-degree curve	24
Curved terminal tracks	15
1/3 curve (10 degree) W	30
*1/8-curve (hand-cut 10-degree curve)	
Right-hand turnout	9
Left-hand turnout	10
Curved right-hand turnout	3
Curved left-hand turnout	3
Wye turnout	2

*Note: These sections must be cut from longer track sections as shown in Chapter 7.

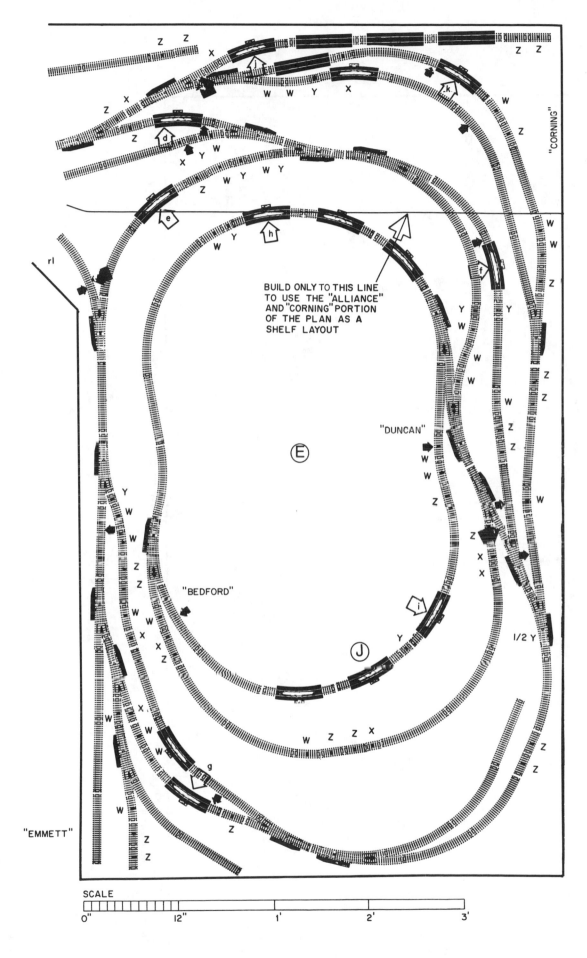

BUILD ONLY TO THIS LINE
TO USE THE "ALLIANCE"
AND "CORNING" PORTION
OF THE PLAN AS A
SHELF LAYOUT

"CORNING"

"DUNCAN"

"BEDFORD"

"EMMETT"

SCALE

0"   12"   1'   2'   3'

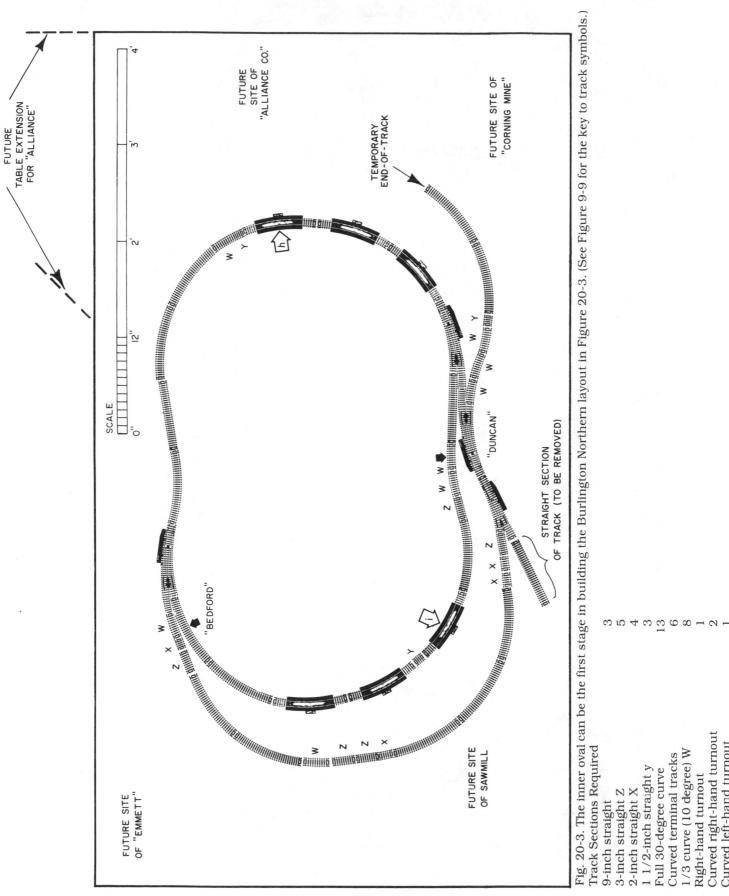

Fig. 20-3. The inner oval can be the first stage in building the Burlington Northern layout in Figure 20-3. (See Figure 9-9 for the key to track symbols.)

Track Sections Required

9-inch straight	3
3-inch straight Z	5
2-inch straight X	4
1 1/2-inch straight y	3
Full 30-degree curve	13
Curved terminal tracks	6
1/3 curve (10 degree) W	8
Right-hand turnout	1
Curved right-hand turnout	2
Curved left-hand turnout	1

Key to Industries and Features
on the Burlington Northern Layout

AA Ford & Sons Ice Co.: meat and other food (reefers) IN; ice (reefers) OUT

AB Mining Supply Co.: timber and hardware (flat cars and boxcars) IN and OUT

AC Farming Tools, Inc.: hardware, tools, and tractors (flat cars and boxcars) IN; empties OUT

AD Company Furniture Co.: lumber and hardware (flat cars and boxcars) IN; furniture (boxcars) OUT

AE Alliance Coal & Fuel: coal and coke (hoppers) IN; empties OUT

AF American Express Co.: paper and cartons (box car) IN and OUT

AX Alliance Co.: coal (hoppers) IN; empties OUT

C Cattle pens (railroad-owned): empties (stock) IN; cattle OUT

CD Coke ovens: coal (hopper or ore) IN, coke (hopper) and empties OUT

D Dwelling or boarding house owned by railroad

DF Duncan Feed & Fuel: seed and coal (box car and hopper) IN; grain (boxcar, C.F. hopper, and covered hopper) OUT

DM Dwellings owned by Corning Mining

DT Duncan Signal Tower for Atchison, Topeka & Santa Fe Railroad interchange

E Engine House

ET Engine, Tool & Supply Co.: engines and tools (box car) IN; empties OUT

FC F. C. Rode & Co.: concrete and steel pipe (flat cars) IN; empties OUT

FT Alliance Freight House: lcl merchandise (box car) IN and OUT

G Grade crossing

GG Grade crossing

ISF Interchange track with Atchison, Topeka & Santa Fe Railroad (every type of car IN and OUT, empty or loaded)

IUP Interchange track with Union Pacific Railroad (every type of car IN and OUT, empty or loaded)

L Lumber Supply Co.: empties (box car) IN; finished lumber OUT

LS Log dump for Lumber Supply Co.: logs (log cars) IN; empties OUT

MX Corning Mining Co.: timber, tools, and empties (flat car, box car, and hopper) IN; coal and empties OUT

O Diesel fuel-oil storage and refueling: oil (tank) IN; empties OUT

PE Trailer Train loading dock (Piggyback Flatcar set): lcl merchandise (trailers on flat cars and box cars) IN and OUT

PL Trailer Train terminal: lcl merchandise (trailers on flat cars) IN and OUT

PT Trailer Train terminal: lcl merchandise (trailers on flat cars) IN and OUT

SA Passenger station at Alliance

SB Passenger station at Bedford (AT&SF inter-change IN)

SD Passenger station at Duncan

SE Passenger station at Emmett

ST Sand house, tower, and bins: sand (gondola) IN; empties OUT

SW Sons Winery: crates (box car) and empties (box car and reefers) IN; empties (box car) and wine (boxcar and reefers) OUT

W Water tower

WW Billboard

NOTE: The types of cars in parentheses, near the IN or OUT traffic pattern of each industry, are the types of cars the industry uses to carry the commodities it receives (IN) or ships (OUT).

Fig. 20-4. A satellite view of the 9 x 9-foot Burlington Northern layout.

3. The railroad can be operated as a point-to-point line (as illustrated in Chapter 2 for the Burlington Northern—to run trains from Alliance to the holding siding F called Points East, then back again). The Burlington Route can be operated as a point-to-point line in a similar manner between Abbott and Chester, using the wye at Abbott to turn the Chester trains as well as the Abbott trains.

4. The Burlington Northern layout can be operated as an Out-and-Back plan from Alliance to Bedford to Emmett and back to Alliance using the left leg of the Alliance wye. Similar operations are possible on the Burlington Route layout starting at Abbott and traveling to the inner oval through Emmett and back out to Chester and across the straight leg of the wye back to Abbott.

5. The Loads-In/Empties-Out trackage can be used through the Corning Mine and the Alliance Co. on the Burlington Northern (between the Duncan Mine and the Tri-State Utility Co. on the Burlington Route) for switching individual cars, as described in Chapter 19, or for complete unit trains.

6. The hidden siding J (the interchange with the Union Pacific) on the Burlington Northern can be operated as a one-track Fiddle Yard, where cars and locomotives are hand-carried to and from the layout. There's really no provision for such a siding on the 7 x 8 foot Burlington Route, although the siding nearest the edge of the 1 x 3-foot extension at Abbott could be used for a hands-on interchange track.

7. The switching operations of the pedlar freight or way freight can be duplicated (with or without the system of waybills in Chapter 19) thanks to numerous industrial sidings.

8. The tracks near the Alliance Station can be used by a locomotive to perform the typical yard operations of making up and breaking down trains. Frankly, the Fiddle Yard area of Figure 20-6 is better for that type of yard work, and you'll probably enjoy operating this layout (Figure 20-2) more by just fiddling new trains on and off the layout by hand on the hidden track J. On the Burlington Route layout (Figure 20-5) there really are not enough sidings at Abbott to allow it to be switched like a yard.

THE BURLINGTON ROUTE, IN STAGES

The Burlington Route layout (Figure 20-5) is designed to be built with Bachmann E-Z Track, Life-Like Power-Loc track or Atlas True Track. Since these types of track have sturdy built-in roadbeds they can be rested on the tabletop or on the floor without nails or glue while you are experimenting to find the best layout for the space. The photos in Chapter 4 (Figures 4-2, 4-3 and 4-4) show how this layout was developed, in stages, from a simple oval with a passing siding to a double-loop mainline, while it can still be operated on the living room floor. The trackage at Abbott was developed after the layout was located on a tabletop as shown in Chapter 4 (Figures 4-5, 4-6, 4-7 and 4-8).

THE BURLINGTON NORTHERN, IN STAGES

Larry Larson built the 9 x 9-foot Burlington Northern layout and detailed it using the techniques you see in Chapters 5, 7, 8, 9, 15 and 16. There are a large number of small sections of track because the operating concept of the layout was developed first, and the track was then fitted into that concept. If Larry were to do it again, he would use pencil lines to locate most of the track centers and then use 3-foot flexible track sections, cut to fit between the turnouts, rather than the dozens of sectional-track pieces. The sectional track, however, does allow you to add just a little bit at a time as your funds allow. The large number of small pieces of track, especially near the turnouts, would make this layout impractical to attempt with track that has built-in

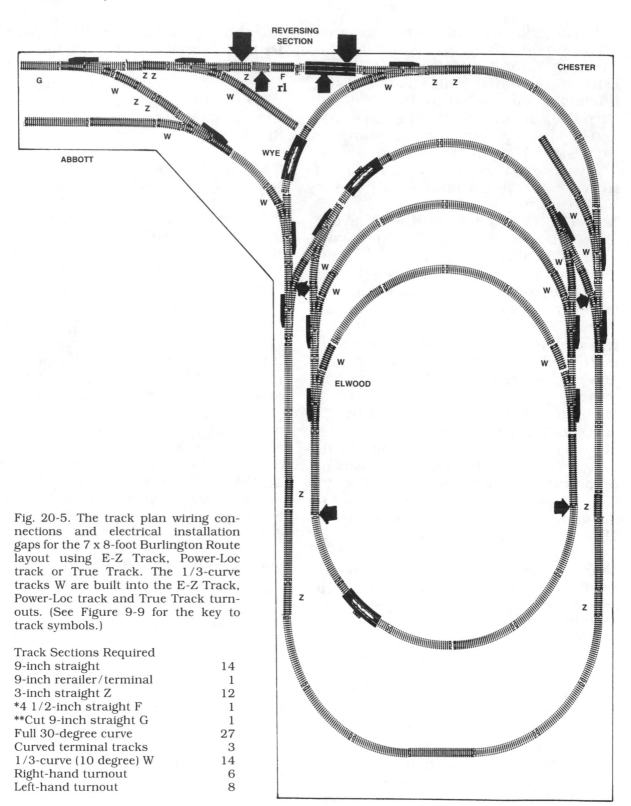

Fig. 20-5. The track plan wiring connections and electrical installation
gaps for the 7 x 8-foot Burlington Route
layout using E-Z Track, Power-Loc
track or True Track. The 1/3-curve
tracks W are built into the E-Z Track,
Power-Loc track and True Track turnouts. (See Figure 9-9 for the key to
track symbols.)

Track Sections Required
9-inch straight	14
9-inch rerailer/terminal	1
3-inch straight Z	12
*4 1/2-inch straight F	1
**Cut 9-inch straight G	1
Full 30-degree curve	27
Curved terminal tracks	3
1/3-curve (10 degree) W	14
Right-hand turnout	6
Left-hand turnout	8

*Note: This sections must be cut from a 9-inch section as shown in Chapter 7. Cut this section 6-1/2
    inches if the layout is built with Life-Like Power-Loc track.
**Note: Cut this section of track from a 9-inch straight to fit between turnout and end of table 20.6.

roadbed like E-Z Track, Power-Loc track or True Track.

The Burlington Northern layout can begin as a simple oval with the minimum-switch allotment (Figure 20-1). I recommend you allow a passing siding, or runaround track, and both a facing-point and a trailing-point stub-end siding. If you want an unusual effect during this early stage, leave the center 2 x 4-foot panel E off the benchwork and operate the layout from a central pit. You'll soon discover why no one makes duck-under layout plans anymore—all that ducking and stooping is tiring. This layout is really designed to be operated from three of the outside edges. You can expand outward from the oval in Figure 20-3 in almost any direction, working toward the final plan in Figure 20-2.

ELECTRICAL WIRING

The track plans on these pages are wired for two-train operation based on the principles of common-rail wiring and blocks for conventional power packs in Chapter 9. There are far more terminal tracks shown on the plan for the Burlington Northern (Figures 20-2) than are needed just to connect wires to individual blocks. The actual block wire connections are indicated with open arrows with the letters "a" through "k", and wiring to the reverse section of the wye is indicated by the letters "r" and "l". All of the remaining rerailer tracks should provide an automatic car-rerailer inside the tunnels. That's why there's a string of straight rerailers inside the tunnel at track J, which is a fiddle track where you'll be taking cars on and off the layout. The rerailers will make the job much easier. One of the rail joiners with a wire soldered to it (as described in Chapter 9) must be used at a, b and c as an electrical connection to one rail, as indicated on the Burlington Northern plan (Figure 20-2), when no terminal track is present. Almost all of the buildings are modified with at least a different shade of paint, but they are all kits or lighted ready-builts. The major building modifications or conversions are described in Chapter 14.

AROUND-THE-WALL LAYOUT PLAN

The around-the-wall type of layout plan (Figure 20-6) offers the greatest possible degree of realism, but the least degree of flexibility in layout planning. The around-the-wall plans are only for really experienced model railroaders who know what type of operation and construction they prefer. It is difficult to provide any type of oval or distorted oval for continuous operation on an around-the-wall layout because the shelf for the layout can't be much more than 24 inches wide or you won't be able to reach the tracks near the rear. To get around this problem, you could extend the 9 x 9-foot layout in Figure 20-2 to the left from the town of Alliance around all four walls of a room. If you have the space, that's one of the ways that any layout plan can grow in the years to come. The general areas and track arrangements in Figure 20-6 could be used to extend any layout into an around-the-wall configuration.

The around-the-wall plan (Figure 20-6) is really three shelf-style layouts combined into one. You could decide to build either one of the 2 x 8-foot portions with or without the 9 x 68-inch Fiddle Yard. The wye in the corner could be used by either plan with a 2-foot extension beyond the 2 x 8-foot limit. One other source of a 2 x 9-foot shelf layout is included. Use only the upper 2 feet of the Burlington Northern plan (Figure 20-2), and eliminate any trace of the inner oval. The five tracks on the upper left of the around-the-wall plan are designed to connect to those at the Corning Mine, and the Alliance wye is extended (with dashed lines) directly out into the center of the room. The resulting layout would fill a 10 x 10-foot area with a 2-foot space in the lower left corner for a doorway or entrance to the layout. Steep mountain scenery and tunnels would be most effective on the 2 x 8-foot portion that includes the wye. The other 2 x 8-foot area could just as well be designed with large industrial

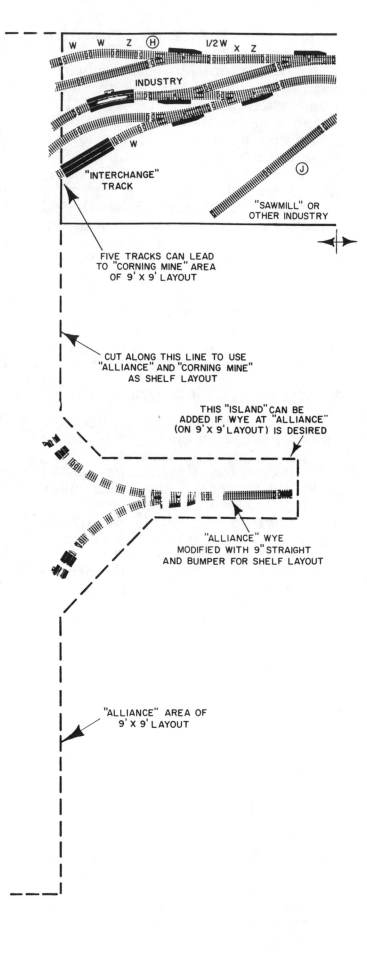

Fig. 20-6. An around-the-wall plan for a minimum
8 x 10-foot or 10 x 10-foot area. (See Figure 9-9 for
the key to track symbols.)

Track Sections Required.

9-inch straight	39
9-inch rerailer/terminal	1
3-inch straight Z	17
2-inch straight X	13
	1
Bumper track	6
Full 30-degree curve	11
Curved terminal tracks	5
1/3 curve (10 degree) W	13
*1/8-curve (hand-cut 10-degree curve)	
Right-hand turnout	10
Left-hand turnout	11
Wye turnout	1

*Note: This section must be cut from longer track
section as shown in Chapter 7.

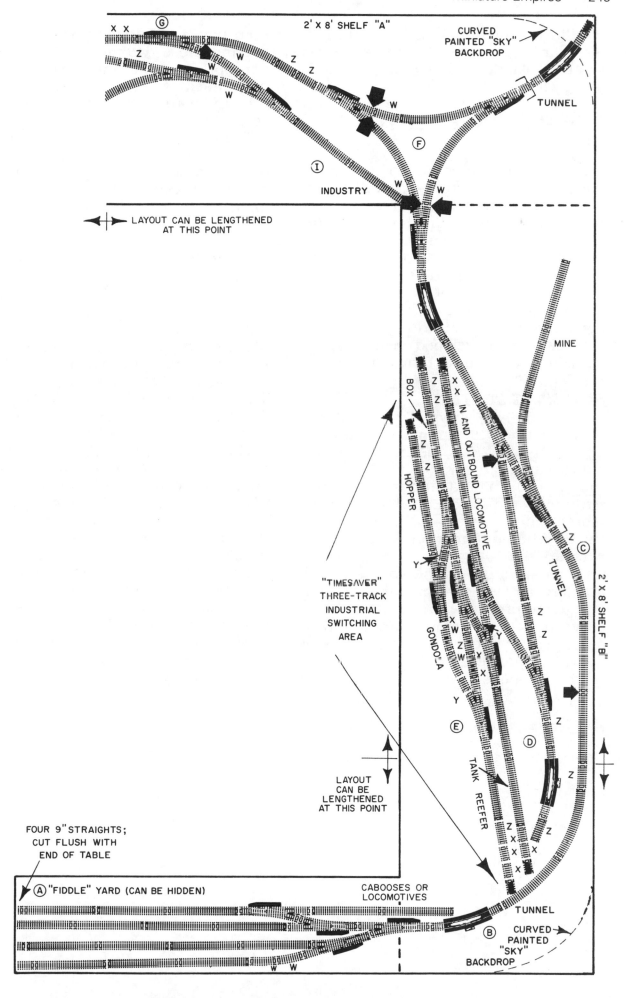

2' X 8' SHELF "A"

CURVED PAINTED "SKY" BACKDROP

X X

Z

W

W

Z   Z

W

TUNNEL

INDUSTRY

← LAYOUT CAN BE LENGTHENED AT THIS POINT

W   W

MINE

BOX

HOPPER

IN AND OUTBOUND LOCOMOTIVE

Z

X X

Z

Z

Z

C

TUNNEL

"TIMESAVER" THREE-TRACK INDUSTRIAL SWITCHING AREA

Y

GONDOLA

X W

Z W Y

W Y

Y

E

Z

Z

D

2' X 8' SHELF "B"

LAYOUT CAN BE LENGTHENED AT THIS POINT

TANK

REEFER

Z

Z

Z   Z

X   X

FOUR 9" STRAIGHTS; CUT FLUSH WITH END OF TABLE

A "FIDDLE" YARD (CAN BE HIDDEN)

CABOOSES OR LOCOMOTIVES

TUNNEL

B CURVED PAINTED "SKY" BACKDROP

W W

buildings. The tunnel leading to the Fiddle Yard could really be a tunnel through plastic buildings that extends into a closet.

THE TIMESAVER LAYOUT MODULE

You can consider any of the three portions of the around-the-wall layout (Figure 20-6) to be a module that can be combined with any other layout. These plans are primarily for those who enjoy the way freight or pedlar freight switching action, so these can be self-contained layouts of their own. The three parallel tracks on the Timesaver portion of the layout are a duplicate of a track plan developed years ago by those who enjoy switching contests.

SWITCHING CONTEST

The switching contest that was developed around the compact Timesaver area (Figure 20-6) begins with two empty cars sitting on the track marked Inbound/Outbound and a locomotive sitting where it says Locomotive. Three more loaded cars rest at any three of the locations that would match the cars' style.

Let's say that a tank car, a boxcar and a reefer (refrigerator) car are sitting on their appropriate tracks. If that's the case, then the two empty cars would be a hopper car and a gondola car. Two of the three loaded cars are picked as "ready to be shipped." The engineer then has the switching problem of delivering those two empty cars to their appropriate spots and picking up the two loaded cars so they end up on the Inbound/Outbound track with the locomotive, where they belong.

The game is run against a clock with the throttle preset to the slowest possible speed so that moves can be made with the directional switch. The switching moves needed to do the job are described in Chapter 18, but in this game, the number of moves are less important than the time it takes to make them all. A different pair of cars should be designated as ready for pickup for the next player/engineer, so he or she does not benefit from the experience of the first engineer. The two cars on the Inbound/Outbound track can always be designated empty for the next game. The cars must all be a scale 40 feet or shorter, and the locomotive must be a small one, such as a GP-20.

The game can be made more complicated by adding up to four more cars, once you've mastered the moves for five. You'll find that switching will be far more enjoyable once you've played the Timesaver game often enough to develop the skill of moving the cars efficiently. When the Timesaver is incorporated into a layout, as it is here, it can also be used for normal switching—but only if each of those sidings serves a structure that would normally use the type of car intended for that spot in the game.

GLOSSARY

AAR: The full-size railroad's trade group; the Association of American Railroads, that establishes their standards for equipment and safety.

Articulated: A steam locomotive with two separate sets of drivers, rods, and cylinders beneath a single boiler. Usually one set of drivers, rods, and cylinders is pivoted so it can swing from side to side around curves while the boiler remains rigidly attached to the rear set of drivers, rods, and cylinders.

Bad Order: The term the real railroads use to describe a malfunctioning part.

Big Hook: The wrecking crane.

Block: A section of track that is electrically isolated from the adjoining sections for multiple-train operation; to prevent short circuits.

Bolster: The portion of a railroad freight or passenger car that runs across the underbody of the car to connect the trucks' pivot points to the body of the car. Sometimes used to describe all the cross members, including the ends, of a car's underframe.

Branch: A portion of a real railroad that branches off from the main line to reach a town or industry or to connect with another railroad.

Bumper: A device placed at the stub end of a track siding so cars or locomotives do not derail.

Caboose: The rolling office and living quarters for the crew of a freight train. Usually identifiable by a small box with windows on the roof (called a cupola) or one on each side (called bay windows) so the crew can see the length of the train from inside. Sometimes called crummy, bobber, or way car.

Catenary: Overhead trolley wires, usually used by prototype interurbans (electric-powered locomotives and self-propelled cars) with diamond-shaped current pick-up devices on the roofs called pantographs.

Coaling Station: Any building where coal for steam locomotives is stored and shoveled or dumped through chutes into the locomotives' tenders. When the storage bins are elevated and the coal hoisted by conveyor belts or buckets, the structure is usually called a coaling tower. When the elevated storage bins are reached by a trestle so the coal can be dumped from the cars or shoveled right into the storage bins, the structure is usually called a coaling trestle.

Crossing: When two tracks cross each other, as in the center of a one-level Figure-8-style model railroad.

Crossover: The pair of turnouts that allows trains to travel from one parallel track to the adjacent one on double-track systems.

Cut: When the railroad has to dig or blast through a hill or mountain to maintain a level roadbed; a few cars coupled together.

DCC: Short for Digital Command Control. A system for controlling model locomotives that sends a signal through the track to a decoder in the locomotive to instruct the locomotive to go forward or backward, to change its speed or to stop or go. With the least expensive systems, a non-equipped standard locomotive and up to nine more locomotives (each equipped with a decoder), can be controlled independently on the same track. More expensive systems can control over 200 locomotives as well as activate sound systems and operate turnouts.

D.P.D.T.: An electrical slide or toggle-type switch that is used for reversing the flow of current to the tracks by wiring across the back of the switch. Some types have an off position midway in their throw and these center-off D.P.D.T. switches are often used for wiring model railroads to allow two-train and two-throttle operation.

Draft Gear: The box under the ends of a prototype car or locomotive (and on most models) where the coupler is spring-mounted to center it and to help absorb shocks and bumps.

Fiddle Yard: A hidden track or series of tracks used by modelers to make up or break down trains by lifting the equipment by hand.

Fill: When the prototype railroad has to haul dirt to fill in a valley with an embankment to bring the roadbed level up to that of the nearest trackage.

Flange: The portion of any railroad wheel that guides that wheel down the rails. The flange extends around the circumference of each railroad wheel as its largest diameter.

Frog: The point where the track rails actually cross at every turnout and rail/rail crossing.

Gap: A break in the rails to electrically isolate some portion of the track from another to prevent short circuits or to allow for multiple-train operation on the same stretch of track.

Gauge: The spacing of the rails as measured from the inside of one rail head to the next. The standard gauge for most American railroads is 4 feet 8-1/2 inches; this distance was also once the standard center-to-center spacing for horse-drawn wagon wheels.

Grade: The angled rise or fall of the track so it can pass over another track or so it can follow the rising or falling contour of the land.

Grab iron: The steel handrails on the sides, ends, and roofs of rolling stock.

Head-end cars: The cars that are normally coupled to the front of a passenger train, including express refrigerator, express baggage, baggage, and mail cars.

Helper: The locomotive that is added to a train to supply extra power that may be needed to surmount a steep grade.

Hostler: Men who service and sometimes move locomotives from one servicing facility to another to prepare the locomotive for the engineer.

Hotbox: A bearing that has become overheated from lack of lubrication.

Interchange: A section of track or several tracks where one railroad connects with another so trains or individual cars can move from one railroad to the next.

Interlocking: A system of mechanical or electrical controls so only one train at a time can move through a junction of two or more tracks like a crossing or yard throat.

Intermodal: The transportation concept of using railroads, trucks and/or ships to carry the same container or trailer from its shipper to its destination without having to unload and reload along the way. If the railroads are carrying just trailers, some refer to it as piggyback service.

Interurban: Prototype railroads and railroad cars that were self-propelled with electrical power pick-up from an overhead wire, catenary, or from a third rail suspended alongside the track. The cars ran from city-to-city as well as inside the city limits and hence the name. (See also trolley and traction.)

Journal: The bearing that supports the load on the end of a railroad car or locomotive axle.

Kingpin: The pivot point for a freight or passenger car truck where it connects to the bolster.

Kit-bash: To combine parts from two or more kits to produce a model different from both. Sometimes called cross-kitting, customizing, or converting. The process is also a kit-conversion.

Kit-convert: See kit-bash.

LCL: Less-than-carload lot; freight shipments that are too small to require an entire car.

Main line: The most heavily trafficked routes of the railroad.

Maintenance-of-Way: The rolling stock or structures that are directly associated with maintaining the railroad or with repairing and righting wrecked trains.

Narrow Gauge: Railroads that were built with their rails spaced closer than the 4-foot, 8-1/2-inch standard gauge. Two-foot and 3-foot spaces between the rail heads were the most common in this country, particularly in the 1880-1900 period.

Pedlar Freight: A freight train that switches cars at most towns along its route from terminal to terminal. Also called a way freight.

Piggyback: The modern railroads' special flatcar service to transport highway trailers. Sometimes called TOFC. Also see intermodal.

Points: The portions of a turnout that move to change the track's route from the main line to a siding. The point where the rails actually cross is called the frog part of the switch.

Prototype: The term used to describe the full-size version that any model is supposed to duplicate.

Pullman: The passenger cars that were owned and operated by the Pullman company, usually sleeping cars, diners, or parlor cars. Sometimes used to describe any sleeping car.

Rail joiner: The pieces of metal that join two lengths of rail together. They slide onto the ends of the rail on a model railroad; they are bolted to the rails on the prototype.

Reefer: The insulated cars, cooled by either ice in bunkers fed through hatches on the roof or, in modern times, by mechanical refrigeration units.

Right of Way: The property and the track owned by the railroad.

r-t-r: Abbreviation for ready-to-run that also includes the simple snap-together and glue-together plastic kits. Some of the brands included are: Accurail, Athearn, Atlas, Bachmann, Bowser, Con-Cor, E & C Shops, IHC, Life-Like, Mantua, Model Die Casting, Model Power, Rivarossi, Stewart and Walthers. Some of the more complex kits are the Life-Like Proto 2000 series and some of the InterMountain kits are also available r-t-r.

Snowshed: The protective buildings that cover the track, usually in mountain areas, so deep snow and drifts won't cover the tracks themselves.

Spot: The switching maneuver whereby a freight or passenger car is moved to the desired position on the track, usually beside some industry's loading platform.

Superelevation: Banking the tracks in a curve so the trains can travel at some designated speed with a minimum of load on the outer wheels and rails and with a minimum of sway.

Switch: Usually used to refer to the portion of the railroad track that allows the trains to change routes, but also used for electrical switches on model railroads, such as D.P.D.T. or S.P.S.T. switches. Track switches are often called turnouts to avoid this confusion.

Switch Machine: The electrical solenoid-type devices that move the track switch from one route to another to allow remote-controlled operation of trains over diverging trackage.

Switch Points: The moving portion of a turnout that changes the route. Also called turnout points.

Talgo: Model railroad trucks with the couplers mounted to them so the couplers swivel with the trucks to allow operation of longer cars on tighter radius curves. Talgo trucks can, however, cause derailments when pushing or backing a long train.

Tangent: Straight sections of trackage.

Tank engine: A steam locomotive without a tender where the coal or fuel oil is carried in a bunker behind the cab and the water in a tank over the top of the boiler. Often used for switching on the prototype and on model railroads.

Tender: The car just behind most steam locomotives that carries the water, coal, wood, or fuel oil.

Throat: The point where the yard trackage begins to diverge into the multiple tracks for storage and switching.

Timetable: A schedule, usually printed, to tell railroad employees and customers when trains are scheduled to be at certain stations or points on the railroad.

Traction: The term used to describe all prototype locomotives and self-powered cars like trolleys and interurbans that operate by electrical power.

Transistor Throttle: An electrical speed control for model railroad layouts that is used in place of the older wire-wound rheostat to provide infinitely better and smoother slow speed and starting control for locomotives.

Transition Curve: A length of track where any curve joins a tangent with gradually diminishing radius to ease the sudden transition of straight-to-curve for smoother operation and to help prevent derailments of extra-length cars that are caused by coupler bind in such areas of trackage. Also called an easement.

Turnout: Where two diverging tracks join; also called a switch. The moving parts that divert the trains from the straight to the curved-path are called turnout points or switch points.

Trolley: Self-propelled, electric-powered cars that ran almost exclusively in city streets as opposed to the interurbans that ran through the country between cities and towns.

Truck: The sprung frame and four (or more) wheels under each end of most railroad freight and passenger cars.

Turntable: A rotating steel or wooden bridge to turn locomotives or cars and/or to position them to align with the tracks in the engine house or round house.

Vestibule: The enclosed area, usually in both ends of a passenger car, where patrons enter the car from the station platform and where they walk to move from one car to the next.

Way freight: See pedlar freight.

Wye: A track switch where both diverging routes curve away in opposite directions from the single straight track. Also, the triangular-shaped track (in plain view) where trains can be reversed.

INDEX